Cavendish
Publishing
Limited

CW00724290

WILLS, PROBATE
& ADMINISTRATION

London Guildhall-Cavendish
Legal Practice Course Companion Series

LONDON GUILDHALL
UNIVERSITY

TITLES IN THE SERIES

Cavendish
Publishing
Limited

WILLS, PROBATE & ADMINISTRATION

Catherine Rendell

London Guildhall-Cavendish
Legal Practice Course Companion Series

LONDON GUILDHALL
UNIVERSITY

First published in Great Britain 1994 by Cavendish Publishing Limited, The Glass House, Wharton Street, London WC1X 9PX.

Telephone: 071-278 8000 Facsimile: 071-278 8080

British Library Cataloguing in Publication Data

London Guildhall University
Wills, Probate and Administration - (LPC Series)
I Title II Series
344.20654

ISBN 1-874241-99-6
Printed and bound in Great Britain

Outline contents

Contents

Table of cases

Table of statutes

Chapter 1

Should a will be drafted for this client?

Introduction

1.1

The purpose of this chapter is to outline preliminary matters which you *may* have to explain to your client before proceeding to take instructions to draft a will; namely:

- Is it necessary/desirable to draw up a will?
- Can the mental elements required of a testator for a valid will be satisfied by the client?
- Have the client's instructions been properly obtained?

Reasons for making a will

1.2

The majority of people die without having made a will. This may be because of a reluctance to contemplate their own death, the mistaken belief that a will is pointless in their case, or simply out of ignorance of the possibilities open to them.

There are many advantages to be gained from making a will, particularly in respect to:

- The rules of intestacy;
- Demonstrating generosity;
- Tax considerations;
- Choice of personal representatives and convenience of administration;
- Extension of personal representatives' powers;
- Appointment of testamentary guardians;
- Providing an opportunity to give directions for burial and disposal of your body.

Finally, and of considerable personal importance, there is the advantage of obtaining *peace of mind*.

The rules of intestacy

1.2.1

If a person dies without leaving a valid will, they are said to have died *intestate* and their estate will be distributed in accordance with the provisions set down in the Administration of Estates Act 1925 (*see* Chapter 7).

While the provisions of the Act ensure that the next-of-kin benefit from the estate of the deceased, the shares which they receive in the estate are arbitrary and consequently often unsuitable. They may be unsuitable from the tax planning point of view or because they provide inadequate provision for the next-of-kin in most need of the assets.

A common problem arises in relation to relatively small estates where the deceased leaves a spouse and children. Under the rules of intestacy, the spouse will only get the deceased's personal chattels, a statutory legacy of £125,000 and a *life* interest in half the residue, the remainder of the estate being divided between the issue. This may be insufficient for the surviving spouse, especially if the matrimonial home forms a major part of the deceased's estate.

1.2.2 Demonstrating generosity

Reliance on the rules of intestacy gives no rights in the deceased estate other than to the next-of-kin. Friends and charities might benefit under a will.

1.2.3 Tax considerations

In planning any will, the intending testator, with their professional advisers, must consider the means by which benefit can be conferred with the greatest taxation advantages. To do this, *all* the circumstances which might arise must be considered, eg. the tax implications on the death of the testator's spouse as well as those on the death of the testator. The main tax which requires consideration in planning a will is inheritance tax (IHT), but capital gains tax (CGT) and income tax considerations may also be important.

1.2.4 Choice of personal representatives and convenience of administration

If a person dies intestate, the person(s) entitled to a grant of letters of administration to administer the estate will be governed by Rule 22, Non-Contentious Probate Rules 1987 (*see* Chapter 8, para. 8.7). The deceased will have no choice in the matter.

Where the deceased has left a will, executors of the deceased's choice can be appointed and they will be entitled to a grant of probate.

An appointment of executors is more convenient than relying on the court to appoint administrators as an executor has authority to administer the estate from the testator's death (the grant of probate merely *confirms* the appointment). In contrast, letters of administration *confer* authority on administrators. They have no authority to administer the estate *until* a grant has been obtained.

Extension of the statutory powers of personal representatives

1.2.5

The Administration of Estates Act 1925, the Trustee Act 1925 and the Trustee Investment Act 1961 all give personal representatives powers in connection with the administration of an estate. Many of the powers are, however, subject to unhelpful limitations. Thus, it is usual for professionally drawn wills to *extend the statutory powers* and *give additional powers.*

Appointment of testamentary guardians

1.2.6

Where a parent has minor children, they may wish to appoint a guardian to take parental responsibility for their children, should they die while the children are minors.

Directions for burial and disposal of one's body

1.2.7

Such directions are not legally binding but do enable a testator to express particular preferences (*see* Chapter 4, para. 4.2.6.)

Capacity to make a will

1.3

Age

1.3.1

A person under the age of 18 has no capacity to make a will unless they have *privileged status*: s.7, Wills Act 1837 as amended by s.3(1)(a), Family Law Reform Act 1969 (*see* Chapter 6, para. 6.5).

Consequently, on death, the estate of a minor will pass in accordance with the rules of intestacy (*see* Chapter 7).

> *Note*
>
> A person aged 16 and over can make a valid statutory nomination of certain types of assets provided the nomination is *in writing* and *witnessed* by at least one person.

Testamentary capacity

1.3.2

Apart from the age restriction, a testator must have testamentary capacity to make a will, ie. they must be *mentally capable* of making a will. In *Banks v Goodfellow* (1870) Cockburn CJ said:

It is essential ... that a testator shall understand the nature of the act and it effects; shall understand the extent of the property of which he is disposing; shall be able to comprehend and appreciate the claims to which he ought to give effect ...

This requires that a testator understands three things:

- The *nature of the act* and its *effect*.

  In other words, a testator should understand that in making a will they are disposing of their property on death. They need not, however, understand the precise legal effect of a will.

- The *extent of the property* of which they are disposing.

  A testator need not be able to remember every detail of the property which they own but must be broadly aware of the extent of their wealth, or lack of it.

- The *nature of the claims* upon them.

  This means that a testator must have a memory to recall 'The several persons who may be fitting objects of the testator's bounty and an understanding to comprehend their relationship to himself and their claims upon him.': *Boughten v Knight* (1873), *per* Sir J Hannen. This does not mean, however, that a testator must distribute their estate to such persons. Provided they have testamentary capacity, they '... may disinherit ... children, and leave property to strangers to gratify spite, or to charities to gratify pride.': *per* Sir J Hannen, *ibid*.

Note

Although a will which takes no account of the testator's moral claims will be valid, persons to whom the testator owes a moral obligation to provide may have a claim under the Inheritance Provision for Family and Dependants Act 1975 (*see* Chapter 14).

Insane delusions

In *Dew v Clark* (1826), it was said that a testator suffers from an insane delusion if they hold a belief on a particular matter which no rational person could hold and the belief cannot be permanently eradicated from their mind by reasoning with them.

Note

The existence of an insane delusion may be proved by extrinsic evidence.

Such an insane delusion does not affect a person's capacity to make a valid will unless it affects the way in which they dispose of their property by will. This will be the case where the insane delusions relates to their property or to the persons who may expect to benefit from their estate.

Example

On the facts of *Banks v Goodfellow* the testator believed that he was being pursued by devils or evil spirits. Nevertheless, the court held that the testator has testamentary capacity because the delusions did not influence the provision of the will.

An insane delusion which impairs testamentary capacity may only affect the validity of *part* of the will. If this is so, probate may be granted of the remainder.

Example

In *Re Bohrmann's Estate* (1938), the testator made a will and three codicils in which he made substantial gifts to charity. He later began to suffer from the insane delusion that he was being persecuted by the London County Council. Shortly before his death, he executed a forth codicil, one clause of which stated that all references to English charities should be read as references to corresponding American charities. This clause alone was omitted from probate.

The time for ascertaining testamentary capacity

As a general rule, a person must have mental capacity *at the time they execute the will*. However, under the rule in *Parker v Felgate* (1883), a testator has sufficient testamentary capacity if:

- They had such capacity at the time when they gave instructions to a solicitor for the preparation of a will; and

- The will is prepared in accordance with their instructions; and

- At the time of executing the will, they were capable of understanding and did understand that they were executing a will for which they gave instructions.

The rule in *Parker v Felgate* is useful in cases where the testator deteriorates in mental capacity after giving instructions for a will.

Note

The rule was extended in *In the estate of Wallace, Solicitor of the Duchy of Cornwall v Batten* (1952) to apply to a will drafted by a solicitor on the basis of the client's own draft. However, in *Battan Singh v Amirchand* (1948) the Privy Council said that the rule in *Parker v Felgate* should be applied with the greatest caution where the testator, in giving instructions, relies upon a lay intermediary to repeat the instructions to a solicitor.

Burden of proof

The *legal burden* of proof lies on the propounder of the will (the person seeking to rely upon the effectiveness of the will) to prove that the testator had testamentary capacity at the relevant time. However, the *evidential burden* may shift from one party to the other in the course of a case where either of the following rebuttable presumptions operate:

- Where the will is rational on the face of it, it is presumed that the testator had mental capacity at the time the will was made. Therefore, the person attacking the will must bring before the court evidence of a lack of testamentary capacity;

- The presumption of continuance operates, eg. if it is proved that on 1 August 1993 the testator had (or had not) sufficient testamentary capacity this is presumed to continue until evidence to the contrary is produced.

Doubtful testamentary capacity

If doubt might be cast upon the testamentary capacity of the client, medical advice should be obtained to avoid allegations at death of lack of capacity. In *Kenward v Adams* (1975) it was suggested that solicitors should take the following steps when a will is executed by an elderly and/or sick testator:

- Arrange for a doctor to examine the testator at the time the will is to be executed and provide a written statement as to the testator's mental capacity; and

- Ask the doctor to witness the will.

In a hospital or nursing home it may not be possible for you to arrange for a resident doctor to witness the will as many hospitals and nursing homes have rules which forbid staff from witnessing wills. If this is so, it may be possible to get the testator's GP to examine the patient and witness the will. If not, non-medical witnesses will have to be used.

Note

In addition, you should make a detailed attendance note for the file in such circumstances.

1.3.3   **Statutory wills**

If a client lacks testamentary capacity, it may be possible for a 'statutory' will to be executed on their behalf.

Under s.96, Mental Health Act 1983 the Court of Protection is empowered to order the execution of a will for an adult patient who is mentally disordered if the court has reason to believe that the patient is incapable of making a valid will for themselves. The patient need not be hospitalised before such order can be made.

Note _____

A 'statutory' will must be executed with the special formalities
set out in s.97, Mental Health Act 1983.

_____

Knowledge and approval   1.4

In addition to having testamentary capacity, a testator must
know and approve the contents of their will. However, a
testator is taken to know and approve the contents of their
will even though they do not understand its precise legal
effect.

Note _____

Statutory wills are an exception to the 'knowledge and approval'
rule.

_____

The point in time at which a testator must know and
approve the contents of their will is when they execute it.
However, a will is valid despite lack of knowledge and
approval at the time of execution provided:

* The testator knows and approves the contents of instructions given to a solicitor to draft a will; and

* The will is prepared in accordance with his instructions;
  and

* At the time of execution the testator understands that
  they are executing a will for which they gave instructions: *In the estate of Wallace* (1952).

The following practical steps should be taken by a solicitor
in order to avoid any allegations on death that the testator
did not know and approve the contents of their will:

* Explain the meaning and effect of each clause in the will
  to the testator;

* Ask the testator to read the will before they execute it to
  see that it complies with their wishes.

Burden of proof   1.4.1

The person propounding the will must prove that the
testator knew and approved the contents of the will. However, once it is established that the testator had testamentary capacity and that the will has been properly executed,
there is a *rebuttable presumption* of knowledge and approval
and the evidential burden shifts to the person opposing the
will to provide evidence to rebut the presumption.

The presumption of knowledge and approval does *not*
apply:

* Where the testator is *blind, dumb or illiterate*, or the will is

signed on *behalf of* the testator. (For the requirements of signature generally and signing on behalf of the testator, *see* Chapter 6, para. 6.1.2.)

Here, Rule 13, Non-Contentious Probate Rules 1987 requires evidence that the testator had actual knowledge of the contents of the will.

Note

In order to avoid at death the need for affidavit evidence from a witness or some other person present at the time of execution, you must ensure that the will is read out to, and approved by, the testator in front of the witnesses and includes an amended form of attestation clause which incorporates a statement that the will was read to the testator and that the testator approved its contents.

Specimen clause

This will having been read over
to the above named testator in our
joint presence and the testator
appearing thoroughly to understand
the same and to approve its contents
was signed by (name of person signing)
in his presence and by his direction
as his last will in the presence of
us present at the same time who at his
request in his presence and in the
presence of each other have hereunto
subscribed our names as witnesses

- Where there are *suspicious circumstances.*

  Where a person who writes or prepares a will takes a substantial benefit under it, this will be regarded as a suspicious circumstance. The same will be true if the will is prepared by a close relative of a substantial beneficiary, or where a person rather than writing/preparing a will themselves, suggests the terms of the will to the testator and takes the testator to a solicitor of that person's choice: *Fulton v Andrew* (1875).

Note

In *Wintle v Nye* (1959) the House of Lords pointed out that the degree of suspicion will vary with the circumstances of each case. The greater the suspicion, the stronger the affirmative evidence of knowledge and approval must be.

1.4.2   Legacies to solicitors

Although, in *Wintle v Nye* the House of Lords stated that the law did not prevent a solicitor from taking a benefit under a will, a solicitor might now be in breach of the rules of professional conduct if they attempt to take such a benefit in certain circumstances.

The Law Society's rules of professional conduct provide that:

... where a client intends to make a gift *inter vivos* or by will to his solicitor, or to the solicitor's partner, or a member of staff, or to the families of any of them, and the gift is of a significant amount, either in itself or having regard to the size of the client's estate and the reasonable expectations of prospective beneficiaries, the solicitor must advise the client to be independently advised as to the gift, and, if the client declines, must refuse to act.

Points to note

1   The rule applies not only to the solicitor drafting the will, but also to partners of the solicitor and any member of their staff, as well as to the families of any of them.

A solicitor must therefore ensure that no member of staff includes in a will (or any other document) a gift to themselves without their approval. Where the solicitor is a relative of the testator, the solicitor should consider whether, in the circumstances, legal advice is essential. The same applies where the client is a relative of a partner or member of the solicitor's staff.

2   The rule only applies where the gift is of 'a significant amount'. This is judged according to the size of the estate and the 'reasonable expectations of prospective beneficiaries'.

Where the gift is not of a significant amount, independent advice is unnecessary. However, the solicitor should satisfy themselves that

- The client does not feel obliged to make the gift to the solicitor; and, in particular
- Where the solicitor is to act as executor, that the client does not include the legacy as payment for the services to be rendered.

Note

Point out to the client that a professional charging clause will be included in the will. This will provide for payment for the services as executor.

3   If the solicitor taking a legacy of a significant amount on the face of the will has agreed with the client to hold the legacy on secret trust, the solicitor will not be in breach of

the rules of professional conduct even if no independent advice is obtained by the testator. This is because the solicitor will not be taking a personal benefit.

Note

The instructions from which the will has been drawn up should be retained and the terms of the secret trust should be embodied in a written document signed by the testator.

4   If the client refuses to seek independent advice and the gift is of a significant amount, the solicitor must refuse to act for them in drawing up the will or any other document by which a gift is made.

1.5   Fraud or undue influence

If a will is made as a result of fraud or undue influence of another, it is invalid. If only part of the will was made as a result of fraud or undue influence, only that part will be omitted from probate.

1.5.1   Fraud

Fraud occurs where the testator has been deliberately misled, eg. by a false representation about a person's character or conduct, which induces the testator either to include or exclude that person from the will.

1.5.2   Undue influence

Undue influence arises where the testator is coerced into making a will they do not want to make.

It is essential to distinguish between persuasion, as a result of which the testator does want to make a will in a particular way, and coercion which overpowers the testator's will without convincing their judgment. Only the latter amounts to undue influence.

Undue influence may take a number of forms, eg. actual violence, fear of injury or extreme verbal pressure. In the case of the latter, it is often very difficult to distinguish between coercion and strong persuasion. The court will be more prepared to find undue influence where the testator is physically and/or mentally weak.

1.5.3   Burden of proof

The legal burden of proof of fraud or undue influence always lies with the person alleging it. This is so even where the donee stands in a confidential relationship to the testator, eg. child to father, client to solicitor, where equity presumes undue influence with regard to *inter vivos* trans-actions. Consequently, where there is no affirmative evi-dence of fraud or undue influence, a will is admissible to probate.

Note

It is important to distinguish between the requirement of knowledge and approval and an allegation of fraud or undue influence in this respect. In the former case the burden of proof lies on the person propounding the will.

Instructions from third parties 1.6

You should take instructions for a will from the *testator*. It is not uncommon to receive instructions from the testator's spouse or bank. If you receive instructions to draft a will from a third party, the Law Society's rules of professional conduct require you to write to the testator to confirm that the testator wishes you to act and to confirm the instruc-tions.

You must make it absolutely clear to the testator that they are completely free to instruct a solicitor of their choice. It is important for you to remember that the intending testator is your client and not the person who initially approached you. This is why it is so important not only to obtain written confirmation that the testator wishes you to act but also written confirmation of the instructions.

Self-assessment questions

1 What are the possible disadvantages of dying intestate?

2 Martin, aged 80, is a client of your firm. He has displayed considerable confusion about the date and time of his appointment with you concerning the making of his will. However, you have at last managed to see him and he tells you that he wishes to revoke his existing will – he cannot remember how long ago he made it – and make a new one. In taking instructions from him, he appears confused about the number of grandchildren he has and you have to remind him about the trust he established for his children five years ago. He tells you he wishes to strike his daughter Mary, who benefited under the old will, out of the new will.

What important considerations will you need to address before any new will of Martin is ready for execution? (Ignore appropriate procedures for execution.)

3   Sandra seeks your advice as to her chances of establishing that a will made by her father, William, two weeks before he died is invalid. The will leaves a substantial part of William's estate to Father Brown, a Roman Catholic Priest with whom William became well-acquainted in the last six months of his life. The will is written in Father Brown's handwriting. William was too weak to be able to write during the month before he died.

Advise Sandra.

4   You are a solicitor drafting a will for John Brown who is of limited means. He tells you he wishes to leave a legacy of £1,000 to your partner who is a friend of his.

What problem, if any, does this raise?

5   Distinguish between the requirement of knowledge and approval on the part of a testator and establishing that there is no fraud or undue influence.

6   You have this morning received a letter from the Moorgate Bank plc, asking you to draft a will for Brenda Conway, a customer of the Bank, on the basis of instructions given by Brenda Conway to an official of the Moorgate Bank plc.

What steps will you take before proceeding to draft the will of Brenda Conway?

Answer guidance to self-assessment questions

1   *See* 1.2.

2   Given Martin's confusion and loss of memory, it is necessary to consider whether there is any doubt as to his testamentary capacity, especially as he wishes to strike Mary out of the new will. There is a possibility she may try to claim on his death that Martin lacked testamentary capacity to make the new will and, consequently, the earlier will is admissible to probate.

Three questions about Martin's mental state will need to be asked.

- Does he understand the nature of a will?

- Does he have sufficient recollection of his assets?

- Does he recall the moral claims his relatives may have upon him (*see* further 1.3.2).

The confusion and forgetfulness displayed by Martin is probably not itself enough for the solicitor to have doubts about Martin's testamentary capacity. However, as there is a possibility that Mary, at Martin's death, may try to deny the validity of any will drawn up, it may be advisable to suggest to Martin that at the time of execution of the will he agrees to an examination by his GP, who would then provide a statement as to his mental capacity.

3 Issues of whether William had 'knowledge and approval' (*see* 1.4) and whether or not he was subject to undue influence (*see* 1.5.2) should be considered. Particular points which need to be made about the requirement of knowledge and approval are that the presumption of knowledge and approval does not apply even if it is clear that William has sufficient testamentary capacity, as this is a 'suspicious circumstance'. Therefore, the party propounding the will will need to provide affirmative evidence of knowledge and approval.

The legal burden of proving undue influence always lies with the party alleging it, even in a confidential relationship such as priest/confessor. Consequently, the will is more easily challenged on the basis of lack of knowledge and approval, and the onus will be on Father Brown to provide affirmative evidence of 'knowledge and approval' on the part of William.

4 This raises a problem of professional conduct (*see* 1.4.2). Given that John Brown is not very wealthy, the gift is likely to be regarded as being one of a significant amount. Unless John Brown seeks independent advice, you must refuse to act, as a gift to a partner is covered by the Law Society ruling.

5 *See* 1.4 and 1.5. Of particular significance is the fact that the burden of proof in a case of fraud or undue influence always lies on the party alleging it, whereas in the case of knowledge and approval it normally lies on the person propounding the will.

6 Your client will be the customer whose will is to be drafted. The instructions have been obtained from a third party, the bank. The instructions should be confirmed with the client, preferably in writing. You should also contact the bank and ascertain who is to pay for the solicitor's services, the bank or the client (*see* 1.5).

Chapter 2

General principles of inheritance tax

Introduction 2.1

The purpose of this chapter is to set out the basic principles of inheritance tax in the context of the death of the taxpayer. These principles are drawn on in subsequent chapters to explain tax considerations in will drafting and in the administration of an estate.

The nature, scope and incidence of inheritance tax 2.2

Inheritance tax (IHT) was introduced by the Finance Act 1986. It is a tax which arises on death and on gifts made within seven years of death and certain other lifetime gifts – mainly those made on trust.

The tax is governed by the Inheritance Tax Act 1984 (IHTA 1984) which was formerly the Capital Transfer Tax Act 1984.

Note

1 References, to capital transfer tax in documents such as wills, made before 18 March 1986 are now taken as references to inheritance tax.

2 All references are to the Inheritance Tax Act 1984 unless otherwise stated.

Definitions 2.2.1

Chargeable transfer
Inheritance tax is *prima facie* payable where there is a chargeable transfer. This is defined as:

... any transfer of value which is made to an individual but is not ... an exempt transfer: s.2(1).

A transfer of value
A transfer of value is defined as:

... a disposition made by a person ... as a result of which the value of his estate immediately after the transfer is less than it would be but for the disposition(s) ...

A transfer of value occurs *inter vivos* as a result of a gift of property or a sale at undervalue.

On death, a person is treated as if they had made a transfer of value immediately before their death, the value transferred being equal to the value of their whole estate immediately before death: s.4.

Estate
Estate is defined as the aggregate of all the property to which the deceased was entitled before death. The term 'estate' is normally used when referring to the property of a deceased person, but for the purpose of inheritance tax it is also used with reference to lifetime gifts and trust property. The amount by which the value of the transferor's estate is less as a result of the disposition is the value transferred. It is on this amount that inheritance tax is *prima facie* payable.

2.2.2   **When is IHT chargeable?**

There are three categories of transfer which can give rise to inheritance tax:

- Chargeable transfers made before death;
- Potentially exempt transfers (PET);
- Transfers on death.

Chargeable transfers made before death
The main categories of chargeable transfers are:

- Transfers of settlements without an interest in possession (*see* 2.6);
- Chargeable events within settlements without an interest in possession (*see* 2.6);
- Transfers by which no property becomes comprised in the estate of another by virtue of the transfer.

   Such transfers occur where the transferor purchases a service for another. A common example is where a grandparent pays school fees for a grandchild. (As the grandparent's estate is reduced in value there is a transfer of value, but there can be no PET (*see* below) as the grandchild's estate is not increased.)

Chargeable transfers are immediately taxable, but at only half the rate which applies on death. However, if the transferor dies *within seven years* of making the transfer, the transferee becomes taxable at the full rate of tax in force at the date of death.

Potentially exempt transfers (PET)
Any lifetime transfer which is made to an individual which would otherwise be chargeable is 'potentially exempt'.

   Where a transfer of value is a potentially exempt transfer, no tax is payable at the time of the transfer but if the transferor dies *within seven years* the transfer becomes chargeable at the rates of tax in force at the date of death. Conversely, if the transferor survives seven years after the date of transfer, the potentially exempt transfer becomes fully exempt.

Example

On 1 June 1990 John makes a gift of £200,000 to his daughter Jane. The gift is a potentially exempt transfer, being an *inter vivos* gift to an *individual*. As such, no IHT is payable at the time that the gift is made. However, on 22 June 1992 John dies. As the gift to Jane has been made within seven years of his death, the PET becomes chargeable. Had John survived beyond 1 June 1997, the PET would not have become chargeable.

Note

The rate of tax is reduced if the transferor survives at least three years after making the transfer (*see* 2.3).

Transfers on death

Transfers on death are charged at the full rates of tax. The chargeable transfer deemed to take place on death has to be cumulated with the deceased's existing cumulative total of lifetime chargeable transfers and PETs.

The calculation of tax   2.3

Rates of tax   2.3.1

In respect of transfers made on or after 15 March 1988, there are only two rates of tax:

- The nil rate band (currently £150,000); and once this has been exhausted;
- 40% on the balance.

This full rate of 40% applies if the transfer is made on death or was made within the three years before the date of death.

If the transfer is a *chargeable transfer* (for definition, *see* 2.2.2) made before death, the tax charged at the time of the transfer is half the full rate: s.7(2).

If the transfer is a potentially exempt transfer or a chargeable transfer and death occurs within seven years but not less than three years of the transfer, tapering relief is available. Table 2.1 shows the percentages of the full rate in force at the time of *death* that are charged on the value of the transfer (at the date it was made): s.7.

Table 2.1 Rates of tax

Years before death	% of full rate
0–3	100
3–4	80
4–5	60
5–6	40
6–7	20

Example

On 1 December 1989 Paul made a gift of £200,000 to Tim. Paul dies on 1 August 1993.

The gift to Tim is a PET which becomes chargeable because Paul has died within seven years of making the gift – he has in fact died between three and four years of making the gift. Assuming that Paul has made no previous lifetime transfers and that no exemptions (*see* 2.4) are available, the tax on the PET will be calculated as follows.

£		Rate %	£
0–150,000	(Nil rate band in force at death)	0	= Nil
150–200,000		40	= 20,000

However, as Paul has survived for three to four years following the making of the gift, only 80% of the £20,000 is payable:

$$\frac{80}{100} \times £20,000 = £16,000$$

Note

There will be no repayment of the difference if the inheritance tax payable, calculated according to the above scale is less than that originally paid on a *chargeable transfer*, eg. if the scale rates have been reduced, or where the tapering rate is less than 50%.

2.3.2 Principle of cumulation

The principle of cumulation takes into account all previous transfers made by the transferor within seven years before the present transfer in order in order to establish whether or not the nil rate band has been exhausted in respect of a particular chargeable transfer: s.7(1).

Think of every taxpayer having a meter which starts at birth accumulating chargeable transfers. Only transfers made within the previous seven years of the present transfer need be cumulated, so seven years after each transfer the meter is wound back cancelling that transfer. On the taxpayer's death the last seven years are re-worked, adding to the meter all potentially exempt transfers and finally adding the taxpayer's estate at the moment of death.

Example _____

(Note: In this example any exemptions and reliefs (*see* 2.4–5) are ignored.)

Between five and six years before his death, D made a *chargeable transfer* of £160,000. Prior to this, D had made no chargeable transfers.

Between four and five years prior to his death D made a potentially exempt transfer of £100,000.

Between one and two years prior to his death D makes a potentially exempt transfer of £20,000.

On D's death, in addition to the tax payable on his death estate, the following will be payable.

Transfers before death	Category of transfer	Nil rate	40% rate	
5 – 6 years	Chargeable transfer 160,000	150,000	10,000 $= (4,000 \times 40\%$ [1]$) - 2,000$ [2] $= -400$ [3]	Nil [4]
4 – 5 years	PET 100,000	—	$100,000 = 40,000 \times 60\%$ [1]	24,000
1 – 2 years	PET 20,000	—	20,000	8,000
				32,000

[1] tapering relief
[2] paid at the date of transfer at 50% of the full rate
[3] no refund where over payment of tax: s.7(5), IHTA 1984.
[4] no additional payment due

Exemptions   2.4

An exempt transfer is not liable to tax. It is not included in the cumulative total of the transferor so that it does not affect the rate of tax on later transfers.

Exempt transfers are:
- Spouse exemption: s.18;
- Gifts to charities etc: ss.23–6;
- Annual exemption: s.19;
- Small gifts exemption: s.20;
- Normal expenditure out of income: s.21;
- Gifts in consideration of marriage: s.22;
- Family maintenance: s.11;
- Death on active or other warlike service: s.154;
- Conditional exemption: ss.33–5.

Note _____

Some of the exemptions do not apply on death. It is important to know all the exemptions as it may be preferable to make a lifetime gift from the tax planning point of view rather than to dispose of property by will in circumstances when only lifetime exemptions are available.

2.4.1 Spouse exemption: s.18

This is available both *inter vivos* and on death. Gifts to the transferor's spouse either before death or on death are generally completely exempt provided that the spouse is domiciled in the UK. If the spouse is domiciled elsewhere, only the first £55,000 of transfers are exempt.

Note

For inheritance tax purposes, 'spouse' has its normal meaning, and this includes a separated spouse.

The spouse exemption is available even though the gift to the spouse is not absolute, provided the spouse takes an immediate interest, eg. if a testator makes a gift of property to 'my spouse for life, with remainder to Y', the exemption will apply.

The exemption is lost, however, if the gift to the spouse does not take effect immediately. For example, if a testator leaves property to 'Y for life, with remainder to my spouse', the gift of remainder will not be an exempt transfer.

If a gift to a spouse is *conditional*, the spouse exemption applies *provided* the condition is satisfied within *12 months* of the transfer. This is significant in relation to 'survivorship clauses' which are commonly included in wills (*see* Chapter 4, para. 4.10). Such a clause will require that a spouse survives the deceased for a certain minimum period of time before they become entitled to the gift made in a will.

Example

Henry makes a will leaving all his property to his wife Wendy if she survives him by 28 days. If Wendy does not survive him by 28 days, his estate is to be divided between their children.

The gift to Wendy does not take effect immediately, but rather vests in her 28 days from Henry's death (if she survives for that period). Despite the fact that it is not an immediate gift if Wendy survives Henry by 28 days, the spouse exemption operates for IHT purposes and no tax is payable on Henry's estate.

Note

To obtain the spouse exemption the period of survivorship required must be *no more than 12 months*. If, in any case, the survivorship period is a period *exceeding six months*, the gift will be treated as creating a settlement without an interest in possession and will result in an immediate chargeable transfer from the deceased to the settlement.

Gifts to charities etc: ss.23–6   2.4.2

This exemption is also available whether the gift is made *inter vivos* or on death and there is no limit to the amount which is exempt.

Transfers of value to the following transferees are exempt in the same way as transfers to charities:

- A transfer to an *exempt political party*.

  A political party qualifies for this exemption if it had at least two members elected to the House of Commons at the last general election or one member elected and a total of 150,000 votes cast for *all* its candidates.

- A *national body* listed in Schedule 13 of the IHTA 1984.

  This includes national museums and art galleries, the National Trust, universities and their libraries, local authorities and government departments.

- Where the *Treasury* directs that an exemption be available.

  This is possible where the transfer is to a non-profit making body (other than a charity, political party, or national body, eg. local historical or preservation societies) provided that the property transferred is within certain specified categories. These cover scenic, historic or scientifically important land, buildings, books, papers or objects.

Note

A transfer to a charity (or other transferee to which the exemption applies) is only exempt if the whole of the property given is to be used exclusively for the purposes of the charity etc: ss.24(3), 25(2), 26(7).

Annual exemption: s.19   2.4.3

The annual exemption of £3,000 only applies to transfers made *inter vivos*. It applies to the first £3,000 of transfers in each tax year. It is available in *addition* to other exemptions (*see* 2.4.7).

To the extent that the annual exemption is not used in a particular year, the unused part may be carried forward to the next tax year but no further. Thus, the exemption from the current year must be used first, and only after the whole exemption has been exhausted can the previous year's unused exemption be used.

Example

Year 1   Tom transfers nothing

Year 2   Tom transfers £5,000

Year 3   Tom transfers £5,600

Tom uses up his £3,000 exemption from year 2 first, and carries forward £2,000 from year 1. However, in year 3, only the £3,000 exemption from that year is available.

2.4.4   Small gifts exemption: s.20

Gifts made by the donor to any one donee are exempt transfers if they do not exceed £250 in any one tax year.

The exemption only applies to outright *inter vivos* gifts, it does not include a transfer to trustees. The exemption does not apply to the first £250 of a gift which exceeds £250; if the figure is exceeded the whole of the gift is chargeable, unless otherwise exempt.

Example

Helen transfers £200 to A, £300 to B and £100 to C. The gifts to A and C are exempt under the small gifts exemption. The gift to B is not exempt under its head but can be set against the 'annual' exemption of £3,000. The gifts to A and C do not use the 'annual' exemption at all.

2.4.5   Normal expenditure out of income: s.21

If gifts are habitually made each year out of income, they are treated as exempt transfers. This exemption can only apply to *inter vivos* transfers.

The following conditions must be satisfied before the exemption applies.

- The gift must be part of the *normal expenditure* of the transferor.

  Normal means typical or habitual. What is normal expenditure is a question of fact but, as a rule of thumb, it involves expenditure occurring for at least three years. Expenditure made under a legal obligation, eg. deed of covenant, or payments made on a life assurance policy, will be treated by the Revenue as normal.

- The gift must be made *out of income* and not capital.

- The transferor must have *sufficient net income* during the year to maintain their usual standard of living after deducting all transfers of value forming part of their normal expenditure. (This is to prevent transferors from giving away all their income every year as normal expenditure, and living off the capital.)

The most common examples for exemption as normal expenditure out of income are payments under deeds of covenant to relatives and premiums on endowment policies on the life of the transferor. In both these cases the first payment made is treated as normal whereas in other cases a retrospective exemption is given once 'normality' is established.

Gifts in consideration of marriage: s.22

2.4.6

The exemption only applies *inter vivos* and is limited to:

- £5,000 from a parent of one of the parties to the marriage;
- £2,500 from a remote ancestor of one of the parties;
- £1,000 in any other case.

Note

The limits apply to each marriage, not to each donee, eg. a mother cannot give £5,000 to her son and £1,000 to her future daughter-in-law and so obtain an exemption of £6,000.

Family maintenance: s.11

2.4.7

Spouses and children

A disposition is exempt, if it is:

- Made by one party to a marriage in favour of the other party and is for the maintenance of the other party; or is
- Made for the maintenance, education or benefit of a child of either party to a marriage. (Exceptionally, where a child is not in the care of its parents, the provision extends to others maintaining the child.)

Note

With regard to the maintenance of a spouse, transfers to a spouse are usually exempt in any case under the spouse exemption (*see* 2.4.1) but the family maintenance provision applies to ex-spouses and to spouses domiciled outside the UK. In the case of ex-spouses exemption does *not* apply while if the transferee is not domiciled in the UK the spouse exemption is limited to £55,000.

Other dependent relatives

Section 11(3) provides that dispositions in favour of dependent relatives other than spouses and children are exempt to the extent that they are 'reasonable provisions for care or maintenance'.

2.4.8 Death on active or other warlike service: s.154

An exemption is available for the whole value of the deceased's estate where the deceased died as a result of active or other warlike service and the deceased was a member of the armed forces or a civilian accompanying armed forces.

2.4.9 Conditional exemption: ss.33–5

A conditional exemption is available on death and on certain *inter vivos* transfers designated by the Treasury as being of national, scientific, historic or artistic interest.

The exemption is conditional on the giving of specified undertakings, eg. an undertaking to preserve the assets, to keep them permanently in the UK, or to make them available for research. If the undertakings are broken, or if there is a disposal and similar undertakings are not given by the transferee, tax becomes payable. Tax will normally become payable, in any event, if the asset is sold.

2.4.10 Cumulative effect of exemptions

Apart from the small gifts exemption (*see* 2.4.4), the exemptions outlined above are cumulative. In addition, after the exemptions have been claimed the transferor is entitled to £150,000 fixed at nil rate (*see* 2.3.1).

Example

In the tax year 1992–93, X who had made no previous gifts, gave £5,000 to his daughter Y on her marriage, £6,000 to his son Z to buy a house and £2,000 to a charity. He died on 23 September 1993. On his death the following exemption from inheritance tax could be claimed:

Annual exemption 1991–92	£3,000
Annual exemption 1992–93	£3,000
Gift in consideration of marriage	£5,000
Gift to charity	£2,000
Nil rate band	£150,000
Total	£163,000

2.4.11 Excluded property

Excluded property comprises:

- Reversionary (ie. future) interests in settled property *unless*:
  - acquired for money or money's worth
  - vested in the settlor or settlor's spouse
  - expectant on a lease for life at a nominal rent: s.48(1);

Example
_____

Property is settled on Peter for life with remainder to Quentin. Quentin's future interest is excluded property, so that if Quentin dies during Peter's life, Quentin's interest in remainder does not form part of his estate (unless one of the two exceptions noted above applies).
_____

- Most types of property situated outside the UK and owned by a person domiciled outside the UK: s.6(1);
- Some types of property situated in the UK but owned by a person not domiciled in the UK: s.6(2);
- Settled property situated outside the UK provided the settlor was domiciled outside the UK at the date the settlement was made: s.6(2).

Reliefs   2.5

Reliefs are available to *reduce* the liability to inheritance tax.

Quick succession relief: s.114   2.5.1

Quick succession relief reduces the amount of tax payable on a deceased person's estate if the deceased received property under a chargeable transfer (*inter vivos* or on death) made to him/her within the five years before s/he died. The relief takes the form of a percentage reduction.

The percentage relief is as follows:

- 100% if the death is within 1 year;
- 80% if more than 1 but not more than 2 years;
- 60% if more than 2 but not more than 3 years;
- 40% if more than 3 years but not more than 4 years;
- 20% if more than 4 years but not more than 5 years.

Example
_____

Mary died leaving £300,000 to her daughter Deborah. Eighteen months later Deborah died leaving her estate worth £500,000 to her friend Ferdinand. Deborah had made no previous lifetime transfers.

		Tax liability (£)
0–150,000	(Nil rate band)	—
150,000–500,000	@ 40%	140,000
Total liability		140,000

QSR = Tax paid on 1st transfer × relevant QSR%

= 40% × £(300,000 – 150,000) = £60,000 × 80% = £48,000 (48,000)

Tax on the deceased's estate =	£92,000

The relief only applies where:

- Tax was paid on the transfer to the deceased; and
- Tax is payable on the deceased's estate.

Note

It is not necessary for the deceased to own the property at the date of death which forms the subject matter of the chargeable transfer.

2.5.2   Agricultural relief: ss.115–24A

The right to agricultural relief applies if the transferor:

- Owned the land ccupied the land for the purpose of agriculture throughout the period of two years ending with the date of transfer; or
- Owned the land throughout the period of seven years ending with the date of transfer and was occupied by the transferor or another for the purposes of agriculture throughout that period: s.117.

Agricultural relief applies whether the transfer of agricultural property is made *inter vivos* or on death.

Rates of relief
In the case of charges to tax arising on or after 10 March 1992 the reduction in value is either 100% or 50%.

100% relief This is generally available where the transferor had the right to vacant possession immediately before the transfer or the right to obtain it within 12 months after transfer: s.116(2).

50% relief This is available on any other qualifying agricultural property.

Example

Immediately before his death, Joe owned a farm which had been let to a tenant farmer for the previous five years. The agricultural value of the farm is £300,000. The value is reduced to £150,000 for IHT purposes.

2.5.3   Business property relief: ss.103–14

As with agricultural relief, business property relief takes effect by means of a percentage reduction in the value transferred. It applies whether the transfer of 'relevant business property' is made *inter vivos* or on death.

What is a business?
The term business includes a profession or vocation, but does not include a business carried on otherwise than for

gain: s.103(3). Neither does it include businesses which consist of dealing in securities, stock and shares, land or buildings or of holding investments: s.105(3). As agriculture is regarded as a type of business, business property relief may be available to the extent that agricultural relief cannot be claimed, eg. on the non-agricultural value of agricultural property.

Qualifying for relief

As a general rule, to qualify the transferor must have owned the relevant business property throughout the two years before the transfer: s.107(1).

Rates of relief

In the case of tax charges arising on or after 10 March 1992 the relief is either 100% or 50%, depending on the category in which the 'relevant business property' falls: Finance (No 2) Act 1992.

100% relief This is available in respect of:

- A business or an interest in a business (this includes the interest of a sole proprietor or of a partner in a business);

- Shares in *unquoted companies* or companies on the Unlisted Securities Market which alone or with other shares owned by the transferor gave the transferor control of the company;

- Shares in *unquoted companies* or companies quoted on the Unlisted Securities Market which alone or with related property, eg. shares owned by the taxpayer's spouse, carry more than 25% of the votes in the company but not more than 50% (*substantial minority shareholdings*).

50% relief This is available in respect of:

- Shares in *quoted companies* which alone or with other shares owned by the transferor or with related property gave the transferor control immediately before the transfer;

- Shares in *unquoted companies* or companies quoted on the Unlisted Securities Market of 25% or less;

- Land or buildings, machinery or plant used immediately before the transfer wholly or mainly for the purposes of a company controlled by the transferor or of a partnership of which the transferor was a member.

Example

Paula has a 20% shareholding in Blocker Ltd (a private company) worth £40,000. The value of the shares in her estate for IHT purposes is reduced to £20,000.

2.5.4   Timber: ss.125–30

Any IHT liability on growing timber on a transfer on death may be *deferred* until the timber is sold either felled or still growing *provided* a claim is made to the Revenue in writing within two years of death.

The deceased must have held beneficial ownership of the relevant woodland for at least five years prior to death or, if the deceased held the woodland for a shorter period, they must have acquired it by gift.

The relief is given simply by excluding the value of the growing timber from the IHT computation at death and so effectively reducing the IHT rate applicable to the rest of the estate.

2.6   Settlements and IHT

To understand the inheritance tax consequences on property comprised in a settlement, it is important to remember that the term 'settlement' has a special meaning for tax purposes (*see* 2.6.1). Next it is important to distinguish between trusts with an interest in possession and those with no interest in possession – the inheritance tax consequences are completely different (*see* 2.6.2).

2.6.1   A settlement for IHT purposes

The definition of a settlement for tax purposes, including inheritance tax, is different from the definition for other purposes. For inheritance tax purposes it is defined by s.43(2) as:

... any disposition or dispositions of property ... whereby the property is for the time being:

(a) held in trust for persons in succession (eg. to Adam for life with remainder to Bill) or for any person subject to a contingency (eg. to Catherine provided she attain 25 years of age); or

(b) held by trustees on trust to accumulate the whole or part of any income of the property or with power to make payments out of that income at the discretion of the trustees or some other person, with or without powers to accumulate surplus income; or

(c) charged or burdened (otherwise than for full consideration ...) with the payment of any annuity or other periodical payment payable for a life or any other limited or determinable period ...

Property is only a settlement for IHT purposes for so long as it is held in one of the ways listed in s.43(2) or (3).

Note _____

There is no settlement for inheritance tax purposes where:

● Co-ownership arises under a statutory trust for sale;

- There is a bare trust, ie. one person is absolutely entitled in equity.

Settlements with an interest in possession

2.6.2

'Interest in possession' is not defined by statute but the basic test of an interest is possession is the *immediate right* to income from, or to use or enjoyment of the property. However, it is clear that normally a life tenant under a settlement has an interest in possession. Conversely, neither beneficiaries under a discretionary trust (as they have no right to any part of the income) nor beneficiaries under an accumulation and maintenance trust (*see* Chapter 5) have an interest in possession.

Charging basis
Section 49(1) provides that:

A person beneficially entitled to an interest in possession in settled property shall be treated ... as beneficially entitled to the property in which the interest subsists.

This means that where a person is entitled to receive the whole income in settled property, s/he is treated as being the owner of the trust asset; where a person is entitled to a part of the income; s/he is treated as being the owner of that part of the trust asset.

> *Example*
>
> Land is held on trust for Judith for life with reminder to XYZ.
>
> As a life tenant Judith is only entitled to the *income* from the land; she has no interest in the capital. However, for IHT purposes Judith is treated as though she is an absolute owner of the land, entitled therefore to both the capital and income.

Chargeable events – settlements with an interest in possession

2.6.3

Creation of the settlement
So long as no exemptions apply if a settlor makes an *inter vivos* transfer of property to a settlement with an interest in possession, the transfer will be a potentially exempt transfer (*see* 2.2). Consequently, no inheritance tax is payable unless the settlor dies within seven years of the transfer.

Conversely, if death does occur within seven years the transfer becomes chargeable at the full rates in force at death but subject to tapering relief (*see* 2.3).

If the settlor creates an *inter vivos* settlement by which the settlor becomes the first life tenant, there will be no charge to tax because the person with an interest in possession is deemed to own the trust assets beneficially (*see* 2.6.2). As the settlor actually owns the property before creation and is deemed to own it beneficially after creation, the value of the settlor's estate has not altered.

If the settlor creates an *inter vivos* settlement and the settlor's spouse is the first life tenant, there will be no charge to tax as the spouse is deemed to own the trust's assets beneficially and the spouse exemption will apply (*see* 2.4.1).

If the settlement with an interest in possession is created on death it will give rise to a charge to tax (unless an exemption applies). The property to be transferred to the trust will be taxed as part of the settlor's death estate before being transferred to the trustees of the settlement.

As with an *inter vivos* settlement, if the spouse exemption applies, no tax will be payable as the surviving spouse is treated as owning the trust assets beneficially because the deceased's surviving spouse becomes the first life tenant.

Liability to IHT after creation

After creation of a settlement with an interest in possession, the following are chargeable events:

- The death of the person with the interest in possession;
- A disposition of the deceased's interest by the person with the interest in possession (whether by gift, sale or surrender).

This is so even though in the case of a sale, the sale is at full value. The reason for this is that the life tenant is treated as beneficially entitled to the trusts assets. However, for the purposes of the sale the interest in possession is actuarially valued and this value will always be less than the value of the settled property itself. Consequently there will be a reduction in the value of the life tenant's estate corresponding to the difference in value between the price paid for the interest in possession and the trust property.

Example

Robert is the life tenant of a fund of £150,000. He sells his life interest to Susan for £45,000 (its full actuarial value). There will be a transfer of value (usually a PET) by which Robert's estate goes down in value to £105,000.

- Any other determining event, eg. where the interest in possession is determinable on the occurrence of a particular event.
- Termination of an interest in possession is taxable as a

disposition of the trust property by the person with an interest in possession. This is because such person is treated as owning the trusts assets beneficially. It therefore follows that the rate of tax payable depends on the cumulative total of the person with an interest in possession and on whether the termination is during that person's lifetime or on death.

Note

Where an interest in possession comes to an end, and the life tenant becomes beneficially entitled to the trust property, there will be no tax to pay. This is because *before* the interest comes to an end the life tenant is deemed to own the trust property beneficially and *after* the interest in possession comes to an end such person actually owns the trust property.

The normal exemptions and reliefs are available on termination of an interest in possession.

Note

The spouse exemption does not apply if the spouse acquired the reversion for money or money's worth.

Advancement of capital

An advancement of capital to a person with an interest in possession does not give rise to IHT liability because such a person is treated as owning the trust property beneficially. However, an advancement to a beneficiary other than the life tenant will give rise to liability as it will either reduce or bring the life tenant's interest in that property to an end.

Example

If property is held on trust for X for life, with remainder to Y, and the trustees make an advancement of capital to Y, tax will be payable on the value of the advancement to Y.

Chargeable events – settlements with no interest in possession

2.6.4

The most common type of settlements with no interest in possession are accumulation and maintenance trusts (*see* Chapter 5) and discretionary trusts.

Note

In the case of a discretionary trust a beneficiary does not have an interest in possession as they do not have a *right* to receive any of the trust property.

You have seen above that where an interest in possession

comes to an end there is generally a charge to tax. The rules for settlements *without* an interest in possession are designed to treat settlements where there is no interest in possession in the same way as settlements with an interest in possession by providing for one full charge to tax every generation.

Creation of the settlement

A transfer to a settlement without an interest in possession is a chargeable transfer by the settlor or testator.

If the transfer is made *inter vivos*, it is a chargeable transfer and inheritance tax is charged initially at half the full rate, but tax will be charged at the full rate, subject to the availability of tapering relief, if the settlor dies within seven years of making the transfer (*see* 2.3.1).

If the settlement is created on *death*, the property is taxed as part of the death estate before being transferred to the trustees of the settlement.

Liability to IHT after creation

Chargeable events after creation fall into one of two categories:

- Periodic charge;
- Exit charge.

Periodic charge Tax is charged on each 10th anniversary of the creation of the settlement throughout the period when there is no interest in possession.

The periodic charge is levied at 30% of the lifetime rate for inheritance tax, ie. 30% of 20% (the lifetime rate).

In calculating the tax payable, the settlor's cumulative total of chargeable lifetime transfers in the seven years prior to the creation of the settlement is the starting point for the settlement's cumulative total.

Exit charge A proportion of the periodic charge may be payable where:

- Property leaves the settlement during a 10 year period, eg. because the beneficiary satisfies a contingency during the period and so becomes entitled to the capital or because the trustees exercise their discretion to distribute capital; and
- Someone acquires an interest in possession in the settled property.

Self-assessment questions

1 Distinguish between a chargeable transfer made before

death and a potentially exempt transfer.

2   X makes a potentially exempt transfer to Y of £200,000. X has made no previous chargeable transfers. X dies between four and five years after making the transfer to Y. Explain the IHT consequences, if any, of the gift to Y.

3   X makes a chargeable transfer to a settlement with no interest in possession of £300,000. X has made no previous chargeable transfers. Four years later X makes a potentially exempt transfer to Y of £50,000 and dies within a year. Explain the IHT consequences, if any, of the above transfers.

4   Which exemptions and reliefs do not apply to transfers on death?

5   In the tax year 1991–92, X (who had made no previous chargeable transfers) made a chargeable transfer to a settlement with no interest in possession of £100,000 and gave £5,000 each to his son and daughter on their respective marriages. In the same tax year he gave £10,000 to his nephew as a deposit on a house and £4,000 to Cancer Research.

In the tax year 1992–93 X gave £3,000 each to his son and daughter and £5,000 to his wife. He also made a chargeable transfer to a settlement with no interest in possession of £80,000.

X died on 25 December 1993.

Explain the IHT consequences, if any, of the above lifetime transfers and their effect, if any, on X's death estate.

6   Compare the occurrence of chargeable events for settlements with an interest in possession with settlements with no interest in possession.

Answer guidance to self-assessment questions

1   *See* 2.2.2.

2   Where a transfer of value is a potentially exempt transfer, no tax is payable at the time of the transfer but if, as in this case, the transferor dies within seven years the transfer becomes chargeable at the rates of tax in force at death. However, as the transferor has survived for between four and five years, tapering relief of 60% of the full rate in force at the date of death is available.

The transfer made to Y, together with any subsequent potentially exempted transfer, will be cumulated with his death estate and the first £150,000 taxed at 0% (nil rate band)

and thereafter at 40% (subject to the tapering relief).

3   A transfer to any type of settlement is a transfer of value by the settlor. A transfer to a settlement without an interest in possession is a chargeable transfer.

Inheritance tax is charged initially at half the full rate but as the settlor has died within seven years, tax will be charged at the full rate subject, in this case, to tapering relief of 60% (four–five years).

The potentially exempt transfer to Y is not taxable at the time of the transfer but becomes chargeable at the full rate of tax in force at X's death because X dies within a year of the transfer.

The lifetime transfer into the settlement, along with the PET to Y, have to be cumulated with X's death estate.

4   *See* 2.4 and 2.5.

5   A transfer to a settlement without an interest in possession is a chargeable transfer. The transfer made into such settlements in the tax years 1991–92 and 1992–93 are therefore initially chargeable at half the full rate. However, as the death of X is within three years, they will become chargeable at the full rate in force at X's death and no tapering relief is available.

Other transfers made in 1991–92

- £5,000 to son and daughter on respective marriages – both transfers are exempt (*see* 2.4.6);
- £10,000 to nephew – £6,000 exempt (1990–91 annual exemption + 1991–92 annual exemption). Remaining £4,000 is taxable at a PET.
- £4,000 to Cancer Research – charities exemption applies (*see* 2.4.2).

Other transfers made 1992–93

- £5,000 to wife – spouse exemption (*see* 2.4.1);
- £3,000 to son or daughter – annual exemption but remaining £3,000 taxable as a PET.

Consequences on death

The transfers to the settlement(s) with no interest in possession together with PETS. £4,000 (1991–92) and £3,000 (1992–93) will need to be cumulated with X's death estate.

6   *See* 2.6.3 and 2.6.4.

Chapter 3

Taking instructions for wills

Introduction 3.1

In order to prepare a will for a client, you will usually find it necessary to interview him/her; this enables you to obtain, in as short a time as possible, all the information you need to draft the will.

When taking instructions your role is not simply to record the client's instructions. In some cases a client will come to you with very specific ideas, in others more vague ideas, as to how they wish to dispose of their property by will. However, the client may not be aware of all or any of the legal considerations which affect their plans. If they were aware of the legal implications, they might wish to change their plans. For example, they may be unaware of the disastrous inheritance tax implications of their plans, or may be unaware that their proposal to exclude a close relative may lead to a claim against their estate under the Inheritance (Provision for Family and Dependants) Act 1975 (see 3.6).

The purpose of this chapter is to make you aware of the information that you will need from a client in order to be able to advise on the best way of drafting the will to give effect to the client's wishes, taking into account any legal implications of those wishes.

To ensure that accurate details of the client's property and intended beneficiaries are established at the interview in as short a period of time as is possible, it may be appropriate to ask the client to bring to the interview written details of their property and intended beneficiaries of their will.

Prior to the interview, you should prepare/use a 'checklist' for taking instructions; this will ensure that none of the information required is overlooked. In some firms the checklist takes the form of a questionnaire which can be used by some other person in the firm to draft the required will. The paragraphs of this chapter provide details of the preliminary considerations you would expect to find on the checklist.

Existing will(s) and codicil(s) 3.2

For two reasons it is important to ask the client whether they have already executed a will and any codicil(s) to the will.

- If the client does not intend substantial changes you may be able to use a (further) codicil to give effect to their wishes.
- In a professionally drawn will, although it is standard practice to include a revocation clause, revoking any earlier will or codicil, it is advisable to ascertain whether any existing will has already been revoked. If a will does not contain a revocation clause, an earlier will is admissible to probate in so far as it is not inconsistent with the later will (*see* Chapter 6, para. 6.7.1).

If the client is married, you should enquire whether their spouse has made a will already and, if not, point out that it is advisable for spouses to make wills at the same time, so that thought can be given to the ultimate destination of their respective estates and to minimising the burden of inheritance tax.

3.3   Nature and composition of the testator's estate

You must form an idea of both the nature and composition of the testator's estate in order to advise on the best way to dispose of property in preparation for death. For example, an idea of the size of the estate is necessary to advise the testator of ways to most effectively avoid the burden of inheritance tax (*see* further 3.5).

You must also consider the type of property which comprises the estate in order to assess the availability of inheritance tax relief (*see* Chapter 2, para. 3.4). The size and nature of the estate are also important factors in assessing the likelihood of successful claims under the Inheritance (Provision for Family and Dependants) Act 1975 (*see* further 3.6).

3.4   Dispositions of property on death without a will

You must explain to clients that there are methods other than the execution of a will for disposing of property on death. It is also important that the client understands that certain types of property will not form part of their estate on death, eg. joint property, so that they are aware of the extent of the property that they have to dispose of by will. Particularly important are:

- Property held as a joint tenant;
- Insurance policies;
- Nominations; and
- *Donatio mortis causa.*

Property held as a joint tenant 3.4.1

Where a person is a beneficial *joint tenant* of any property, whether real or personal, their interest will automatically pass to the surviving joint tenant(s) on their death under the rule of survivorship.

If the joint tenancy has been *severed during the lifetime* of the testator, however, the property is held as *tenants in common*, and the deceased's share can pass under their will.

You should ascertain what property is held by the client as a joint tenant, and it may be appropriate in some circumstances to advise the client to sever a joint tenancy *inter vivos*.

Insurance policies 3.4.2

On the death of the life assured, the insurance company will pay the sum assured to the deceased's personal representatives. This will then form part of the deceased's estate and will be discounted by the personal representatives in accordance with the terms of the deceased's will or the rules of intestacy. However, by making use of s.11, Married Woman's Property Act 1882, or by *expressly* assigning or writing a policy in trust for a person, the assured can ensure that the proceeds of the insurance policy are paid *directly to the intended beneficiary*.

This may be desirable for two reasons. First, if the assured sum is to be paid to the deceased's personal representatives, they will not be able to get access to the money until they have a grant of representation. This is because the insurance company will not pay over the assured sum to the personal representatives until they have proof of their title by the production of a grant of representation (*see* Chapter 8, para. 8.3.3). From the practical point of view, as the beneficiary of the insurance policy is likely to be a close relative of the deceased, eg. spouse, the delay in receiving the assured sum may cause serious financial problems for the beneficiary, especially as inheritance tax due on the estate of the deceased has to be paid before a grant of probate can be obtained (*See* Chapter 9, para. 10.1.4).

Second, it may be desirable because if the assured sum is payable to the deceased's personal representatives it will form part of the death estate and will potentially attract inheritance tax. It may well be, however, that the estate of the deceased is so small that the assured sum falls within the nil rate band or that an exemption applies, eg. the beneficiary of the policy is the deceased's spouse. In these circumstances inheritance tax is not a consideration. However, if the beneficiaries of the policy are the deceased's children the position may be different.

Section 11 policies

Under s.11, Married Women's Property Act 1882, the assured may expressly provide that their policy be fore the benefit of their spouse and/or children (which includes children of a relationship outside marriage). The effect of this is to create a *trust* in favour of the spouse and/or children on the death of the assured under which the proceeds of the insurance policy are payable directly to the trustees of the policy for the benefit of the named beneficiary/beneficiaries.

If the assured wishes to benefit someone other that their spouse or children, the same effect as a s.11 policy is achieved if the policy is expressly written in trust for them or expressly assigned to them.

From the inheritance tax point of view, as the deceased had no beneficial interest in the assured sum, it cannot be taxed as part of the deceased's estate. However, when a testator pays premiums on such a policy, they are making lifetime gifts to beneficiaries – but such payments will probably be exempt as part of normal expenditure out of income (*see* Chapter 2, para. 2.4.5).

From the practical point of view, as the proceeds are payable by the trustees of the policy directly to the beneficiaries, the assured sum can be paid over immediately after the assured's death without need for a grant of representation. This can provide a useful fund for payment of the inheritance tax which is due before a grant of representation can be obtained. Without a grant of probate to prove their title, the personal representatives may not have access to assets of the deceased's estate to raise the money to pay the tax in order to obtain the grant of probate to administer the estate.

Note the following points about use of s.11.

- Before the proceeds can be applied for the payment of IHT, the consent of the beneficiaries is required.

Note

Remember that the beneficiary under the trust, eg. a spouse, may not be the person who bears the burden of IHT.

- So long as the trustees of the policy hold on trust for the beneficiary absolutely (and not subject to any contingency), the beneficiary takes an *immediate interest* in the policy. Consequently, if the beneficiary predeceases the assured, the beneficiary's estate will be liable to tax on the value (or appropriate portion of the value) of the policy.

- Where the beneficiary has an immediate absolute interest in the policy, the assured is no longer free to *assign or surrender* the policy.
- Where the beneficiaries of a s.11 policy are the assured's children it may be advisable to appoint trustees to hold the money until the children reach majority or other suitable age. If no such trustees are appointed the deceased's personal representatives will hold the proceeds of the policy on trust for the deceased's children. This would not have an adverse effect from the inheritance tax point of view as the proceeds of the policy still do not form part of the deceased's estate.

Nominations 3.4.3

A nomination is a direction by an individual (the nominator) to the person holding investments on their behalf to pay the funds to a nominated person (the nominee) on the nominator's death. The direction is made by the nominator during their lifetime but, like a will, the gift only takes effect on death.

A nomination differs from a *gift* by will in that the funds which form the subject matter of a nomination do not form part of the nominator's estate on death (except for inheritance tax purposes, in the case of a statutory nomination (*see* below)) and therefore do not vest in the nominator's personal representative but pass directly to the nominee. As a consequence, the payer will not require a grant of representation before paying the funds to the nominee but the payer will want to see the nominator's death certificate.

In contrast to a beneficiary under a s.11 policy, the nominee does not have an interest in the funds until the death of the nominator who may deal freely with the property during their lifetime.

Note

Although a minor cannot make a will (except a privileged will), a minor of 16 years or over can make a nomination.

A nomination is revoked by:

- The subsequent marriage of the nominator;
- A later nomination; or
- The death of the nominee prior to the death of the nominator.

Note

A nomination is *not* revoked by a subsequent will. For this reason you should ascertain whether the client has made any nominations when taking instructions.

Nominations either operate:

- By statute; or
- In connection with discretionary pension schemes.

Statutory nominations
The following deposits may form the subject matter of a statutory nomination up to a limit of £5,000 each: ss.2 and 6, Administration of Estates (Small Payments) Act 1965; and Administration of Estates (Small Payments), Increase of Limit Order 1984 No 539 para. 2:

- Trustee savings banks;
- Friendly societies; and
- Industrial and provident societies

Note

Until May 1979 it was also possible to make nominations up to an unlimited amount in respect of trustee savings bank deposits and until 1 May 1987 in respect of national savings certificates and National Savings Bank deposits. Nominations made before these dates remain valid.

A statutory nomination must be made in writing and attested by one witness.

Discretionary pension schemes
Discretionary pension schemes may allow the contributor to nominate a third party to receive benefits after the former's death in the form of either a *lump sum* or as a *pension*.

Such nominations are different from statutory nominations in that the nomination is *not binding* on the trustees of the pension fund but merely an indication of the deceased's wishes.

As with a statutory nomination, funds paid by the trustees of a pension fund to a third party do not form part of the deceased's estate as they are paid by the trustees to the nominee directly. Neither are they treated as part of the deceased's estate for inheritance tax purposes as the deceased has no absolute right to the funds.

Note

To maximise the tax advantages, the contributor may have to

request that the benefits are paid to a non-exempt beneficiary for IHT purposes, eg. children rather than spouse.

Donatio mortis causa   3.4.4

Meaning

A *donatio mortis causa* is a gift made by a person during their lifetime which is conditional upon their death.

The property is delivered by the donor to the donee during the donor's lifetime and once the condition of dying has been satisfied, the gift takes place retroactively from the date of the gift. Thus, it cannot be revoked by a subsequent will.

As a *donatio mortis causa* is *not* a testamentary gift, the subject matter does not form part of the deceased's estate on death (except for inheritance tax purposes). However, if the estate proves insufficient to pay the deceased's debts, the subject matter of a *donatio mortis causa* may be used.

Conditions

The onus lies on the *donee* to establish that *all* four of the following conditions have been satisfied:

1   The gift was made *in contemplation of the donor's death.* The death need not be imminent but the donor must believe that they are dying or likely to die in some specific way, eg. serious illness, dangerous expedition. It is irrelevant that the donor dies from some cause other than the one within their contemplation, *unless* the gift is made conditional on death from a *specific cause.*

Example

In *Wilkes v Allington* (1931) a valid *donatio mortis causa* was made where the donor made a gift knowing that he was suffering from cancer but not knowing exactly how long he had to live. A month after making the gift he died of pneumonia.

2   The gift must be *conditional upon death.* If the donor does not die, the gift will not take effect and the donor will be entitled to recover possession of the property.

3   The subject matter of the gift *must be delivered to the donee.* The donor must have handed over the subject matter to the donee (or an agent of the donee) or the means of control to it, eg. keys.

In the case of choses in action, there must be delivery of the evidence of title to the chose in action.

Example

Handing over a post office savings book, national savings

certificates and a cheque payable to the donor (not a cheque drawn by the donor, *see* below) have all been held to create a valid *donatio mortis causa*.

If the donor at a later date resumes possession of the property, the *donatio mortis causa* is revoked.

4   The subject matter must be capable of forming a valid *donatio mortis causa*. In *Sen v Headley* (1991) the Court of Appeal held that land is capable of passing by *donatio mortis causa*.

Doubtful cases

Some forms of personal property are possibly not capable of passing by *donatio mortis causa*. There is doubt whether shares can pass in this way and it is clear that a cheque drawn by the donor cannot pass by means of a *donatio mortis causa* as it is merely an order to the donor's bank to pay which is automatically revoked by the donor's death: *Re Beaumont* (1902).

3.5   Tax considerations

Before drafting a will for a client you should:

1   Ascertain the *size of the client's estate* to decide whether it is large enough to make tax-planning *inter vivos*.

2   Obtain information from the client about *inter vivos* gifts to estimate the *testator's cumulative total of transfers* in order to calculate the inheritance tax effects on the client's death estate.

3   In the light of the information obtained in stages 1 and 2, consider *financial planning* with regard to the will itself.

> *Example*
>
> Where a client is married and has children, but expresses a wish to leave all their estate to their surviving spouse, it may be appropriate to suggest making use of the nil rate band (if not already used) to make legacies to the children who (in contrast to the spouse) would be non-exempt beneficiaries. (The various tax planning options in the drafting of wills in the family cases are considered in more detail in 3.9.)

4   In the light of the information obtained in stages 1 and 2, consider *inter vivos* tax planning and suggest to the client that some *inter vivos* gifts are made rather than leaving all gifts to be made on death.

> *Note*
>
> This is usually only viable where the client is fairly wealthy and can afford to dispose of property before their death.

Inter vivos tax planning   3.5.1

If *inter vivos* tax planning is worthwhile, you must ensure that the client has no need of the property or no wish to keep the property to be given away.

Potential inheritance tax savings

An *inter vivos* gift can be potentially beneficial in the following ways:

1   An *inter vivos* gift (unless a chargeable transfer) will be a *potentially exempt transfer*. Thus, provided the donor survives *seven years* after the date of the gift, no inheritance tax will be payable. Even if the donor does die within seven years, tapering relief may be available.

However, you must weigh up whether the inheritance tax saving is outweighed by any *capital gains tax considerations*. Capital gains tax is not paid on death but may be payable on an *inter vivos* gift where no exemption or relief applies. You must therefore consider whether the annual exemption can be used, or whether spouse relief, retirement relief, hold-over relief and indexation allowance can be relied upon to reduce or cancel out liability.

2   An *inter vivos* gift may be advantageous where the assets transferred are likely to *increase in value in the short term*. This is because the inheritance tax payable on death is calculated on the value of the property *at the time the gift was made*. Thus, even though the transferor may die within seven years and tax therefore becomes payable on the potentially exempt transfer, and even though no tapering relief is available, the liability will be less.

3   It may be possible to take advantage of *exemptions* available only on *inter vivos* gifts, eg. the annual exemption, the small gifts exemption and gifts made in consideration of marriage (*see* Chapter 2, para. 2.4).

4   Where one party to a marriage owns substantially more property than the other party, it may be beneficial for that party to make *inter vivos* gifts to the other.

This potential benefit only applies where the parties are sufficiently wealthy that, first, they are able to make *inter vivos* gifts to the other and, second, by doing so it will mean that the surviving spouse need not be left the whole of the deceased spouse's estate. Because of the existence of the nil rate band, one large estate attracts greater liability to inheritance tax than two small estates. Thus, if spouses equalise their estates and each spouse leaves their respective estates to their children, advantage can be taken of two nil rate bands.

Example

H has an estate of £360,000 and W an estate of £40,000. Assuming that neither H or W have made any chargeable transfers *inter vivos* or potentially exempt transfers within seven years of death, and W survives H who leaves all his estate to W, the inheritance tax liability is as follows.

- On the death of H no inheritance tax is payable because of the spouse exemption.

- On the death of W the cumulative estates of H and W amount to £400,000, the first £150,000 is taxed at 0%, but the remaining £250,000 is taxed at 40% giving a liability of £100,000.

If H and W were to equalise their estates by H making *inter vivos* transfers to W, so that each estate comprised £200,000 and they were to leave their respective estates to their children (assuming, again, nil lifetime cumulative totals) the position would be as follows.

- On the death of H £150,000 would be taxed at 0% and the remaining £50,000 at 40% giving a liability of £20,000.

- On the death of W the position would be the same as for H, and the liability £20,000.

- The total liability of the joint estates would then be £40,000 compared with £100,000 had the estates not been equalised.

Business property

A gift of a business or an interest in a business is eligible for business relief for inheritance tax purposes. However, *inter vivos* planning can reduce the inheritance tax liability still further. The following are common ways in which this can be done.

1 *Partnerships*

- A provision for *automatic accrual of goodwill in a partnership agreement.*

   Such an agreement means that when a partner dies their interest in the goodwill of the business automatically passes to the surviving partners and so reduces the value of the deceased partner's interest. To the extent that consideration in money or money's worth was given for the accrual clause, the agreement for automatic accrual will not be regarded as a transfer of value for inheritance tax purposes.

- An alternative is for the partnership agreement to provide for an *option to purchase the goodwill of the deceased partner at a fixed price.*

The value of the goodwill to the partner on death is then the price that their estate is paid on the exercise of the option.

Note

An agreement that a partner's share in the goodwill must be purchased by the surviving partners on their death is not desirable as the Inland Revenue takes the view that such a contract of sale may disentitle the deceased's partner to business property relief.

2   *Companies*

- When a company is formed *pre-emption rights* can be provided whereby if a shareholder disposes of their shares or dies owning shares, the other shareholders have a right to buy at a fixed price or a price fixed in accordance with the articles of the company.

  Such a pre-emption right would operate for inheritance tax purposes in the same way as an option to purchase the goodwill in the case of a partnership.

Inheritance (Provision for Family and Dependants) Act 1975   3.6

As a general rule a person may give their property on death to the person(s) of their choice. Although the Inheritance (Provision for Family and Dependants) Act 1975 (I(PFD)A) does not alter this principle, it does allow certain categories of person to make a claim against the estate of a deceased where they can establish that the deceased's will or the rules of intestacy, or a combination of both, do not make 'reasonable financial provision' for them (*see* further Chapter 14).

You must therefore get a picture of the testator's family and mention the I(PFD)A to ascertain whether there may be possible claimants. If you then believe that a claim under the I(PFD)A may be a possibility, you should point out the possible effects of the Act (*see* Chapter 14).

It may be appropriate for you to suggest that the client should avoid a potential claim against their estate by a particular person by making a lifetime gift(s) and/or a suitably sized gift by will. If the client decides to act on this suggestion, details of the particular form of provision made should be recorded by the client in order to provide evidence of the client's belief that they have made 'reasonable financial provision' for the potential claimant.

If the client does not wish to make provision for a potential I(PFD)A applicant, they should be encouraged to write a letter to their executor explaining their motives. This letter should then be signed by the client and kept with their will. If a claim is then brought under the I(PFD)A at the client's death, the statement is admissible evidence to the court in considering the applicant's claim under the Act.

Note

1   It is inadvisable to explain the motives for not making provision in the client's will itself as a will is a public document and as such is available for public inspection. (The client may not wish their motives to be read by persons generally.)

2   You should make a file note of any advice given to the client with regard to possible claims under the I(PFD)A as this is also admissible evidence if claim is made.

3.7 Choice of executors and trustees

You should explain the various options open to your client in the choice of executors and assist them in making a suitable appointment (*see* further Chapter 4, paras. 4.3.2–3).

3.8 Making gifts by will

You should determine the client's priorities as between particular beneficiaries and advise accordingly on the type of gift which should be made (*see* further Chapter 4, paras. 4.5–5).

You should also ascertain whether the client's aim is to give a particular item of property to a given beneficiary (in which case a specific gift will be appropriate), or whether they wish a given beneficiary to have a certain measure of financial advantage (where a pecuniary legacy may be appropriate) (*see* further Chapter 4, para. 4.5.1).

Note

1   It is important to obtain precise details of:

●   The property forming the subject matter of the gift; and

●   Names and addresses of the beneficiaries.

2   The Law Society rules about gifts to solicitors etc and the need for independent advice where the gift is of a significant amount must be followed (*see* further Chapter 1, para. 1.4.2).

3.9 Possible dispositions in family cases

Where the client is married and has children, you must ascertain the client's priorities as between spouse, children and any other intended beneficiaries. You may then have to advise on the suitability of the proposals bearing in mind the likely size of the client's estate at death, the intended beneficiaries own resources, and inheritance tax implications.

You have already read (*see* 3.2) that you will need information about the estate of the client's spouse and that if the spouse has not already executed a will you should advise the client to persuade their spouse to do so. The client's own will should then take into account the provision for beneficiaries made by their spouse's will and you should consider the effects on the client's will of each spouse dying first and of the possibility of a common accident in drafting the client's will (*see* Chapter 4, para. 4.10 and Chapter 13, para. 13.1.3).

The rest of this section considers the most common types of dispositions in the will of a married person and reflects the different priorities as between spouse and children, and when their use is appropriate. The types of disposition explained are not necessarily mutually exclusive, in that, say, 50% of an estate may be disposed of by way of absolute gift to the surviving spouse, with the remaining 50% giving the spouse only a life interest with remainder to the children. (The drafting of dispositions is considered in Chapter 4.)

Absolute gift to spouse with substitutional gift to children should the gift to the spouse fail

3.9.1

If a will leaves everything to the testator's spouse, this will ensure that the surviving spouse is provided for to the fullest extent possible. However, the client should decide whether they have to provide for their surviving spouse to this extent bearing in mind the following two potential disadvantages.

1 *Loss of control* If the client makes an absolute gift to their spouse and the spouse survives, the client has lost control over the ultimate destination of the property and must hope that their spouse makes appropriate provision for their children or other intended beneficiaries. If the surviving spouse remarries, there is a danger that they may execute a new will with altered priorities, or alternatively, fail to realise that their will has automatically been revoked by marriage (*see* Chapter 6, para. 6.7.2).

You should point out the possibility to the client that their spouse may only survive them by a very short period as they might die as a result of a common accident. In such circumstances the client may wish to ensure that their property passes under the terms of their own will, and not their spouse's. You can achieve this by means of a *survivorship clause* which makes the gift conditional upon the spouse surviving a specified period, eg. 28 days, (*see* Chapter 4, para. 4.10).

2 *Inheritance tax* If a will leaves the testator's entire estate to their spouse, no inheritance tax will be payable on the death of the first spouse as the spouse exemption will apply (*see* Chapter 2, para. 2.3.1). However, if the estate is large enough, inheritance tax will be payable on the death of the surviving spouse. Because it will only be possible to take advantage of one nil rate band and because the surviving spouse's estate is likely to be swollen by the property inherited from the first spouse, the amount of inheritance tax payable is likely to be greater, ie. bunching will potentially occur (*see* further 3.5.1). You can mitigate this problem, however, by *inter vivos* tax planning – the surviving spouse may make *inter vivos* gifts taking into account the various lifetime exemptions.

Note

Where an absolute gift is made to a surviving spouse, there should be a substitutional gift to the children in the event of the primary gift failing (*see* Chapter 4, para. 4.9).

3.9.2 Legacies to children, residue to spouse

The feasibility of giving legacies to children with the residue to the spouse will depend upon the independent financial resources of the surviving spouse. The residue of the estate after the payment of legacies to the children must be sufficient to provide for the surviving spouse bearing in mind the spouse's own assets.

If the surviving spouse has limited wealth, it may be appropriate only to make legacies to children sufficient to exhaust the nil rate band in force from time to time, to take advantage of two nil rate bands. (For the drafting of such a clause *see* Chapter 4, para. 4.5.4.)

The advantages of this type of disposition are that it enables immediate provision to be made for children and if the extent of the legacies to the children does not exceed the nil rate band no inheritance tax liability will arise on the death of the first spouse.

3.9.3 Life interest to spouse, remainder to children

Where a testator only gives a life interest to their surviving spouse, the testator retains control over the ultimate destination of their property. However, as the surviving spouse will only be entitled to the income from the estate, you must consider whether, in the light of the surviving spouse's own independent property, this makes sufficient provision. To a certain extent, any possible problems can be mitigated by including powers for the trustees to make advances of capital and/or loans to the surviving spouse (*see* Chapter 4, para. 4.11.4).

Where a gift of a life interest only to the spouse may create problems for this spouse's continued occupation of the matrimonial home (where the surviving spouse is not a joint tenant who takes by survivorship), consider the following three alternatives:

- Make a *specific gift of the matrimonial home* to the surviving spouse and leave the rest of the estate to the spouse for life with remainder to children; or

- Give the surviving spouse a *right of residence in the matrimonial home*; (For drafting and the precise effect see Chapter 4, para. 4.6.)

- *Include the matrimonial home in the successive interest trust*, but require the trustees for sale to obtain the consent of the spouse before selling or simply express the wish that the trustees shall not sell so long as the spouse wishes to remain in occupation.

The inheritance tax consequences of a successive interest trust are broadly the same as for an absolute gift to a spouse as the surviving spouse has, for tax purposes, an interest in possession in the whole of the settled property and the spouse exemption therefore applies.

Legacy to spouse, residue to children   3.9.4

It is only appropriate to leave the residue to the children and simply a legacy to the surviving spouse if the surviving spouse is wealthy in their own right – even then caution is needed. The legacy may become inadequate due to inflation and/or changes in circumstances.

Although the spouse exemption is lost except to the extent of the legacy, in the long term there may be inheritance tax savings through the effects of equalising estates (*see* 3.5.1).

Giving effect to instructions   3.10

You will be in breach of your professional duty, if after taking instructions for a will, you fail to carry out those instructions without delay. You will be liable in damages to compensate the intended beneficiaries: *White v Jones* (1993).

3.11   The need to review a will

You should advise the client that their will may need reviewing if there are significant changes in tax law or where the client's personal circumstances change, eg. they are divorced.

Self-assessment questions

1 Why might it be important to know whether a client or their spouse has already executed a will?

2 What are the potential advantages of a s.11, Married Woman's Property Act 1882 policy?

3 What are the potential advantages of a statutory nomination and why is it important to know whether a client has made any statutory nominations before drafting the client's will?

4 In 1990, at a time when Joan knew that she was seriously ill with cancer, she handed over some valuable paintings to her son Robert saying 'When I die these will be yours'. Robert immediately hung the paintings in his house. Joan died in September 1993, having executed a will a month before in which she left the paintings to an art gallery.

   Advise Robert.

5 What is the potential advantage of spouses equalising their estates?

6 Why may it be advantageous for inheritance tax purposes to make *inter vivos* gifts rather than gifts on death?

7 Explain in broad terms the inheritance tax position on the death of:

   (a) The testator; and

   (b) The testator's surviving spouse, where the testator leaves:

   (i) his estate to his surviving spouse absolutely;

   (ii) the residue of the estate to his surviving spouse absolutely, with legacies to his children;

   (iii) a life interest to his spouse with remainder to his children;

   (iv) a legacy to his surviving spouse and the residue to his children.

   In what circumstances may each of these arrangements be disadvantageous?

Answer guidance to self-assessment questions

1 *See* 3.2.

2 *See* 3.4.2.

3 *See* 3.4.3

4 *See* 3.4.4. Provided that Joan did not recover from cancer between 1990 and her death in 1993, this would appear to be a valid *donatio mortis causa*. Once Joan dies the gift takes effect retroactively from the date of the gift, ie. in 1990. Consequently, the subsequent execution of the will leaving the paintings to the art gallery is of no effect.

5 *See* 3.5.1, point 3.

6 *See* 3.5.1, points 1–3.

7 *See* 3.7.

Chapter 4

Planning and drafting a will

Introduction

Chapter 3 was concerned with the need for you to establish a general picture of:

- The extent of the client's property;
- The value of the estate to be disposed of by will;
- Any tax planning considerations; and
- Any persons for whom the client may need to provide by will.

This chapter is concerned with the planning and drafting of the individual terms of the will. In drafting a will, you will normally rely upon precedents which, in most cases, have to be adapted to fit the particular needs and wishes of the testator. It is not the intention of this chapter to provide you with a set of precedents, but you will have access to precedents during your course and the drafting exercises you will undertake are intended to familiarise you with the use of precedents,

The aims of the chapter are to:

- Provide a full explanation of the *background to the wording* of the precedents commonly used in the drafting of wills; and
- Explain the detailed information which, on the one hand, you need to obtain from the client and, on the other, you may need to give to the client in order to draft a will effecting the client's wishes.

Your aims

In drafting a will, you must aim to:

- Produce a *valid will*;
- *Effectively dispose of all the property* owned by the testator at the date of their death which is capable of passing by will;
- *Provide expressly for all foreseeable events* which may arise after execution of the will, eg. birth of more children, beneficiaries predeceasing the testator, divorce etc.

Note _____

Where a will does not expressly provide for what is to happen in given circumstances, the law will determine the consequences in most cases. Although the law may provide for what the client intended, you must *always* expressly specify the position to ensure the testator fully understands it.

4.2 Conventions

4.2.1 Structure

A will is usually structured as follows:

1 Words of commencement (including date if not at the end of the will).

2 Revocation clause (this may be part of the words of commencement).

3 Disposal of body.

4 Appointment of executors (and trustees).

5 Appointment of guardians (if appropriate).

6 Specific gifts (if any).

7 General legacies (if any).

8 Residuary gift.

9 Extension of powers of executors and trustees (as appropriate).

10 Attestation clause.

11 Date (if not in the words of commencement).

4.2.2 Essential clauses

A will need not necessarily contain all the clauses outlined above but it must always contain:

● Words of commencement;

● A revocation clause;

● A clause appointing executors;

● A clause(s) setting down the gifts to be made;

● An attestation clause; and

● The date.

Note

The purpose and content of a *revocation clause* and an *attestation clause* are discussed in Chapter 6. The remainder of the clauses are discussed below.

4.2.3 Punctuation, capital letters, numbering and figures

Traditionally wills have been drafted without punctuation. This practise is still often followed and is intended to avoid possible ambiguity in construing a will. An alternative view is that punctuation makes a will easier to read and understand and on this basis should be included.

You should set out important words and phrases in capital letters, eg. names of the testator, executors and beneficiaries, as this facilitates the reading of the will. It is, however, a matter of personal style as to whether any words, and if so which, are capitalised.

There is general agreement that the clauses of a will should be numbered to make it easier to read and refer to.

Where a specified sum of money is given to a particular beneficiary, the sum paid must be put in words *and* numbers to avoid ambiguity.

Specimen clause

I GIVE five hundred pounds (£500) to my niece Sarah Jane Bell.

Identifying the beneficiaries   4.2.4

The beneficiaries must be identified fully and accurately or the gift may fail for uncertainty (*see* Chapter 13, para.13.1.6). The full name and address of the beneficiaries must be given or, if the beneficiary is a relative, their relationship followed by their name must be included, eg. 'my daughter, Elizabeth Mary Stott'. (For class gifts *see* 4.7.2.)

Words of commencement   4.2.5

The words of commencement are included to clearly identify the testator. They may include the date the will is executed, although this often appears after the attestation clause. They may also include words revoking any earlier will or codicil (*see* Chapter 6, para. 6.7).

The testator's full name and address must be stated and, if you wish, the testator's occupation. Traditionally non-working women were described by reference to their marital status, eg. spinster. This practise should no longer be followed as it serves no real purpose and may cause offence.

If a testator holds property in a name different from their full name or generally uses a name which is not their true and proper name, you must refer to this in the words of commencement, eg. 'sometimes known as ...'.

The words 'last will and testament' or reference to 'will' are included to indicate that the testator understands the nature of the document.

Specimen clauses

1 This is the last will and testament of me (full name of testator) of (current address of testator).

2 This will dated (X) day of (month) (year) is made by me (full name of testator) of (current address of testator).

4.2.6   Disposal of the body

A will need not refer to the method for disposing of the testator's body but some testators are concerned about the precise method or wish their body to be donated in whole or in part to medical education, research or for the treatment of patients.

Provisions concerning the disposal of the testator's body do *not* have a legally binding effect on the executors; they only have the status of a *request* to the executors to comply with the testator's wishes.

Note

Requests as to the method of disposal may be set out in a separate non-testamentary document.

Where a testator wishes to donate their body (or part of it) to medical education, research or the treatment of patients, certain forms have to be completed before the request can be complied with. These forms should be kept with the will to enable the formalities to be quickly dispensed with after the testator's death.

Specimen clauses

I desire that my body shall be (shall not be) cremated (and my ashes deposited at ...).

I request that my body or any part may be used for therapeutic purposes including corneal grafting and organ transplantation or for the purpose of medical education or research in accordance with the provisions of the Human Tissue Act 1961 and the Anatomy Act 1984 and in due course the institution receiving it should have it cremated.

4.3   Appointment of executors and trustees

4.3.1   General points

Express and implied appointment

A will must *expressly appoint* executor(s), otherwise the court will appoint administrators and the choice of administrator will be governed by Rule 22, Non-Contentious Probate Rules 1987 (*see* Chapter 8, para. 8.6). This may not coincide with the choice of the testator. Moreover, the administration of the estate may be delayed because an administrator's authority dates only from a grant of representation whereas the executor's authority dates from the death of the testator (*see* Chapter 8, paras. 8.5.3 and 8.6.3).

An executor may be *impliedly appointed* in which case

they are known as *an executor according to the tenor of the will*.

An executor is impliedly appointed where the will shows an intention that a particular person should perform the functions of an executor although it does not actually describe the person as an executor, eg. if the will instructs the person to pay the debts of the estate, as this is an important function of an executor.

Note

It is undesirable to impliedly appoint an executor as it may be open to interpretation whether the words show an intention that the person is to perform the functions of an executor.

Specialists

A will may appoint different executors to deal with different parts of the estate. Where the estate comprises certain types of property, it may be desirable to appoint specialists as executors of that part of the estate, eg. valuable literary works or settled land (*see* Chapter 8, para. 8.10.1).

Settled land

Section 22, Administration of Estates Act 1925 provides that where the deceased is a tenant for life of settled land, the trustees of settled land are deemed to be appointed executors in respect of the settled land alone (although under Rule 29, Non-Contentious Probate Rules 1987, as amended, they act as administrators and not executors).

Executors and trustees

If a will creates or may possibly give rise to a trust (*see* 4.8.1), trustees as well as executors must be appointed. It is usually administratively convenient to appoint the same persons as executors and trustees.

Specimen clause for appointment of executors and trustees

I appoint (full name) of (full address) and (full name) of (full address) (hereinafter called 'my Trustees' which expression shall include the trustees for the time being) to be the executors and trustees of my will.

Note

This clause appoints *two individuals* executors and trustees.

If persons are appointed executors and trustees of a will, a transition in their role takes place when the administration of the estate has been completed and the executors are distributing the assets of the estate. The executors transfer any part of the estate which is to be held on trust to themselves as trustees to hold on the terms of the will.

Nominations

A will may appoint someone to nominate an executor rather than the appointment being made in the will itself. This is seldom advantageous. If such a clause is used it should impose a time limit within which the nominator must make the appointment.

4.3.2   ## Numbers of executors and trustees

There are no limits to the numbers of executors who may be *appointed* but only four executors may *take out a grant* in respect of the same property. Power may be reserved in the grant to any others appointed (*see* Chapter 8, para. 8.5.4).

One executor is always sufficient, but it is desirable to appoint more than one in case the executor appointed either predeceases the testator or dies before completing the administration of the estate. Alternatively, or even where more than one executor is appointed, a substitutional appointment may be made in case the appointed executor(s) predeceases the testator or does not wish to take out a grant of probate.

Where the executor is a spouse, remember that the s.18A (as substituted), Wills Act 1837 provides that, in the event of a subsequent divorce, the will takes effect as if the appointment of a former spouse as executor (and trustee) were omitted. It may therefore be vital to have a substitutional appointment.

Where the executors are also to be trustees, two must be appointed because two trustees are required to give a good receipt for capital money unless the trustee is a trust corporation.

4.3.3   ## Choice of executors

The testator must consider the relative merits of appointing singularly or jointly one or more of the following four categories of executors.

Individual friends/relatives

The obvious advantage of appointing a friend or relative as executor is that it ensures that the administration of the estate is completed by someone who the testator knows and who will not charge for the work to be done. However, in advising a client who proposes to appoint such a person(s) it may be appropriate for you to draw any of the following points to their attention.

1   If the proposed executor lacks expertise, *professional advice/help* in the administration of the estate may be necessary. As the costs of such professional advice are taken from

the deceased's estate, the apparent advantage of cheapness may be illusory. The testator must bear in mind the nature and size of the estate in deciding on the degree of expertise required to administer the estate.

2   Are the individual(s) *willing and available to act*? They may be willing but if they do not have the time to administer the estate, they will need to delegate much of the work to a professional, again with the financial penalty.

3   Should the client propose to appoint *a minor, a bankrupt, a criminal, a person suffering from a mental disorder, or an alien* as executor, you must explain that although the appointment will be valid, such a person either will not or may not be able to take out a grant of probate depending on the circumstances (*see* Chapter 8, paras. 8.4 and 8.9).

4   The client should be aware of the possibility of a *conflict of interest* where a beneficiary of the estate is appointed executor. A beneficiary may be a good choice of executor because their personal interest in the estate will encourage them to see that the estate is efficiently administered. However, if a specific legatee (*see* 4.5.1) was appointed a sole executor, for example, they may be tempted not to act in the best interests of a residuary beneficiary.

5   The client should be aware of causing *difficulties in the administration of the estate* by disputes where several individuals are appointed and they are unable to agree as to what steps should be taken when dealing with assets. This is especially likely to be a problem where the individuals are beneficiaries under the estate with competing interests.

6   Where the client proposes an executor who is about the *same age as the client or older*, a substitutional appointment should be included in case the executor predeceases the testator.

7   The client should check with the intended appointees that they are *prepared to act* as executors (and trustees).

Specimen clause for appointment of individuals as executor

I appoint (full name) of (full address) and (full name) of (full address) to be the executors of my will.

Note

If a trust may arise under the will, the individuals must be appointed executors and trustees (as shown in the specimen clause in 4.3.1).

Solicitors or other professional persons

The advantage in appointing a professional person such as a solicitor or accountant as executor is their knowledge and expertise. The disadvantages, as compared to the appointment of a friend or relative, are the cost and the fact that a professional executor will have no personal interest in the estate.

Bearing in mind these advantages and disadvantages, the client, taking account of the nature and size of the estate, must weigh up whether a professional executor should be appointed.

Often a client will express a wish that a particular individual within a firm of solicitors or accountants should be appointed executor. You should point out that problems will arise if the individual dies, leaves the firm or retires. You should suggest that the client appoints the firm to act rather than named individuals. However, you could include words expressing a *wish* that particularly named persons should act in the administration of the estate.

Specimen clause for the appointment of a firm of solicitors as executors and trustees (expressing a wish for particular individuals to act)

I APPOINT the partners at the date of my death in the firm of (name of firm) of (address) (solicitors) or the firm which at that date has succeeded to and carries on its practice to be executors and trustees of my will (hereinafter called 'my Trustees' which expression shall include the trustees or trustee for the time being) and I express the wish that John Smith and Brian Brown shall prove my will and act initially in its trusts.

When drafting a clause which appoints a firm as executors and trustees take care over the following points:

- Although a firm may be appointed executors of a will, the office of executor is a personal one and so the appointment of a firm is treated as the appointment of all the individual partners in that firm. In the absence of clear words to the contrary, such an appointment is treated as an appointment of the partners in the firm at the date the will is made rather than the partners at the date of death. Since partners may die, retire or leave the firm and thus be unable or unwilling to act, it is undesirable for partners at the date the will is made to be appointed. Reference must therefore be made to appointment of partners *at the date of the testator's death* (as per the clause above).
- It is usual to express the wish that only two of the partners in the firm should take out a grant.
- As executors are in a fiduciary position they must not, unless expressly authorised, make a profit from their position. A charging clause will consequently need to be included in the will (*see* 4.11.1).

- To avoid the risk of the appointment being ineffective if the firm changes its name or amalgamates with another firm, reference to change of name, amalgamation etc must be made. It may also now be a possibility that a firm will be incorporated under the Solicitors' Incorporated Practice Rules 1988. If this is a risk then the following words must be included.

Specimen clause (covering the possibility of an amalgamation)

I appoint the partners at the date of my death in the firm of (name) Solicitors of (address) or in the firm or incorporated solicitors' practise which at that date carries on its practise (hereinafter called 'my Trustees') to be the executors and trustees of my will ....

Note

When advising a client about the appointment of executors, you must bear in mind Rule 1, Solicitors' Practise Rules 1990. This provides, *inter alia*, that a solicitor must not do anything in the course of practising as a solicitor, or permit another person to do anything on their behalf which will impair the solicitor's independence and integrity, a person's freedom to instruct a solicitor of their choice or the solicitor's duty to act in the best interests of the client. Therefore, you must not allow your own interests to distort the advice you give to the client in advising on the appointment of executor. This means that you must objectively state all the relative advantages and disadvantages of the appointment of different types of executors.

Trust corporation/bank

A client may wish to appoint a trust corporation, such as the trustee department of a bank, as executor, either alone or in addition to an individual or professional adviser. In this event you must point out the following to the client:

- Trust corporations usually insist that the appointment is made on the corporation's standard terms and conditions which are incorporated into the will; these include a scale of charges which the client may wish to compare with a solicitor's fees.
- If difficulties occur in the administration of the estate, it may be necessary for a trust corporation to instruct a solicitor. This can be expensive as there may be an element of double charging.

Specimen clause for the appointment of a bank jointly with an individual

(a) I APPOINT the (X) Bank plc (hereinafter called 'the Bank') and (name of individual) of (address of individual) (hereinafter together called 'my Trustees' which expression shall include the trustees for the time being) to be the executors and trustees of my will.

(b) The Bank's standard terms and conditions for acting as executor and trustee (including the scale of remuneration) last published before the date of my death shall apply with power to charge remuneration in accordance with any later published terms of the Bank for the time being in force.

(c) It is my wish that the firm of (name) of (address) shall be employed as solicitors in connection with my estate.

Note

1   It is common for a client to approach their bank directly over the appointment of the bank as executor. The bank may then approach you on behalf of the testator and ask you to draft the will. Remember that the testator and not the bank is your client. Consequently, it is your professional duty to ensure that any will prepared complies with the testator's wishes by contacting the testator directly in order to confirm the instructions.

2   You must obtain the bank/trust corporation's published terms and conditions and explain the meaning of the wording to the testator and obtain the testator's authority to include the terms and conditions in their will.

The chosen bank's standard clauses must be used.

Public Trustee
Where a client has difficulty in finding someone willing to act as executor, the Public Trustee may be appointed. However, the Public Trustee can refuse to accept any appointment (except on the sole ground that the estate is too small.) He will not normally accept the trust if it involves the management of a business. The Public Trustee can act alone or jointly with others.

A fee will be charged for the service and the client may wish to compare this with a solicitor's fee.

4.4   Appointment of guardians

Where a testator has a minor child(ren) or may have such a child(ren) they may wish to appoint a guardian for the child(ren) after their death. The appointment may be by will or in writing: s.5(5), Children Act 1989.

A parent with parental responsibility may appoint a guardian. A mother of a child automatically has parental responsibility as does the father of the child if he was married to the mother at any time later than the date of conception of the child. If the father has never been married to the mother of the child he can acquire parental responsibility by court order or by an agreement with the child's mother.

Where the parents of the child are married, the appointment of a guardian by one spouse will normally only take effect after the death of the surviving spouse: ss.5(7) and 5(8), Children Act 1989. If the surviving spouse also appoints a guardian, the guardians appointed by each of the spouses will act together after the death of the surviving spouse.

Where a residence order is in force in favour of a spouse, the appointment of a guardian by the spouse can take effect immediately despite the existence of a surviving spouse. However, the surviving spouse can apply to the court to have the guardianship terminated: s.6(7), Children Act 1989.

From the practical point of view it is better for parents (whether spouses or cohabitees) with parental responsibility to appoint the same people as guardians for their minor children. Appropriate choices of guardian are persons with experience of bringing up children who are perhaps relatives or close family friends who are already liked and known well by the children.

The testator should consult the proposed appointees to find out whether they are prepared to act as guardians and the testator should also consider any additional expense that the guardian will incur in caring for the child(ren). It may be appropriate to make the guardians trustees of a trust fund for the benefit of the children.

Specimen clause for appointment of guardians

I appoint (full name) of (address) (and (full name) of (address) jointly) to be the guardian(s) of any of my children who are under eighteen years (at the date of my death) (at the date of the death of my wife/husband).

Note

An appointment of a guardian can be revoked, whether or not the appointment is made in a will, provided the revocation is in writing and signed and dated.

Beneficial gifts 4.5

Types of gifts 4.5.1

A gift by will may be of realty or personalty. In the past a gift of realty was always termed 'a devise' and in drafting a gift of realty the phrase 'I devise ...' was used. For personalty, the gift was always referred to as a 'legacy' and the term 'I bequeath ...' adopted. Today the term 'legacy' is used more generally to refer to a gift of any type of property by will and in drafting it is acceptable to simply write 'I give ...'. If the term 'I devise' is used, it must only be used in connection with a gift of realty.

Specific gift

A specific gift is a gift of property forming part of the testator's estate and distinguished in the will from other property of the same+ kind, eg. 'my Georgian oak corner cupboard'.

Section 24, Wills Act 1837 provides that, as regards property, the will speaks from the date of death unless a contrary intention is expressed. If the subject matter is described so specifically that it shows that only an object in existence at the date of the will was intended, a contrary intention is shown by the will. The use of the word 'my' followed by the description of the item, eg. 'my Georgian oak corner cupboard', is likely to be construed as showing a contrary intention. You must decide whether a contrary intention exists because, if the words of the will are taken to apply to property in existence at the date of the will, and that property is destroyed, sold or given away, the legacy is said to fail for ademption and the beneficiary will receive nothing. This is so even if the particular item is later replaced by a similar item fitting the description in the will.

On account of s.24, you must ascertain whether the client only wishes the beneficiary to take the particular item in existence at the date of the will, as opposed to any item corresponding to a particular description at the date of death. If the client's intends the former, the principle of ademption must be explained to the client. If the testator intends the latter, clear wording to this effect must be used.

Specimen clause

I give to my nephew John Crank any Georgian oak corner cupboard which I own at the date of my death.

In drafting specific gifts take care to clearly identify the property. For example, confusion may arise where a testator leaves 'my MG motor car' to a particular beneficiary, but in fact the testator owned two MG motor cars.

Specimen clause

I give to my niece Sarah Todd my 1964 MG motor car registration number FAB 1.

Special care is needed in drafting gifts of shares because of the possibility of:

- Changes in the testator's shareholding between the date of execution of the will and the date of death as a result of, for example, bonus issues or rights issues; and

- The company in which the shares are held being taken over or amalgamated with another company.

For these reasons – unlike other specific gifts – it is wise not to describe shares too precisely and also to anticipate the possibility of take-overs and amalgamations.

Specimen clause

(a) I GIVE to (full name of beneficiary) all my shares in (name of company).

(b) Any charge on the shares existing at my death shall be paid out of my Residuary Estate.

(c) If any of the shares referred to in the gift in paragraph (a) above are as a result of take-over amalgamation or reconstruction represented by a different holding paragraph (a) above shall take effect as a gift of that holding.

> *Note*
>
> Para (b) is included to counter the effect of s.35, Administration of Estates Act 1925 which provides that debts charged on particular assets during the deceased's lifetime are payable out of those assets (*see* 4.5.5).

General

A general gift is a gift of property which is not in any way distinguished in the will from other property of the same kind.

A general legacy is usually a *pecuniary legacy*, but it need not be. For example, a gift of 500 shares in British Telecom is a general legacy unless there are indications in the will, construed as a whole and in the light of relevant circumstances, to show that a testator intended to refer to shares belonging to them. Furthermore, a gift of a sum of money need not be a general legacy. For example, a specific gift would be created if a testator left 'all the cash in the safe in my study at the date of my death' to a particular beneficiary.

Where a general gift is made the personal representatives will have to purchase property satisfying the description if the testator does not own the property described at the date of death.

Demonstrative

A demonstrative gift is a gift which is in its nature a general gift but which is expressed to be payable out of a particular fund or property, eg. 'I give £500 out of my current account with Barclays Bank'. The important point is that the gift is valid even if the particular fund or property does not exist at the testator's death.

However, if the gift is directed to be satisfied *only* out of the particular fund or property, eg. 'I give £500 payable out of my current account with Barclays Bank', it cannot be demonstrative as the essential characteristic of a demonstrative gift is that it operates as a general gift in so far as it cannot be satisfied out of the specified fund or property.

Pecuniary legacies

A gift of money, whether specific, general or demonstrative is known as a pecuniary legacy.

The term 'pecuniary legacy' has a special meaning for the purposes of the Administration of Estates Act 1925. It is widely defined by s.55(1)(ix) to include:

'an annuity, a general legacy, a demonstrative legacy so far as it is not discharged out of the designated property, and any other general direction by a testator for the payment of money, including all death duties free from which any devise bequest or payment is made to take effect'.

This definition is relevant, for example, where the statutory order for the payment of debts is applied to an estate (*see* Chapter 12, para. 12.4.2), although the statutory order is normally excluded.

Residuary gift

A residuary gift is a gift of the property which remains after the payment of other legacies and usually all debts, liabilities and expenses (*see* 4.8).

4.5.2   Gifts to unincorporated associations

Note the following points when taking instructions and drafting gifts to unincorporated associations.

Receipt clause

As an unincorporated association has no legal identity separate from that of the individual members, a gift to an unincorporated association is construed as a gift to all the individual members. Consequently, in the absence of an express provision in the will to the contrary, the personal representatives would theoretically have to obtain a receipt from each individual member of the association. To avoid this a clause must be inserted into the will providing that the receipt of the person appearing to be the treasurer or other appropriate officer will be sufficient to give good discharge to the personal representatives. The words 'appearing to be' are important to relieve the personal representatives of the need to check whether the appointment of the treasurer or other officer was properly made.

Confirm existence and correct name

Where a testator intends to make a gift to an unincorporated association, you must confirm that the name and address of the association given by the client is correct and that the association exists.

Provision for change of name etc

To prevent a gift from failing if the unincorporated association changes its name and/or objects, or amalgamates with another similar body, you must make provision to allow the gift to take effect to the association in its altered form.

Provision must also be made to cover the possibility of the association dissolving before the testator's death.

Charitable associations

If the testator believes that they are making a gift to a charitable association, you must confirm the association's charitable status to ensure the inheritance tax exemption (*see* Chapter 2, para. 2.4.2). In addition, it may be desirable to include words showing a general charitable intention to enable the gift to be applied *cy-près* should the charity cease to exist during the testator's lifetime. Where there is an initial failure of a charitable gift, property can only be applied *cy-près* if the testator shows a general charitable intention. The gift must therefore be expressed as being for the 'general charitable purposes of the association'.

Specimen clause for a gift to an unincorporated association which is a charity

(a) I GIVE £(X) to (name of charity) ('the Charity') for its general charitable purposes.

(b) The receipt of a person who appears to be a proper officer of the Charity shall be a sufficient discharge to my Trustees.

(c) If at my death the Charity has ceased to exist or has amalgamated with another charity or has changed its name my Trustees shall pay it to the charitable organisation which they consider most nearly fulfils the objects of the Charity.

Gifts of chattels to be divided by agreement   4.5.3

It is common for a testator to want to leave it up to the beneficiaries to agree as to how certain chattels are to be divided between them. The potential difficulty with this is the beneficiaries may not be able to agree. To overcome this problem, the clause should include some mechanism for resolving any dispute.

Specimen clause

I give all my personal chattels as defined by s.55(1)(x), Administration of Estates Act 1925 to my children living at the date of my death in equal shares to be divided between them as they shall agree but so that in default of agreement such division shall be made by my Trustees in their absolute discretion and according to their estimation of the values of the items comprising my personal chattels and shall be final and binding.

> *Note* _____
>
> '... personal chattels as defined by s.55(1)(x), Administration of Estates Act 1925' refers to the definition of personal chattels for the purpose of the application of the rules of intestacy (*see* Chapter 7, para. 7.4.1). It is common to adopt this definition in making gifts by will in order to pass all property fitting the description owned by the testator at the date of death without the term personal chattels being uncertain in meaning.

4.5.4   Legacies taking advantage of the IHT nil rate band

Where a testator leaves their estate to their surviving spouse, no IHT will be payable on their death because of the spouse exemption (*see* Chapter 2, para. 2.4.1). However, on the death of the surviving spouse, if the surviving spouse's estate passes to non-exempt beneficiaries, eg. children, IHT will be payable and only one nil rate band, ie. that of the surviving spouse, will have been used. In circumstances where a testator wishes to leave their estate to their surviving spouse, but where the surviving spouse is likely to be sufficiently wealthy to manage on less than the entire estate, it may be appropriate to make legacies equivalent to the nil rate band to non-exempt beneficiaries (which may or may not be the testator's children) so as to make use of the testator's nil-rate band.

Specimen clause

I leave to (my children) such sums which at my death shall equal the maximum sum which can be given to (my children) by this will without inheritance tax being payable in respect of such sums after taking into account any lifetime gifts that may be taxable at my death and any legacies given by this will or any codicil hereto.

4.5.5   Relieving provisions

You must ensure that the client is clear as to which gifts are to bear any inheritance tax due, and any other debts and expenses incurred in the administration of the estate, and draft the will accordingly. You must consider the following three categories of liabilities.

Inheritance tax

Inheritance tax on gifts of UK property which is free estate and which vests in the personal representatives is usually regarded as a testamentary expense and as such is payable out of the residue of the estate. However, in order to draw the position to the testator's attention, and for the sake of clarity, it is usual to expressly provide that a non-residuary gift is made free of tax. In any case, the testator may wish the specific beneficiary to bear the tax, in which case the clause must be drafted to express this wish.

Mortgages and other charges existing on property during the deceased's lifetime

Section 35, Administration of Estates Act 1925 provides that where a gift is made of property which was charged with a mortgage or other debt during the testator's lifetime, the property passes to the beneficiary subject to the debt unless the will provides otherwise.

You must, when taking instructions, enquire whether the testator has any property charged with mortgages or other debts and if so how they are to be discharged. You must then ascertain whether the testator wishes the beneficiary to take the property free from the mortgage or other debt and, if so, to expressly provide for this in the will by stating that the gift is made free from the mortgage etc. This places the burden of paying the mortgage debt on the residue.

Note

Where the debt is a mortgage, the testator may have taken out a *mortgage protection policy* under which, on the mortgagor's death, either a fixed sum (equal to the original loan), or an amount sufficient to pay off the sum outstanding on the loan at the date of death, becomes payable. You should therefore enquire whether such a policy exists and, if it does, ensure that the client takes this into account when deciding which part of the estate should bear the mortgage debt.

Expenses

In the case of a specific gift, the costs of insuring, packing and transferring the asset(s) to the beneficiary is borne by the specific beneficiary unless the will expressly provides to the contrary. You must therefore ask the client whether they wish such costs to be borne by the residuary estate or by the specific beneficiary where the gift is bulky and/or a valuable item. If the costs are not to be borne by the specific beneficiary, the will must expressly provide that the gift is made free of expenses and costs of transfer.

Specimen clause (with relieving provisions)

I GIVE free of mortgage tax and costs of transfer Flat No 3 Oakdene House Herbert Road Torquay Devon to my son George Alexander Thorpe.

4.6   Gift of occupational rights only

It may be that a testator does not want to make an absolute gift of a particular house to a given beneficiary or even give that beneficiary a life interest under a trust in the house. The testator may simply want to protect the beneficiary's occupation of the house. It is quite common for a testator to wish to protect a surviving spouse's occupation of the matrimonial home in this way, without making a gift of home to the spouse.

Another common use of such a clause is to protect the occupation of an adult child of the testator who has been living with the testator until the testator's death, with the intention that other children of the testator are to share in the proceeds of sale of the house when the occupying adult child has died or decided to give up residency. The following clause illustrates the type of conditions which might be attached to a right of residence.

Specimen clause

I give my house or flat known as (name and address of property) ('the House' which includes any house or flat acquired pursuant to clause (a)(ii)) to my Trustees to hold on trust for sale but with power to postpone the sale and in accordance with the following directions:

(a) (name of beneficiary) ('the Occupant') may live in the House and use it as his/her principal place of residence (so long as he/she wishes and without any charge) (until he/she remarries/marries or co-habits) and so long as this paragraph applies:

> (i) the Occupant shall pay all rates and outgoings and keep the House in good repair and insured to the satisfaction of my Trustees;

> (ii) the House shall not be sold without the consent of the Occupant but my Trustees may sell it at the request of the Occupant and buy another residence to which the provisions of this paragraph shall then apply.

(b) On paragraph (a) ceasing to apply the House or any proceeds of sale of the same shall form part of my Residuary Estate.

Note _____

1 *Possible variations to (a)(i).* The testator may not wish the Occupant to pay all rates and outgoings or, alternatively, it may be difficult to anticipate whether the Occupant will be able to

pay all the rates and outgoings. In the event of the latter, where Trustees are holding the residue of the estate, the trustees could be given discretion to pay rates etc with a power to pay them out of income or capital from the residuary estate generally.

2   The wording of (a)(ii) is such that, although the house cannot be sold without the occupying beneficiary's consent, if the Occupant requests that the trustees sell the house the discretion lies with the trustees in the purchase of another house.

Special considerations in drafting gifts to children   4.7

The considerations discussed below may apply to a gift to the testator's children or to a gift by the testator to someone else's children. Some of them may also be relevant considerations in drafting gifts to beneficiaries other than children but they are explained together here because they are likely to be encountered in relation to drafting gifts to children in the context of the will of a family person.

Meaning of the 'children'   4.7.1

Unless the will expresses a contrary intention, the use of the word 'child' or 'children', whether used in connection with children of the testator or of someone else, includes adopted children (Adoption Act 1976) and illegitimate children (Family Law Reform Act 1987). Thus, if a testator wishes for any reason to exclude an adopted or illegitimate child from benefit, this must be done so expressly.

Individual gift or class gift   4.7.2

Further children
First it is important to decide whether further children whom the testator wishes to benefit are likely to be born. If this is so, it may be appropriate to make the gift a *class gift* rather than naming each child. A class gift is a gift of property to be divided among persons who fulfil a particular description, eg. 'all my children'. The size of each child's share depends upon the number of children falling within the class.

Class closing rules
The making of a class gift can potentially cause problems in distributing the estate. For example, if a gift is made by X to 'the children of A', but for the *class closing rules* (*see* further Chapter 13, para. 13.3.5). it would not be possible to distribute the property to any of the children of A until A's death, as it is only then that the maximum number of persons within the class is certain.

The class closing rules are rules which were developed for administrative convenience to enable the subject matter of a class gift to be distributed at an artificially early date. The basic principle is that beneficiaries who are born after the date that the class closes are excluded from the class although a child who is *en ventre sa mere* at the date the class closes is treated as living for the purpose of the application of the rule. (For details and examples of the class closing rules *see* Chapter 13, para. 13.3.5.)

It is possible to exclude the class closing rules but if this is done the effects of the perpetuity rule have to be borne in mind. In order to facilitate the administration of the estate, you should suggest to the testator that they restrict a class gift to members of the class living at the testator's death.

Specimen clause for class gift to children

SUBJECT to the payment of my debts executorship expenses and all taxes on any gift made free of tax I GIVE all my estate not otherwise specifically disposed of to such of my children as may be living at my death and if more than one in equal shares ....

Specific amounts

Where a testator makes a gift of a specified amount to each person fulfilling a particular description, eg. £5,000 to each of the children of X, the gift will not be a class gift as the amount each child receives does not vary according to the number of people within the class. However, if X is still alive at the testator's death the personal representatives will not know how much property needs to be set aside to cover the possibility of further children being born to X, and this therefore causes similar problems as with class gifts. A rule of construction has therefore developed to facilitate the distribution of an estate where this type of gift is made. This states that unless a contrary intention is shown, only persons alive at the testator's death who fulfil this description can take. If there are no such persons at the testator's death, the entire gift fails.

You must bear this rule of construction in mind when a testator wishes to specify the amount to be received by each person fulfilling a specified description and it may be appropriate to express a contrary intention to the rule of construction. Even where no contrary intention is intended, for the sake of clarity it is advisable to expressly provide that only persons alive at the testator's death fulfilling the specified description qualify.

Specimen clause

£5,000 to such of the children of my brother John Cox as are living at the date of my death.

Vested or contingent gifts   4.7.3

Vested gifts

A gift is said to be vested if the beneficiary *does not have to satisfy any preconditions* before entitlement. An example of a vested gift is '£10,000 to my son, James'.

Where a vested gift is to be made to a child of the testator it is particularly important to consider the possibility of the child being a minor at the testator's death. If the child is a minor, unless the will provides otherwise by means of a receipt clause (*see* 4.11.3), a minor cannot give a good receipt for money nor can a parent or guardian on the minor's behalf. Consequently, with reference to the above example, even though there are no preconditions to James's entitlement to the £10,000, he will not be able to receive the money before he reaches 18, although the trustees may be able to use income or capital for his benefit under their powers of maintenance and advancement (*see* 4.11.3). However, if James dies before 18, but after the testator, the £10,000 will pass into James's estate.

In the light of this, if the testator wishes a child to be able to claim their gift before reaching 18, a receipt clause must be included (*see* 4.11.3). If the testator does not so wish it may be better that the gift is made contingent upon the child attaining 18 or some greater age.

Contingent gift

A contingent gift is one where the beneficiary *has to satisfy some precondition* before they become entitled to the gift. The precondition is usually the attaining of a specified age. An example of a contingent gift is '£10,000 to my son James if he attains the age of eighteen years', where James is less than eighteen years at the testator's death. Once James reaches 18 his gift becomes vested. If James dies before he reaches 18, the £10,000 will not pass into his estate.

Where a contingent gift is made, it may be possible to make it in such terms as to be an *accumulation and maintenance* trust falling within s.71, Inheritance Tax Act 1984 (*see* Chapter 5). The inheritance tax advantages of so doing are significant although the income tax position is not necessarily advantageous.

General considerations in drafting residuary gifts   4.8

Bear the following in mind in the drafting of any residuary gift:

- Is a trust required (*see* 4.8.1)?

- Provision for payment of debts, funeral and testamentary expenses (*see* 4.8.2);
- Provision for payment of legacies (*see* 4.8.3);
- Substitutional gifts (*see* 4.9).

4.8.1 Is a trust required and, if so, what type?

Whether a trust is required will depend on the form the gift of the residue takes and also who the beneficiaries of the gift are to be.

As regards the form of th*e gift*, if there are to be successive and/or contingent gifts as opposed to an absolute gift of the residue, a trust will be required. Thus, for example, if the testator's surviving spouse is to have a life interest in the residue, with remainder to the children of the testator, a trust will be required. Likewise, if the residue is to be divided between the children of the testator contingent upon attaining the age of, say, 25, a trust will be required.

As regards the *beneficiaries* of the residue, if the beneficiaries include persons who are or may be minors at the testator's death, a trust of the residue must be established. Remember that even if the primary beneficiaries of the residue are all adults, you must consider whether the beneficiaries under any substitutional gift (if the primary gift fails) may be minors.

Example

Frank wishes to leave the residue of his estate to be divided between his children in equal shares. All his children are over 18 at the time of the execution of the will and it is improbable that he will have further children. There is to be a substitutional gift to grandchildren or remoter issue should any children predecease Frank. As there is a possibility that a grandchild or remoter issue may be a minor at Frank's death and take by substitution, a trust must be included.

Having decided that a trust is needed, you must then decide *what type of trust* to create. Section 39, Administration of Estates Act 1925 gives personal representatives a power to sell assets of the estate for the purposes of administration. However, you must consider whether a *trust for sale* should be established. This imposes a *duty* on the trustees to sell as opposed to giving them merely a power of sale. Where the residuary estate does or may include land and either there are successive and/or contingent interests or potential minority interests, it is usual to establish a trust for sale to avoid the creation of a strict settlement which is unlikely to be the testator's intention. If a strict settlement arises the tenant for life, ie. the beneficiary entitled in possession, is entitled to call for the legal estate in the land and has all the powers of management and administration which cannot be vested in anyone else (effects of the Settled Land Act 1925).

Where there are or will be no minority, successive or contingent interests it does not normally matter whether or not a trust for sale of the residuary estate is established but it is common to include such a trust as a method of providing expressly for the payment of debts etc and legacies (*see* 4.8.2–3).

It is not advisable to set up a trust for sale of the residue where there is only one beneficiary of the residuary estate and the testator wishes the beneficiary to enjoy the property *in specie* (which basically means in the form that it is left).

Provision for payment of debts 4.8.2

Where there is not express provision in the will, the statutory order for payment of debts set out in Part II, First Schedule, Administration of Estates Act 1925 (*see* Chapter 12, para. 12.4) will apply. This provides that unless there is undisposed of property, debts are normally paid out of the residue. Although this usually complies with a testator's own wishes, you should include an express provision that debts are to be paid from the residue in order to draw the matter to the testator's attention and so give the opportunity for the testator to request otherwise.

Section 35, Administration of Estates Act 1925 provides for payment of debts secured on specific property during the deceased's lifetime to be paid out of that property unless a contrary intention appears in the will (*see* Chapter 12, para. 12.4.1). If a testator wishes such a secured debt to be paid out of this residue, the residuary gift must expressly provide that debts, including debts charged on specific property, are to be paid out of residue.

Specimen clause

I GIVE the residue of my estate SUBJECT TO the payment of my debts funeral testamentary and administrative expenses including any mortgage or charge affecting my freehold property ....

Provision for payment of legacies 4.8.3

The rules which establish which property is to be applied for the payment of legacies in the absence of an express provision in the will are complex (*see* Chapter 13, para. 13.8.1). and for this reason, as well as for the purpose of drawing the matter to the attention of the testator, you must expressly provide for legacies to be paid out of the residue, if this is the testator's wish.

4.8.4   Drafting a residuary gift with and without a trust

Residuary gift with a trust for sale

Taking into account the issues discussed in 4.8.1–3, the following is one example of a residuary clause incorporating a trust for sale.

Specimen clause

I give all the rest of my estate to my Trustees UPON TRUST to sell call in and convert the same into money with power to postpone such sale calling in and conversion for so long as they in their absolute discretion think fit without being liable for loss and after payment there out of my debts funeral and testamentary expenses and legacies TO HOLD the residue ('my Residuary Estate') on the following trusts ....

> *Note*
>
> Although a duty to sell is important, a trust for sale gives the trustees unlimited discretion to postpone sale and they will not be liable for their decision to postpone sale. The net effect is that they need only sell assets of the residuary estate to pay debts etc and legacies.

Residuary gift not involving a trust

Taking into account the issues discussed in 4.8.1–3, the following is one example of a residuary clause not incorporating a trust.

Specimen clause

SUBJECT to the payment of my debts executorship expenses and all taxes on any gifts made free of tax I GIVE all my estate not otherwise specifically disposed of to such of my brothers and sisters as may be living at the date of my death and if more than one in equal shares.

4.9   Substitutional gifts

4.9.1   Substitutional gifts generally

A substitutional gift is a gift which is to take effect if the gift to the primary beneficiary fails for any specified reason. The doctrine of lapse is the most common reason why the primary gift may fail (*see* Chapter 13, para. 13.5.1). Under the doctrine, subject to exceptions, if a beneficiary predeceases the testator their gift lapses. If the gift which lapses is a specific, general or demonstrative gift, the subject matter of the gift will normally fall into residue and pass to the residuary beneficiary. If a residuary gift lapses the property will *prima facie* pass on partial intestacy. In order to avoid a partial intestacy it is vital to include a substitutional gift in a residuary gift.

Example ⸻

Jane wishes to leave her residuary estate to her husband. There is a possibility that Jane's husband may predecease her. The doctrine of lapse cannot be excluded. To avoid a partial intestacy a substitutional gift must be made, say, to their children.

Substitutional gifts may also be desired by the testator in the case of a non-residuary gift because the testator does not wish the property to pass into residue, but to pass elsewhere.

Example ⸻

Robert leaves legacies of £10,000 to each of his nephews. The residue of the estate is to pass to his surviving spouse. If one or more of his nephews predecease Robert, he wishes any issue of those nephews to share equally the £10,000 their parent would have taken had they not predeceased.

Substitutional gifts are particularly common where the primary beneficiary is a surviving spouse or a child of the testator. Where the primary beneficiary is a *child of the testator*, it is common to make a substitutional gift to grandchildren or remoter issue. Where the primary beneficiary is a *surviving spouse*, the substitutional gift is normally to the testator's children, with a further substitution to grandchildren or remoter issue.

Substitutional gifts to children   4.9.2

In the case of a gift to a child of the testator to a certain extent a substitutional gift is automatically provided for by s.33, Wills Act 1837 (as substituted by the Administration of Justice Act 1982). This will normally save from lapse a gift made to a child of the testator where the child predeceases the testator (*see* Chapter 13, para. 13.5.1), It is, however, better to include an *express* substitutional gift to grandchildren and remoter issue for the following reasons.

● An express provision draws the effects of s.33 to the testator's attention and gives the testator the opportunity to vary the terms of the statutory substitutional clause. For example, although it would be unusual, a testator may wish for a distribution *per capita* so that any issue of a deceased child share equally with surviving children, rather than taking *per stirpes* the share their deceased parent would have taken (*see* Chapter 13, para. 13.5.1).

● Where the primary gift is contingent the effects of s.33 are unclear in that there is doubt whether the substituted beneficiary has to satisfy the contingency required of the primary beneficiary to come within s.33.

Note

Section 33 only operates where the gift is made to the testator's children or remoter issue and not where the gift is made to the children of someone else. In the latter case a substitutional gift is necessary to save a gift from lapse when the beneficiary predeceases the testator.

4.9.3   Drafting points

When drafting substitutional gifts there are two very important points to remember.

1   If a class gift is made to beneficiaries as *joint tenants* (as opposed to tenants in common), because of the principle of survivorship, the gift *will not lapse* so as to bring a substitutional gift into operation unless *all* the joint tenants predecease the testator. In contrast, if a gift is made to the beneficiaries as *tenants in common* (as tenants in common have a distinct, although undivided share, in the property forming the subject matter of the gift), the share of any tenant in common who has predeceased the testator *will lapse*.

Example

1   *Joint tenants.* David leaves his residuary estate 'to my children'. As there are no words of severance, the children take as joint tenants. If one of David's children predeceases him, any children of that deceased child cannot take by substitution whether any express clause is included in the will or by placing reliance on s.33.

2   *Tenants in common.* Bill leaves his residuary estate 'to such of my children as are living at the date of my death, if more than one in equal shares'. 'Equal shares' are words of severance, consequently Bill's children take as tenants in common and if one of them predeceases Bill, any children of the deceased child will be able to take by substitution either under s.33 or by a suitably worded express clause.

2   Where the *primary beneficiary is a surviving spouse*, a divorce will cause a gift to the spouse to fail (*see* Chapter 6, para. 6.7.3). Consequently, if a will leaves the residue of the testator's estate to his surviving spouse and provides only for a substitutional gift to the children if his wife predeceases him, there will be a partial intestacy if his wife survives him but has divorced him prior to his death. The clause therefore has to be drafted to provide that the substitutional gift takes effect not only if the spouse predeceases the testator but also 'if the gift fails for any other reason'.

Specimen clause for substitutional gift to children and remoter issue

I give all the rest of my estate to my Trustees UPON TRUST to sell … and after payment of my debts funeral and testamentary expenses and legacies TO HOLD the residue ('my Residuary Estate') on the following trusts:

1 to pay my Residuary Estate to my husband if he survives me by twenty-eight days but if he does not so survive me or if his gift fails for any other reason then;

2 to pay my Residuary Estate to such of my children as are living at my death and if more than one in equal shares provided that if any child of mine shall die before me leaving children living at my death then such children shall on attaining eighteen take by substitution and if more than one in equal shares the share of my estate which their parent would have taken if he or she had attained a vested interest.

Note

In 1 above the reference to surviving by 28 days is a survivorship clause (*see* 4.10).

You should always explain the doctrine of lapse to a testator so that they can consider whether they wish to make a substitutional gift. You should point out in particular the inconvenience of a partial intestacy where a residuary gift lapses and no substitutional gift is made.

Survivorship clauses 4.10

A survivorship clause is a provision in a will which requires the beneficiary to survive the testator by a specified period before they become entitled to their gift. For an example, *see* the Specimen Clause (substitutional gift to children and remoter issue) in 4.9.3.

As the doctrine of lapse will not prevent a beneficiary from being entitled to their gift under a will if they survive the testator for so much as a second in time, survivorship clauses are included to ensure that the beneficiary may only benefit if they survive the testator for a reasonable period of time. If the beneficiary does not survive the specified period of time, a substitutional gift takes effect.

Survivorship clauses are often used in relation to a residuary gift made to a surviving spouse. The gift must be an absolute gift as opposed to a life interest of residue before such a clause is relevant because, by definition, where a beneficiary has a life interest they can only benefit so long as they are alive. The reasons for the popularity of survivorship clauses in gifts of residue to a surviving spouse are twofold.

1   An absolute gift of residue to a spouse means the *loss of control* over the ultimate destination of the testator's property. Many testators consider that this is undesirable where their spouse only survives them by a very short time because, for example, they die in a common accident. (The possibility of death in a common accident is greatest in the case of spouses.) Furthermore, the doctrine of commorientes (under which a beneficiary who dies in a common accident involving the testator may be *deemed* to have survived the testator: *see* Chapter 13, para. 13.5.1) makes the loss of control over the ultimate destination of the testator's property all the more unacceptable. Where the doctrine of commorientes applies, as no survivorship clause has been included, the testator's property will pass under the terms of their will into their spouse's estate as if their spouse survived them and from there under their spouse's will or the rules of intestacy (as appropriate).

2   A survivorship clause may be beneficial from the inheritance tax point of view where each spouse owns a substantial amount of property. If the spouse fails to survive the specified period (usually 28 or 30 days), the property passes to other beneficiaries by means of a substitutional gift. Although the spouse exemption is lost, it means that there will be two estates rather than one for inheritance tax purposes. If there were no survivorship clause, the testator's property would fall into the surviving spouse's estate. No tax would be payable from the testator's estate on the gift to the surviving spouse but the surviving spouse's estate would be swollen by the property of the combined estates; one large estate attracts more inheritance tax than two smaller estates (*see* Chapter 3, para. 3.5.1).

Note _____

A survivorship clause must never require survivorship for more than six months because it will give rise to a settlement for inheritance tax purposes and this may give rise to additional tax liability.

From the practical point of view it will probably be undesirable to have a survivorship period exceeding six months because the personal representatives cannot distribute the estate until the primary beneficiary survives the specified period or dies before (when the substitutional gift can take effect).

Administrative powers 4.11

Personal representatives and trustees have statutory powers to enable them to administer an estate. These powers can be excluded, extended or restricted by the terms of a will, and additional powers can be conferred by the will. In this section we consider:

- The terms which might be included in a will to facilitate the administration of an estate;

- The circumstances in which it is appropriate to include each type of clause;

- The elements which need to be included in such clauses.

It is not normal practise to replace the statutory powers, but rather to widen them. The opening words of the clause conferring powers of administration should make this clear.

Specimen clause

My trustees shall have the following powers in addition to their powers under the general law.

What administrative clauses should be included depends to a certain extent on the nature of the gifts in the will and the status of the beneficiaries. The following paragraphs discuss the appropriateness of particular clauses.

Clauses to be considered in relation to any will 4.11.1

Insurance
Under s.19, Trustee Act 1925 personal representatives (and trustees) can insure the assets of the estate up to 75% of their value against the risk of fire and pay the insurance premiums out of income. It is usual to extend this limited power by an express term which allows them to insure to any amount against all risks and to pay premiums out of capital or income.

Specimen clause

To insure any asset of my estate on such terms as they think fit and

(i) to pay premiums out of income or capital

(ii) to use any insurance money received either to restore the assets or as if it were the proceeds of sale.

Appropriation
Under s.41, Administration of Estates Act 1925 personal representatives can appropriate assets in or towards any legacy, share or interest in an estate *provided* no specific gift is prejudiced and consent is given by the beneficiary. It is usual, however, to insert a term into a will dispensing with the need for consent to an appropriation. This is administratively convenient.

Specimen clause

To exercise the power of appropriation conferred by s.41, Administration of Estates Act 1925 without obtaining any of the consents required by that section.

Power to carry on a business

Where the will is silent, personal representatives have implied power to continue the business of a sole trader but *only* for the purpose of enabling the business to be sold as a going concern. In *Re Crowther* (1895) it was said that this would not normally exceed one year. Thus, where the testator is a sole trader it is usual to expressly provide that the personal representatives:

- May continue to run the business as a going concern for as long as they see fit;
- May use assets of the estate as they see fit;
- Will not be personally liable for any loss which results in running the business;
- May be reimbursed out of the testator's residuary estate if this business is carried on at a loss.

Where the client is a sole trader you should discuss with them whether it would be better to make provision for the running of the business after the client's death by creating a partnership or limited company rather than giving the personal representatives power to carry on the business. You should point out that the personal representatives selected must be prepared to carry on the business and that professional persons are often reluctant to do so. Furthermore, if the business is to be transferred to a beneficiary, it may be helpful to appoint the beneficiary a personal representative.

Where the client is a partner or runs a business through a limited company, you should discuss how the partnership agreement (partnership) or Articles of Association (limited company) are to operate on death.

Power to charge

If the personal representatives are to be professional persons as opposed to relatives or friends, they will want to be paid for their services. However, because of the rule that a fiduciary must not make an unauthorised profit from their position, you must include a clause giving an express power to charge, otherwise the personal representatives will only be able to claim expenses.

In drafting the clause you must state that the personal representative may charge for everything done in connection with the estate whether or not the act could have been done by a lay person. If such words are not included, the clause is strictly construed to allow the personal representative to charge for work done only by a person in the particular profession of the personal representative.

If a bank or a trust corporation is appointed personal representative, the charging clause will probably be required to be in the institution's approved form.

A charging clause is a *legacy*. Legacies abate proportionately if there are insufficient funds to pay them in full unless a contrary intention is shown. Thus, it is quite common to include a clause providing that the fees of personal representatives and trustees are to be paid in priority to other legacies.

Specimen clause

If any of my TRUSTEES is a solicitor or other person engaged in any profession or business then that trustee shall be entitled to charge and be paid without abatement all his usual professional or other charges for any services provided or time spent by him or his firm in connection with the administration of my estate or trusts of my will including anything which a trustee not engaged in a profession or business could have done personally and on the same basis as if he were not one of my Trustees but had been employed to carry out work on their behalf.

Note

A charging clause may either be placed earlier in the will as part of the clause appointing the executors and trustees or it may appear along with the administrative powers towards the end of the will.

Clause to be considered where the will contains or potentially contains a trust   4.11.2

A will may only *potentially* contain a trust because whether a trust arises depends on whether a substitutional gift comes into operation involving a trust. A common example is where the residuary estate is left to a spouse provided they survive by 28 days and if they do not so survive it is held on trust for the testator's children.

Investment

Where the will is silent as to the investment, the position is governed by the Trustee Investment Act 1961. This gives very limited power of investment and sets up a complex and expensive scheme by which investments have to be administered. You should therefore insert an express power to extend the trustees' power of investment. Usually the power is very widely drafted to enable the trustees to invest as if they were sole absolute and beneficial owners.

Note

An investment involves the trustees in purchasing property for the sake of its income, it will not be within the trustee's power to purchase a house as a residence for a beneficiary. If the testator wishes to provide for such a power, there must be an express clause to this effect.

Specimen clause

To invest as freely as if they were absolutely entitled and this power includes the right to use trust money in or towards the purchase or improvement of property for occupation as a residence by a beneficiary.

4.11.3 Clauses to be considered where minority interests may arise under the will

Receipt clause

As a general rule a minor has no statutory power to give a good receipt to personal representatives for the income or capital and neither can a parent or guardian on the minor's behalf. By way of exception a married minor can give a good receipt for *income*: s.21, LPA 1925.

A testator may wish to include a term in the will which expressly authorises the personal representatives to accept the receipt of a minor's parent, guardian or spouse, and which discharges the personal representatives from further liability in respect of the property handed over. Alternatively, or in addition to, the testator may wish to provide that the receipt of a minor over a specified age, eg. 16, will give a good discharge to the personal representatives.

A clause giving power to accept receipts from or on behalf of minors may be incorporated into a specific or pecuniary legacy left to the minor or may be included in the list of administrative powers. It may be worded so as to cover only absolute gifts to a minor or more generally to cover interests of a minor under a trust. Even if such a provision is included, the executors are *not bound* to transfer the property to the minor but are simply relieved from liability if they do.

Specimen clause 1

I GIVE to my nephew JAMES ROBERTS the sum of one thousand pounds (£1,000) absolutely AND I DIRECT that if he should be a minor at the date of my death the receipt of his parent or guardian should be sufficient discharge to my trustees.

Note

This clause is incorporated into a particular pecuniary legacy and has been made specific to a particular beneficiary.

Specimen clause 2

In any case where they have an obligation or a discretion under the provisions of my will or under the general law to pay income or capital to or for the benefit of a minor to discharge that obligation or to exercise that discretion if they think fit by making payment either to a parent or a guardian of the minor or to the minor personally if of the age of sixteen (16) at least and so that their respective receipts shall be a full discharge to my Trustees who shall not be required to see to the application of any income or capital so paid.

Note

This clause applies to any specific or pecuniary legacies to a minor as well as to the interest of a minor under a trust. The reference to a *discretion* to pay income or capital to a minor refers to powers of maintenance and advancement (*see* below).

Extension of the statutory power of maintenance

Under s.31, Trustee Act 1925 trustees can apply the income of a minor's interest for their maintenance, education or benefit, *provided* that the gift carries intermediate income (*see* Chapter 11, para. 11.4.5 and Chapter 3, *Introduction to the Legal Practice Course* Companion in this series).

The trustees can apply the whole or part of the income as may in all the circumstances be reasonable but they are required to have regard to specified matters set out in s.31, namely:

- The age of the minor;
- The minors actual requirements;
- Other income applicable for the same purpose; and
- All the circumstances of case.

As the test of reasonableness is an objective test, the testator may wish to extend the statutory power by an express clause giving the trustees *absolute discretion* to apply income as they think fit.

You may need to consider the trustee's powers of maintenance whenever a beneficiary under the estate could possibly be a minor, whether the minor's interest is vested or contingent. In the case of a *vested interest*, this is because the minor will not be able to give a valid receipt to the personal representatives who will therefore not be prepared to transfer the property to the minor unless the testator decides to include a receipt clause (*see* above). Section 42, Administration of Estates Act 1925, however, gives statutory power to personal representatives to appoint trustees to hold a *legacy* for a minor who is absolutely entitled (*see* Chapter 11, para. 11.4.3).

Specimen clause

Section 31, Trustee Act 1925 shall apply to the income of my estate as if the words 'as the trustees in their absolute discretion think fit' were substituted for the words 'as in all the circumstances be reasonable in para (i) of subsection (1) thereof'.

Note

This clause does not totally replace s.31, it simply allows the trustees to act in their absolute discretion in the exercise of their powers, rather than according to the objective standard of reasonableness.

Extension of the statutory power of advancement

Under s.32, Trustee Act 1925 trustees have discretion to apply up to half of the presumptive share of a beneficiary with an interest in capital for the beneficiary's advancement or benefit, provided the consent of any holder of a prior interest is first obtained, the consent being *in writing* and by a beneficiary who is of *full age* and *mental capacity*.

Section 32 applies to both minor and adult beneficiaries and the ways in which the provision may be extended by the terms of a will are discussed in 4.11.4.

4.11.4   Clauses to be considered where a will contains a trust involving a life interest with remainders

Extension of the statutory power of advancement

Under s.32, Trustee Act 1925 (*see* further Chapter 11, para. 11.4.6) trustees can advance capital to beneficiaries (adult or minor) with a vested or contingent interest in *capital* provided that the payment is for the *advancement or benefit of the beneficiary*. The testator may wish to consider enlarging the power to give the trustees absolute discretion in advancing capital and remove one or more of the three *limitations* laid down in s.32 on the statutory power. Specifically, the testator can:

- Extend the amount that may be advanced beyond the one half presumptive share of the beneficiary;
- Remove the requirement that an advancement be brought into account when or if the beneficiary becomes absolutely entitled;
- Remove the requirement that the written consent of a beneficiary (who must be of full age and mental capacity)

with a prior interest must be obtained by the trustees.

Specimen clause 1

To apply for the benefit of any beneficiary as my trustees think fit the whole or any part of the capital to which the beneficiary is entitled or may in future be entitled and I leave it within the discretion of my trustees whether and to what extent the beneficiary shall bring into account any payments received under this clause.

Note _____

1   This clause removes the statutory limitation of an advancement of up to one half of the presumptive share of the beneficiary and also gives the trustees discretion as to whether a beneficiary has to account for an advancement when made.

2   In *Henley v Wardell* (1989) where the trustees were given 'absolute and uncontrolled discretion to advance ... the whole ... of the beneficiary's share', it was held the words 'absolute and uncontrolled' did not allow them to dispense with a life tenant's consent. Clear words to this effect were needed.

3   A testator may also wish to consider giving the trustees an express power to *lend* money to beneficiaries on whatever terms they think appropriate.

Power to advance capital and make loans to a life tenant

The statutory power of advancement only applies to beneficiaries with an interest in *capital* and therefore not to a life tenant who only has an interest in *income.*

A testator may wish to give an express power to advance capital or to lend money to a life tenant, just in case the life tenant finds the gift of income insufficient. Such a power especially needs careful consideration where the life tenant is a spouse.

Specimen clause 2 (In a will in which a wife has a life interest in the residuary estate with remainder to children.)

... absolute discretion to raise capital by way of advancement to any extent for one or more of the following purposes:

(i) to pay or apply it for the benefit of my wife or (subject to not exceeding the expectant or presumptive share of any particular individual) any one or more of my children or of the children of any of my children who may have died;

(ii) to lend it to my wife or any one or more of my children or children of my children who may then have died without charging interest or taking security and on such terms as to repayment and otherwise as my Trustees in their absolute discretion (without being liable for loss) think fit.

Note

You must consider two possible tax implications of the trustees exercising an express power to make advances to a life tenant.

1   Such payment may amount to a disposal for capital gains tax purposes if assets are advanced *in specie* or if assets are sold to raise cash for the advancement.

2   If advancements are regularly made to a life tenant in order to supplement the life tenant's income, they may be regarded as annual payments for the purpose of income tax and will have to be grossed up and included in the life tenant's income tax returns as part of total income.

Exclusion of the rules of apportionment

The rules of apportionment are designed to achieve impartiality between beneficiaries, especially where there is a succession of interests (eg. to X for life, with remainder to Y), but in today's circumstances the effect of the apportionments is rarely such as to warrant the expertise required to make them and for this reason it is usually better to exclude the rules. The rules are as follows (*see* Chapter 3, *Introduction to the Legal Practice Course* Companion in this series).

1   *Howe v Lord Dartmouth* (1802), which imposes a duty on trustees to sell residuary personalty and to apportion between capital and income actual income received from the date of death to the date of sale.

2   *Re Earl of Chesterfield's Trusts*, which requires an apportionment between capital and income on the sale or date of falling in, of a reversionary interest or other non-income producing interest.

3   *Allhusen v Whittell* (1867), which requires debts and immediate legacies to be paid out of capital together with so much income there from as from the date of death to the time of payment as will produce the required amount.

4   Apportionment Act 1870, which treats, *inter alia*, rents, annuities and dividends as accruing from day to day and they are apportioned accordingly.

Specimen clause

To treat as income all the income from any part of my estate whatever the period in respect of which it may accrue (whether in relation to my death or the death of [life tenant]) and to disregard in this respect the Apportionment Act 1870 and any Act replacing it and the rules of equity relating to apportionments (including those known as the rules in *Howe v Dartmouth* and *Allhusen v Whittell* in all their branches).

Self-assessment questions

1 Your client is a successful small businessman. He runs a number of retail businesses as a sole trader and his estate at death is likely to be worth in excess of £200,000. He proposes appointing an elder brother as sole executor. What comments would you make to him about this choice?

2 Your client has told you that she wishes to appoint you to act personally as executor of her will, and she wishes to give you a legacy of £500 'for the trouble it will cause you'. What advise should you give her?

3 Harry and Wendy are happily married with two infant children. Harry has asked you to draft his will, and tells you he wishes to appoint Sidney as guardian of his children alongside Wendy should she survive him. What advice would you give Harry?

4 Are the following gifts specific, general or demonstrative?

   (a) All my property to A.

   (b) £10,000 to B.

   (c) 200 shares in ICI to C.

   (d) £400 out of my current account at Lloyds Bank to D.

5 Prepare a checklist of the drafting considerations where a testator wishes to make a gift to a charitable body which is an unincorporated association?

6 Why is it advisable to include an express substitutional clause in the will where the testator wishes to make a substitutional gift in the event of a gift to his child failing?

7 When is it absolutely necessary to provide for the residuary estate to be held in trust for sale?

8 Why are survivorship clauses usually inserted into gifts made to a spouse by will?

9 Divorce revokes a gift by will to a spouse. In consequence of this, what must you remember when drafting a substitutional gift to a spouse?

10 What administrative clauses would it normally be appropriate to include in a will containing a gift of the residuary estate to the testator's surviving spouse for life, with remainder to the testator's children?

Answer guidance to self-assessment questions

1 It may not be advisable to appoint an individual:

- If the estate is complex to administer and expert assistance will be needed (if this is so consider appointing a professional person, perhaps along with a relative);

- As sole executor, especially where the individual is older than the testator and there may be a danger of the individual predeceasing the testator (this could be remedied by a substitutional appointment);

- If this will gives rise to a conflict of interest in the administration of the estate (this will depend on whether the brother is a beneficiary of the estate and, if so, to what extent).

Whether an individual or a professional person is appointed, if the will is to give the personal representatives power to carry on the testator's business, you must check whether the personal representatives are prepared to do this.

2 *See* 4.3.3 generally.

Explain the problems if an individual solicitor dies, retires or leaves the firm.

Suggest that the firm should be appointed.

With regard to the £500 explain if you or your firm are to act as executors a charging clause will need to be inserted in the will. If the client is aware of this and wishes you to have the £500, as an extra you will need to consider whether such a payment would be in breach of the rules of professional conduct unless you first advise the client to obtain independent advice, ie. is it a gift of a significant amount (*see* Chapter 1, para. 1.3.2).

3 Explain that this is not possible, unless a residence order is in force at the date of his death (*see* 4.4). The appointment will otherwise only take effect after Wendy's death.

4 (a) specific; (b) general (pecuniary legacy); (c) general; (d) demonstrative.

5 *See* 4.5.2.

(a) Check that the charitable body exists and that you have its correct name and address.

(b) Check its charitable status.

(c) Provide for a possible change of name.

(d) Include a receipt clause.

6 *See* 4.6.3

Section 33, Wills Act 1837 (as substituted by the Administration of Justice Act 1982) may save a gift to a child (or remoter issue) from lapse but:

- It may not be in the form the testator wishes;

- It is desirable to draw the existence of a substitutional gift to the testator's attention; and

- The operation of s.33 is ambiguous in some circumstances.

7 Where the residuary gift is to a minor, contingent, or successive and is or includes land. This is because if an express trust for sale is not established a strict settlement of land will arise.

8 *See* 4.10.

9 *See* 4.8.

The clause must contain the words, 'if the gift fails for any other reason ...' to cover the possibility of failure of the gift due to revocation by divorce.

10 Bearing in mind that such a gift will give rise to a trust, and that the children (or any remoter issue under a substitutional gift) may be minors, you should include the following:

- Extension of power of investment;

- Power to purchase a house for the residence of the beneficiaries;

- Receipt clause;

- Extension of statutory power of maintenance;

- Extension of statutory power of advancement;

- Power to advance the capital and make loans to the life tenant;

- Exclusion of:
  - *Howe v Dartmouth*
  - *Re Earl of Chesterfield's trust*
  - *Allhusen v Whittell*
  - Apportionment Act 1870.

Chapter 5

Accumulation and maintenance settlements

Introduction 5.1

In Chapter 2 we considered the basic principles of inheritance tax including taxation of settlements. An accumulation and maintenance settlement is an example of a settlement with no interest in possession (*see* Chapter 2, paras. 2.6.2 and 2.6.4). Where an accumulation and maintenance settlment falls within s.71, Inheritance Tax Act 1984, there will be special tax advantages.

The purpose of this chapter is to explain the operation of accumulation and maintenance settlements, in terms of the availability of income and capital, and to provide an understanding of the inheritance tax, capital gains tax and income tax consequences of the creation of such a settlement.

Availability of income 5.2

An accumulation and maintenance trust may be created *inter vivos* or on death and takes the form of trust property being held for beneficiaries contingent upon attaining a specified age, eg. 25.

Apart from the tax advantages, the creation of an accumulation and maintenance trust is advantageous as it prevents young, and thus potentially imprudent beneficiaries, from having access to capital too soon, but at the same time enables capital and income to be available if it is *needed*. Income may be made available up until the age of 18 either under the statutory power of maintenance (s.31, Trustee Act 1925) or under an express power of maintenance, the latter being more common because of the undesirable limitations of the statutory power (*see* Chapter 4, para. 4.11.3). From the age of 18 onwards, income is available as of right provided that the provisions of s.31(1)(ii), Trustee Act 1925 have not been excluded.

Availability of income up until 18 5.2.1

Up until 18 beneficiaries under an accumulation and maintenance trust will not have a *right* to the income from the trust but, provided the gift carries intermediate income (*see* Chapter 3, *Introduction to the Legal Practice Course* Companion), the trustees have discretion to apply all or part of the income for the maintenance, education or benefit of the beneficiaries.

If the statutory power of maintenance is operating, the making of payments to the beneficiaries is subject to the objective standard of 'reasonableness in all the circumstances', and the trustees are required to take certain specified matters into account (*see* Chapter 4, para. 4.11.3). Where the power is express no such limitations may exist.

To the extent to which income is not applied for the maintenance, education or benefit of the beneficiary under a trustee's power of maintenance, the income must be accumulated and added to the capital. Under s.31(2)(i), beneficiaries are entitled to accumulated income at 18 if their interest is:

- Vested during infancy or until marriage under 18; or
- Contingent on attaining 18 or marriage under that age and the beneficiary is entitled to a capital interest in the property from which the income arose.

5.2.2   Availability of income from 18 onwards

Provided that s.31(1)(ii), Trustee Act 1925 has not been excluded, beneficiaries who have attained 18 will have a right to all the income from the trust until their interest vests in possession (or fails) for so long as they have a contingent interest in such income (*see* Chapter 3, *Introduction to the Legal Practice Course* Companion).

This condition will be satisfied in the case of an accumulation and maintenance trust where the contingency is the attaining an age greater than 18.

5.3   Availability of capital

Where beneficiaries under an accumulation and maintenance trust have not yet satisfied the age contingency, capital will be available at the discretion of the trustees either under the statutory power of advancement set down in s.32 or under an express power of advancement.

It is normal to incorporate an express power of advancement because of the limitations of the statutory power, particularly, in this context, the statutory limitation of advancing up to a maximum of half the beneficiaries' presumptive share in the trust property (*see* Chapter 4, para. 4.11.3).

5.4   Inheritance tax

An accumulation and maintenance settlement is subject to

special and more advantageous tax rules if it satisfies all *four* of the conditions set out in s.71, Inheritance Tax Act 1984. These conditions are explained in paras. 5.4.1–4.

One or more persons etc 5.4.1

One or more persons will, on or before attaining a specified age not exceeding 25, become beneficially entitled to the property of the settlement or to an interest in possession in it.

The reference to 'one or more persons' being entitled 'on or before a specified age ...' refers to a class gift (*see* Chapter 4, para. 4.7.2) by way of an accumulation and maintenance settlement.

Note that s.71(7), Inheritance Tax Act 1984 provides that the conditions for an accumulation and maintenance settlement are not satisfied 'unless there is or has been a living beneficiary'. This means that although 'persons' can include an unborn person, there must be a living person who falls within the class at the date the settlement is created.

Example

If Bharti creates a settlement in favour of her children who attain 25, and Bharti is childless when the settlement is made, the settlement will not be an accumulation and maintenance settlement. If Bharti has a child at the date of creation of the settlement, however, even if that child subsequently dies, the requirement will be satisfied.

The 'one or more persons' must be entitled on or before a specified age not exceeding 25. If such persons may be so entitled the settlement will not be an accumulation and maintenance settlement. For example, if the beneficiaries become entitled 'contingent on attaining twenty-five years *or on earlier marriage*' the requirement will not be satisfied.

Section 71 provides that it is sufficient that on attaining a specified age not exceeding 25 the beneficiaries become entitled to an interest in possession in the settled property. They do not have to become entitled to the settled property itself on or before attaining 25. This means that they do not have to have an interest in capital on or before attaining 25. Thus, if the contingency is attaining the age of 30 for example, the requirement will still be fulfilled provided that s.31(1)(ii), Trustee Act 1925 (*see* 5.2.2) has not been excluded as this gives the right to income from the age of 18 until the interest vests in possession.

Such a right to income is an 'interest in possession' in the settled property for the purpose of s.71.

Note

Even though, technically speaking, the right to income under s.31(1)(ii) does not involve an age of 25 or lower being *specified*, the Inland Revenue has stated that it regards the entitlement to income under s.31(1)(ii) as satisfying the requirement.

5.4.2   No interest in possession subsists in it

Once there is an interest in possession in the settled property, whether an interest in capital or income, the property ceases to be subject to the special rules for accumulation and maintenance settlements: s.31(1)(ii). Where there is more than one beneficiary you must consider each part of the settled property separately.

Example

Ranjit by will creates a settlement in favour of 'such of my children as shall attain the age of twenty-five years'. He dies leaving two children Parveen and Hansa, who are 16 and 12 years old respectively at Ranjit's death. When Parveen reaches 18 years she will become entitled to an interest in possession under s.31(1)(ii) and her one half share in the fund will cease to be subject to the rules for accumulation and maintenance settlements.

5.4.3   The income from the settled property

The income from the settled property is to be accumulated so far as it is not applied for the maintenance, education or benefit of the beneficiaries.

This third requirement will be satisfied provided that:

● The power of maintenance contained in s.31, Trustee Act 1925 has not been excluded (*see* 5.2.1); or

● There is an express power of maintenance giving the trustees power to apply income for the maintenance, education or benefit of the beneficiaries *under the settlement*, ie. those entitled at 25 or some specified lower age, as opposed to any other beneficiaries.

5.4.4   25 year/common grandparent rule

Either (a) *Not more than 25 years has elapsed since the creation of the settlement (or later time when it satisfied all of the first three conditions) or (b) all the beneficiaries had a common grandparent.*

Two points particularly need to be noted about this requirement.

● The common grandparent need not be the settlor.

- Where the settlement is made on persons who do not have a common grandparent, the settlement will only remain an accumulation and maintenance settlement for 25 years. Thereafter adverse tax consequences will apply.

Note _____

Where the beneficiaries did not have a common grandparent the settlement remains a settlement after the elapse of 25 years and tax becomes payable. The rate depends on the length of time the property has been in the settlement and is normally a much higher rate than for settlements either with or without an interest in possession.

_____

The inheritance tax consequences of accumulation and maintenance trusts   5.4.5

If the settlement is created *inter vivos*, it will be a potentially exempt transfer (*see* Chapter 2, para. 2.2.2) and tax will only be payable if the settlor dies within seven years.

Where the accumulation and maintenance settlement is created by will or as a result of the operation of the rules of intestacy, tax will be payable on its creation.

After the creation of an accumulation and maintenance settlement there is no charge to tax on each tenth anniversary. This is so whether the settlement is created *inter vivos* or on death and is in contrast to other settlements where there is no interest in possession (*see* Chapter 2, para. 2.6.4) In fact, there is usually no charge to tax other than on creation of the settlement until the beneficiary gives their interest away or dies after acquiring a vested interest in it. Thus, there is no charge to tax where:

- A beneficiary dies before acquiring an interest in possession; or

- An advancement of capital or income is made to a beneficiary; or

- A beneficiary becomes entitled to an interest in possession in capital or income.

Note _____

For the purposes of the first of these situations above, if s.31(1)(ii) has not been excluded, the beneficiary will have an interest in possession at 18, consisting of the right to the income from the settled property. This means that if the beneficiary dies after reaching 18 but before satisfying the age contingency giving entitlement to the capital, a charge to inheritance tax will arise.

_____

5.5   Income tax

Trust income is taxed in two stages:

● First, in the hands of the trustees;

● Second, the position is adjusted (if necessary) when the income is paid to the beneficiaries, either by charging further tax or by refunding tax.

You must consider income which is paid at the discretion of the trustees separately from the situation where the beneficiaries have a right to the income from the trust property. Paragraph 5.5.1 sets out how income is taxed in the hands of the trustees, para. 5.5.2 income paid at the discretion of the trustees, and para. 5.5.3 income paid to beneficiaries as of right.

5.5.1   Income tax liability of the trustees

The income tax liability of the trustees is calculated in broadly the same way as income tax for individuals. There are, however, two differences:

● Basic rate is payable on all the income from the trust (other than dividends where the rate is 20%) regardless of the amount of income received;

● No deductions can be made for personal reliefs available to 'individuals'.

Section 686(2), Income and Corporation Taxes Act 1988 requires that the trustees pay an 'additional rate' (totalling 35%) on so much of the income of the trust as exceeds the expenses of managing the trust grossed up at basic rate:

● Where the income is to be accumulated (under s.31, Trustee Act 1925 or under the trust instrument) or where the income is payable at the discretion of the trustees: s.686(2)(a); *and*

● It is not income of any person other than the trustees, nor treated as income of the settlor: s.686(2)(b).

The trustee's special rate of 35% is payable in respect of an accumulation and maintenance trust where the beneficiary has no right to the income from the trust. The expenses are grossed up at basic rate to reflect the fact that they were paid from taxed income. When the trustees make a payment to a beneficiary they pay it net of both the basic rate and the additional rate of tax. The beneficiary, therefore, receives a tax credit of 35%.

5.5.2   Beneficiaries with no right to income

Where income is paid to a beneficiary at the discretion of the trustees, such as under a statutory or express power of maintenance (*see* 5.3.1), the beneficiary only pays income tax on income actually received. The trust income is taxed at 35% in the hands of the trustees as it arises.

The income received by the beneficiary has to be grossed up because it has been received net of tax (*see* 5.5.1). It is then included in the beneficiary's statutory income of receipts for the appropriate tax year and the beneficiary can then claim a tax credit of 35%, as this has been paid by the trustees. If the beneficiary is not even liable to pay basic rate tax, they can claim a rebate on all tax paid to the Revenue by the trustees.

These rules can operate favourably where the beneficiary is a higher rate tax payer as the maximum rate will be 35%. (Work through the example on the next page *now*.)

Beneficiaries with a right to income   5.5.3

In the case of an accumulation and maintenance trust falling within s.71, Inheritance Tax Act 1984, so long as s.31(1)(ii), Trustee Act 1925 has not been excluded (*see* 5.2.1), beneficiaries have a right to the income from the trust from the age of 18 until they attain a vested interest or their interest fails.

The trustees will pay basic rate tax on the income. Beneficiaries then include in their 'statutory income' for the appropriate tax year the income available to them, ie. the gross trust income less the trustees' expenses grossed up at basic rate. If the beneficiary is a basic rate payer, they can claim a basic rate tax credit. If the beneficiary is not liable to pay basic rate tax, they can reclaim all the tax paid by the trustees to the Revenue. If, however, the beneficiary is a higher rate tax payer, the difference between the basic rate tax paid by the trustees and higher rate tax, will have to be paid by the beneficiary.

Capital gains tax (CGT)   5.6

Trustees normally pay CGT at a rate equivalent to the basic rate of income tax. In the case of accumulation and maintenance settlements the trustees pay an additional rate of CGT (currently 35%; basic rate 25% plus additional rate 10%) where:

- Income is being accumulated;
- Income is paid at the trustee's discretion.

Note

Tax is payable at 35% on all trust gains whenever any part of the trust income for the year of assessment is liable to the additional rate of income tax.

Example

The trust income is £10,000 and the trustees incur £375 trust expenses.

Tax in the hands of the trustees	£	£
Gross trust income		10,000
Less: trust expenses grossed up (basic rate tax 25%)		
$\dfrac{£375}{75} \times 100\ =$		(500)
Income liable to additional rate		9,500
Additional rate (£9,500 × 10%)		950

The income available to the beneficiaries

	£	£
Trust income		10,000
Less: income tax		
basic rate	(2,500)	
additional rate	(950)	
		(3,450)
Income after tax		6,550
Less: expenses paid		375
Net available income		6,175

Tax in the hands of the beneficiary X

Net income available is £6,175

Statutory income (trust income grossed up at 35%)

$\dfrac{£6,175}{65} \times 100\ =$	9,500
Less: personal relief	(3,445)
Taxable income	6,055

Tax liability is:

£2,500 @ 20%	500
£3,555 @ 25%	888
Personal tax liability	1,388
35% tax credit: (£9,500 − £6,175)	3,325
Tax rebate claimable by X	1,937

Self-assessment questions

1 By her will Joyce left her residuary estate to be divided
between 'such of my children as reach the age of twenty-
five years ...'.

At Joyce's death she had two children, William aged 10
and Sarah aged 19.

(a) Explain in broad terms the availability of capital and
income for each child.

(b) Does the gift give rise to an accumulation and maintenance trust within s.71, Inheritance Tax Act 1984?

2 What are the inheritance tax consequences of an accumulation and maintenance trust within s.71, Inheritance
Tax Act 1984?

3 Compare the income tax position of trustees and beneficiaries where:

(a) The beneficiary has no right to income; and

(b) Where the beneficiary has a right to income.

Answer guidance to self-assessment questions

1   (a) *Capital*

Assuming Joyce's will contains no express power of advancement, the trustees will have power to advance up to
one half of each beneficiary's presumptive share for their
advancement or benefit: s.32, Trustee Act 1925 (*see* 5.3).

Income

Assuming Joyce's will contains no express power of maintenance and s.31, Trustee Act 1925 has not been excluded,
the trustees have discretion to pay all or any part of the trust
income generated by William's share in the trust for his
'maintenance, education or benefit' until he reaches 18.

Sarah will be entitled to all the income generated by her
share of the trust property under s.31(1)(ii).

(b) *See* 5.4. All four requirements are satisfied for William's
share of the fund, but if Sarah has a right to income under
s.31(1)(ii), her part of the fund will not be within s.71 as she
will have an interest in possession, ie. in the income from the
trust, at the date of creation of the settlement.

2   *See* 5.4.5.

3   *See* 5.5.1–3.

Chapter 6

Formalities and revocation

Formal requirements for making a will　　　6.1

A solicitor must know the detail of the formalities for executing a will in order to:

- Ensure that a client executes their will in such a way that there can be no question that the formalities have not been complied with; and

- Be able to decide whether or not a home made will fulfils the statutory requirements.

The requirements for a valid will are set out in s.9, as substituted by s.17, Administration of the Justice Act 1982. *All* must be satisfied.

These are:

- The will must be *in writing*.

- The will must be *signed* by the *testator* or by *some other person* in his presence and under his direction.

- It must appear that the testator *intended* by his signature to give effect to the will.

- The signature must be made or acknowledged in the presence of two or more *witnesses* present at the same time.

- Each witness must either *attest and sign* the will or *acknowledge his signature* in the presence of the attestator (but not necessarily in the presence of any other witness).

Note ⎯⎯⎯⎯⎯⎯⎯⎯⎯⎯⎯⎯⎯⎯⎯⎯⎯

All references in this chapter are to the Wills Act 1837 or to the Non-Contentious Probate Rules 1987 unless otherwise stated.

In writing　　　6.1.1

The will may be handwritten, typed or in a printed or lithographed form. The writing may be that of the testator or of any other person. The writing may be in any language or even in code, so long as the code can be deciphered.

There is no restriction as to the materials with which and on which it is written, provided that the materials produce a visible form.

Note ⎯⎯⎯⎯⎯⎯⎯⎯⎯⎯⎯⎯⎯⎯⎯⎯⎯

If a combination of ink and pencil are used, there is a rebuttable presumption that any pencil writing is merely deliberative, ie.

not the final form, and such parts will be excluded from probate unless evidence can be produced to show that the testator intended the pencil writing to be final.

While professionally drawn wills are produced in typed form, home made wills come in a variety of forms. A common form is for the testator to use a commercial will form which includes standard printed clauses and to complete the remaining sections in hand writing or typed form.

6.1.2   Signature

The will must be signed by the testator or by some other person in his presence and under his direction

What constitutes a signature?
To avoid complications, clients should be advised to sign the will with their normal signature. However, any mark of the testator which is intended as a signature will be valid. Thus a thumb print, initials, a mark made by a rubber stamp with the testator's name on it, and a mark taking the form of broken lines, have all been held to be valid signatures. It follows that a signature need not consist of a name at all. For example, in *Re Cook's Estate* (1960) the court accepted that the words 'your loving mother' at the end of a document, constituted a valid signature.

Part of a signature may be sufficient to validate a will provided the testator intended the mark actually made to be his complete signature.

Example

In *Re Chalcrafts's Goods* (1948) it was held that a signature was valid where a testatrix on the point of death started to sign her normal signature 'E Chalcroft' but after writing 'E Chal' became too weak to continue. The court held that she had decided to end her signature at that point and the signature was, therefore, completed.

Signature by another person
The will need not be signed by the testator provided that it is signed by another person in the testator's presence and under his direction. This involves both mental and physical presence. It may well be that a will is signed on behalf of the testator in circumstances where he is too weak through illness to sign for himself.

In order for the signature of the person signing on the testator's behalf to be valid, the testator must be physically present at the time of signing and also capable of understanding what is being done on his behalf. The person who signs on behalf of the testator may sign in their own name or in the name of the testator, and the person may be one of the witnesses to the will. It is better for such a person to sign in their own name and to say that they are signing on behalf of the testator in his presence and by his direction. (*See* specimen clause in Chapter 1, 1.4.1.)

Intention to give effect to the will   6.1.3

It must appear that the testator intended by his signature to give effect to the will

It is advisable to place the signature at the end of the will, but a signature placed elsewhere will be acceptable if its position suggests that it was intended by the testator to give effect to the will. If a court accepts that a signature wherever placed was intended to validate the will, all of the will will be admitted to probate even if parts of the will appear physically after the signature.

Common problems encountered are a signature on a separate sheet of paper placed either at the beginning or end of the will, or a signature placed on an envelope containing an otherwise unsigned will. In both cases the will is validly signed, provided the signature is intended to validate the will rather than merely to identify it.

Example _____

In *Wood v Smith* (1990) a testator wrote a will in his own handwriting headed 'My Will by Percy Winterbone' but he did not sign his name at the foot of the document. Evidence from the witnesses showed that he regarded the writing of his name at the top to be a signature. The Court of Appeal held that, despite the fact that the will had been signed before the dispositive provisions had been written, by writing his name and the dispositive provisions in one single operation, the deceased had provided clear evidence that he intended the signature to give effect to the provisions. Thus, the will was held to be duly executed.

_____

Witnessing the signature   6.1.4

The signature must be made or acknowledged in the presence of two or more witnesses present at the same time.

Choice of witnesses

There are no special rules as to who may witness a will but 'presence' requires that witnesses are capable of *seeing* the signature as well as *understanding* what they are doing. Thus, a blind person cannot be a witness and an illiterate person is an undesirable choice. Similarly, young children, drunks or those of unsound mind should not be chosen as

witnesses in case they are unable to understand the significance of what they are doing.

In selecting witnesses, a solicitor should be aware that
they may be required to give evidence as to the validity of
the will. Consequently persons of a fixed residence who
will be easy to trace, and persons of such an age that they are
unlikely to predecease the testator should be chosen.

Although the validity of the will itself will not be affected,
s.15, Wills Act 1837 deprives an attesting witness or the
spouse of an attesting witness of any benefit under the will.
In *Ross v Caunters* (1980) a solicitor was held liable in negli-
gence to a beneficiary who witnessed a will and in consequence lost his legacy under the will in circumstances where
the solicitor had not advised the testator of the effect of s.15.

Note

The Wills Act 1968, s.1 provides an exception to the provision
in s.15. It allows the signature of a witness who is also a
beneficiary and/or whose spouse is a beneficiary to be
disregarded provided that there are at least two other
independent witnesses who are unaffected by s.15. The signature
is regarded as superfluous and the beneficiary/witness may
receive their gift under the will.

As a professional charging clause is a benefit for the purpose of s.15, solicitors should not witness the will themselves if the will appoints them, or a firm in which they are
a partner, as executor. If they do, the charging clause will be
void even though the appointment of the solicitor or firm as
executors, and the will, are both valid.

Note

It is possible to use non-partners from the firm as witnesses.
Many firms prefer to suggest to their clients that witnesses are
selected from their non-legal staff, although trainee solicitors
may be used even though they may have become partners by
the date of the client's death.

Presence of witnesses

The testator must either sign in the presence of two witnesses
present at the same time or acknowledge his signature in the
presence of two witnesses present at the same time.

To be present at signing, the witnesses must be capable
of seeing the testator sign, although they need not actually
look at the signature or know that the document is a will.
However, if a witness is present in the same room but is
unaware that the testator is writing, or leaves the room

before the testator completes his signature, this is not sufficient.

Acknowledgement may be by words or conduct. Express acknowledgement, by saying 'this is my signature' for example, is desirable but not necessary.

There will be acknowledgement (by conduct) if the testator (or someone else in his presence and under his direction) asks the witnesses to sign a document and the witnesses see, or have the opportunity of seeing, the signature. They need not know that the document is a will. Thus, provided that the signature is visible it does not matter that the rest of the document is covered up.

Attestation 6.1.5

Each witness must either attest and sign the will or acknowledge his signature in the presence of the testator, but not necessarily in the presence of any other witness. However, in order to reduce the possibility of a later dispute, it is normal practice for both witnesses to be present and to sign after the testator has signed.

Attesting the will requires that the witnesses have placed their signatures on the will with the intention of validating the testator's signature.

The signature of the witness may be anywhere on the will although it must be in such a position to show an intention to attest.

Although a testator may have someone else sign on his behalf, witnesses must sign the will for themselves. However, as with the testator, the term 'signature' is widely interpreted to mean any mark intended by the witness as a signature (*see* 6.1.2).

Attestation clauses 6.2

An attestation clause recites that the proper formalities for the execution of a will have been complied with, and a possible form of drafting is as follows:

Specimen clause

Signed by the above-named)
(testator) as his last will in)
the presence of us present at)
the same time who at his)
request in his presence and)
in the presence of each other)
have hereunto subscribed)
our names as witnesses:)

Although the substituted s.9 provides that no form of attestation is necessary, it is highly desirable because it facilitates a grant of probate as such a clause raises a presumption of due execution.

If the will does not contain an attestation clause, expense and delay will occur as the registrar will require an affidavit of due execution from one of the witnesses or, if this is not possible, any other person present at the time of execution: Rule 12(1). If such an affidavit cannot be obtained the registrar may accept evidence on affidavit from any other person to show that the signature on the will is the handwriting of the testator, or any other evidence of due execution: Rule 12(2). If no evidence of any kind is available a hearing before a judge is usually necessary and the court may apply the maxim *omnia praesumuntur rite ac solemniter esse acta* (all the required formalities are presumed to have been complied with) and admit the will to probate.

Where the will contains an attestation clause, but there appears to be some doubt as to the due execution of the will, eg. if the signature of the testator appears below the signature of the witnesses, the registrar will require an affidavit of due execution, because an attestation clause merely raises a *presumption* of due execution.

It is particularly important that such clauses make clear that the testator knew and approved the contents of the will at the time of execution. (*See* specimen clause in Chapter 1, para. 1.4.1.)

Note

Special forms of attestation clause will be necessary where the testator is blind or illiterate or where the will has been signed on behalf of the testator.

6.3   Execution procedures

6.3.1   At your office

You should take the following steps for the execution of a will:

- Ask the client to attend your office and to sign the will in the presence of two witnesses (you should also be present at the time to see that the correct procedure is adopted);
- *Explain* the will, which has been drafted on the basis of their instructions, to the client;
- Ask the client to confirm that they have read the will, understood its provisions, and that it complies with

their wishes.

- Ensure all the pages of the will are *securely fastened* together in order to prevent loss of parts of the will and to avoid doubt as to precisely what has been attested;

- Keep an *attendance note* containing details of the time and place at which the will was executed together with the names and addresses of the witnesses;

Note _____

You should keep a *full* attendance note where there is the possibility that the testator's capacity may be challenged at a future date.

_____

- Keep a *copy* of the will – this is admissible evidence should the original later be lost.

Away from your office   6.3.2

If the will has to be sent to the client for execution it should be accompanied by detailed instructions as to precisely how the will should be executed. It is especially important to tell the testator:

- That they should re-read the will to see that they thoroughly understand it and that it complies with their wishes and that they should contact you if they have any queries or changes of mind;

- That neither a beneficiary under a will nor their spouse should witness the will (see 6.1.5);

- To contact you if they have any queries about any aspect of the procedure.

- To return the original will for checking, and not to clip, pin or staple anything to it.

A copy of the will should be sent to the client for their reference. Appropriate storage arrangements for the original will should be suggested, eg. the firm's strongroom.

Note _____

If the will has to be executed in hospital it is advisable for the solicitor to take witnesses to the hospital, as some hospital authorities do not allow medical staff to witness a will and other patients may be difficult to trace or lack capacity.

If, at a later date, doubt could be cast on the testator's capacity to make a will it is advisable to get a doctor to examine the testator at the time of execution and to provide a statement of the testator's mental capacity at the time of execution. If possible, the doctor should also witness the will.

_____

6.4   The doctrine of incorporation by reference

A testator may incorporate into his will an unexecuted document and so make the document part of the will provided it is:

- In *existence* at the date of execution of the will;
- *Referred to* in the will as already being in existence;
- Clearly *identified* by the will.

All three conditions must be satisfied.

> *Note*
>
> A document incorporated into a will is treated as a part of the will and must be filed at the probate registry with the rest of the will.

You should avoid the practice of incorporating a document by reference because of the chance that the document referred to might be lost before the testator dies. Where the will refers to a document to be incorporated, the registrar may require affidavit evidence of incorporation: Rule 14(3).

6.5   Privileged wills

The Wills Act 1837, s.11 provides that 'any soldier being in active military service, or any mariner or seaman being at sea, may dispose of his personal estate' without any formalities whatever. The Wills (Soldiers and Sailors) Act 1918 extends this privilege to realty.

> *Note*
>
> A minor can make a will while privileged.

6.5.1   Terms defined

The term 'soldier' includes a member of the RAF and naval or marine personnel serving on land. In *Re Wingham* (1949) it was said that the term 'soldier' includes 'not only fighting men but also those who serve in the Forces as doctors, nurses, chaplains, WRNS, ATS, and so forth ...'

'Active' military service was also explained in *Re Wingham*. It was said to arise where a soldier is serving in the armed forces 'in connection with military operations which are or have been taking place or are believed to be imminent'. In *Re Jones* (1976) a soldier serving in Northern Ireland was held to be on active military service.

The term 'mariner or seaman' includes all ranks of the merchant navy and of HM naval and marine forces. 'Being at sea' has been generously interpreted to include making a will on land when under orders to join a ship.

Note _____

It is beyond the scope of the course to know any further details about privileged wills.

Nuncupative wills

6.5.2

Where the testator is privileged the will can be made in any form including orally – a nuncupative will. The person making the statement need not know that they are making a will, all that is required is that the statement shows an intention to dispose of property at death.

Codicils

6.6

A codicil is a testamentary document which modifies or varies a will and which complies with the formal requirements set down for a valid will (*see* 6.1).

A codicil has the effect of 'republishing' a will so long as some indication to republish is shown. This may simply be by referring to an earlier will in the codicil. When a will is republished by a codicil it 'speaks' from the date of the codicil. This may affect the construction of the will with regard to persons or property (*see* Chapter 13, 13.3.3).

Revocation of wills and codicils

6.7

So long as the testator has testamentary capacity, a will or codicil is revocable until the testator's death. However, where a *mutual will* is made, a constructive trust will be imposed to frustrate the effect of revocation of a will.

A mutual will arises where two (possibly more) people make wills in similar terms and agree not to revoke their wills without the consent of the other(s). If the first to die has kept to the agreement, and the survivor revokes the mutual will, their property will be subject to a trust on the terms of the mutual will.

Note _____

Mutual wills should be distinguished from 'mirror' wills. These are wills made in similar terms but in circumstances where there has been no agreement not to revoke the will.

A will or a codicil, or any part of them, may be revoked by:

- Another will or codicil or duly executed writing declaring an intention to revoke: s.20;
- Marriage: s.18;
- Divorce: s.18A (as substituted by the Administration of Justice Act 1982);

- Destruction: s.20.

6.7.1   By another will or codicil or duly executed writing declaring an intention to revoke

Revocation by another will or codicil may be express or implied. For the sake of clarity, it is desirable that the revocation be express. Thus, a new will which deals with the whole of the property of the testator should contain an express revocation clause.

Specimen clause

I revoke all former wills and testamentary dispositions heretofore made by me.

A codicil may be used when only parts of a will are to be revoked. As little as a single clause or even a single word may be revoked by this means. However, it is important when drafting to ensure that only those parts which the testator intended are in fact revoked.

A will or codicil is *impliedly* revoked by a later will or codicil in so far as the latter contains provisions which are inconsistent with the former.

Conditional revocation

Whether revocation is express or implied, the doctrine of conditional revocation may save a will (or codicil) or part of it from revocation. The doctrine applies where the revocation is conditional upon the effectiveness of the revoking instrument.

Example

In *Re Finnemore (Dec'd)* (1991), the deceased made three wills, each with a revocation clause, and each containing a gift to C. C's husband witnessed the second and third wills. By virtue of s.15 (*see* 6.1.4), C could not take under the second or third will. However, the court held that the revocation clauses in the second and third will were conditional on the validity of the gifts contained in them. C could therefore take under the first will. (Note that the revocation clause in the third will was effective in its revocation of the rest of the first two wills.)

Privileged testators

Where a testator has privileged status (*see* 6.5), the will may be revoked whether or not the will has been made formally. Where a minor is privileged they can revoke a will whether or not they are still privileged – s.3(3), Family Law Reform Act 1969 – but if they are no longer privileged they must do so formally.

Express revocation

Under s.20, the whole or part of a will or codicil may be revoked without executing a later will or codicil by 'some writing declaring an intention to revoke the same' and duly executing it in the same way as the will.

Example

In *Re Spracklan's Estate* (1938), this requirement was satisfied where a testatrix wrote a letter addressed to the manager of a bank which had custody of her will saying 'will you please destroy the will already made out', the letter being signed by the testatrix and attested by two witnesses.

By marriage   6.7.2

A new s.18 was substituted by the Administration of Justice Act 1982 and applies to wills executed after 31 December 1982.

Section 18 provides that the marriage of the testator will automatically revoke a will – subject to following three exceptions.

1 'A disposition in a will in exercise of a power of appointment shall take effect notwithstanding the testator's subsequent marriage unless the property so appointed would, in default of appointment pass to his personal representatives': s.18(2).

2 'Where it appears from a will that at the time it was made the testator was expecting to be married to a particular person and that he intended that the will should not be revoked by the marriage, the will shall not be revoked by his marriage to that person': s.18(3).

It must 'appear from the will' that the testator intended that the will should not be revoked by the marriage, extrinsic evidence of the testator's intention is not admissible for this purpose. The following is a suitable form of words:

I make this will in the expectation of my marriage to (full name) and I intend that this will shall not be revoked by that marriage.

Note

1 Although it is unnecessary for the testator to be engaged to be married, he must contemplate marriage to a particular person at the time of execution of the will, and it must also appear from the will that the testator has a particular person in mind. It is therefore desirable to expressly name the person the testator is to marry. If the testator marries any other person than the one he was expecting to marry, the marriage will revoke the will.

2 It is uncommon for a client to require that a will be executed in contemplation of their marriage to a particular person. The reasons for making such a will is to provide for the testator's partner if the testator dies before the marriage takes place. Usually, such a will is an interim measure and a substantive will is drafted after the marriage has taken place.

3 Where it appears from a will that at the time it was made the testator was expecting to be married to a particular person and he intended that a disposition in the will should not be revoked by his marriage to that person:

- That disposition shall take effect notwithstanding the marriage;
- Any other disposition in the will shall take effect also, unless it appears from the will that the testator intended the disposition to be revoked by the marriage: s.18(4).

Provided that it 'appears from the will' that at the time it was made the testator was expecting to be married to a particular person, a *disposition* in the will shall not be revoked by the marriage. A professionally drawn will should contain express words that the disposition is not to be revoked upon marriage, eg. 'I give £3,000 to each of my nephews and declare that this gift is to take effect notwithstanding my forthcoming marriage to Gertrude Felicity Bowden-Smith'.

If the testator includes a declaration that one or more dispositions are *not* to be revoked by his forthcoming marriage, it is arguable that he has shown in the will his intention that other dispositions are to be revoked. However, for the sake of clarity, it is advisable to include an express declaration to this effect, eg. 'I declare that all the gifts contained in this will other than the gifts to my nephews are to be revoked by my forthcoming marriage to Gertrude Felicity Bowden-Smith'.

6.7.3 Revocation by divorce: s.18A

Under s.18A (as substituted by the Administration of Justice Act 1982), if a marriage is dissolved or annulled by the decree of a court, the will takes effect as if any appointment of the former spouse as executor (and trustee) is omitted. Moreover, any gift to a former spouse lapses.

Section 18A(3) provides that if the gift to the spouse is a gift of a life interest, the interest of the remainderman is accelerated so that they take an immediate interest, even if their interest is contingent on surviving the life tenant.

Note the following points:

- Section 18A applies subject to a contrary intention expressed in the will and s.18A(2) provides that the lapse of gifts to spouses is 'without prejudice to any right of the former spouse to apply for financial provision under the Inheritance (Provision for Family and Dependants) Act 1975' (*see* Chapter 14).

- As s.18A only causes gifts to a former spouse to lapse, the rest of the will remains valid. The will may therefore still need reviewing generally in the light of the testator's changed circumstances.

- A separation (including a judicial separation) does not affect the testator's will in any way. Thus, it is necessary to review whether a new will needs to be drawn up.

- Care is needed in the drafting of substitutional gifts.

Example

In *Re Sinclair (Dec'd)* (1985) a gift was made to the Cancer Research Fund which was expressed to take effect 'if my said wife shall predecease me or fail to survive me for one month ...' The testator divorced then died and his former wife survived him by more than a month. Under s.18A the gift to the wife lapsed and the Court of Appeal decided that the word lapse meant no more than 'fail'. Consequently, as the divorced spouse was not deemed to have predeceased the testator, the conditional gift to the Cancer Research fund could not take effect.

Because of the decision in *Re Sinclair*, to enable conditional gifts to take effect, it is necessary to state that a substitutional gift is to take effect 'if the gift to my spouse shall fail for any reason'.

Specimen clause

If my husband/wife does not survive me for (a specified period) or if the gift fails for any other reason ...

By destruction   6.7.4

Under s.20, Wills Act 1837 the whole or part of a will or codicil is revoked 'by burning, tearing or otherwise destroying the same, by the testator, or by some person in his presence and by his direction with the intention of revoking the same'.

Two distinct elements are necessary:

- Actual destruction;
- An intention to revoke.

One without the other is insufficient.

Actual destruction
Cancelling a will by striking out its clauses and the testator's signature with a pen is not 'otherwise destroying' for the purpose of s.20.

Example

In *Cheese v Lovejoy* (1877) there was held to be no act of destruction where a testator drew his pen through some lines of the will, wrote on the back of it 'All these are revoked' and threw it in a pile of waste paper in the corner of a room. In contrast, in *Re Adams* (1990) the parts of a will scored through heavily with a ball-point pen were held to have been destroyed.

If there is actual destruction of part of the will this may be sufficient to revoke the whole will. Whether this is the case depends on whether the part actually destroyed impairs the whole of the will, eg. if the testator's signature is destroyed, this will revoke the whole will. However, if the parts destroyed are less important, only that part will be treated as revoked. This was so in *Re Everest* (1975) where a testator cut off the part of the will containing trusts of the residue. It was held that the parts cut off were revoked but that the rest remained valid.

To establish actual destruction, it is necessary to show that the acts of destruction were *completed* by the testator.

Example

In *Doe D Perkes v Perkes* (1820), a testator tore his will into four pieces in a rage with a devisee named in the will. He was then calmed down and fitted the pieces together saying 'It is a good job it is no worse'. The court held there was no destruction as the testator had not completed all that he intended to do by way of destruction.

The act of destruction must be by the testator or by some other person in his presence and under his direction. Thus, there will be no revocation if a testator telephones his solicitor and asks the solicitor to destroy his will and the solicitor destroys the will without the testator being present.

Note

It is not possible for a destruction in the absence of the testator or without his direction to be ratified by him. Consequently, it will be necessary to revoke expressly by a further testamentary disposition.

Intention to revoke
The testator must have the same mental capacity as is

necessary to make a valid will to form an intention to revoke a will.

Where a will is destroyed by accident, there is no intention to revoke. Similarly, where the testator destroys a will under some mistaken belief, eg. that it is invalid, or that it has already been revoked, there is no intention to revoke.

A will is *presumed* to have been destroyed by the testator with an intention of revoking where:

- The will is last known to have been in the testator's possession;

and

- Either the will cannot be found at the testator's death; or
- The will is found torn or otherwise mutilated.

If a will last known to be in the testator's possession cannot be found at his death, it is presumed to have been destroyed by the testator with the intention of revoking it. Likewise, a will which has been in the testator's possession which is found to be torn or mutilated at his death is presumed to have been destroyed by the testator with the intention or revoking it in whole or in part. In either circumstance, the presumption may be rebutted by evidence to the contrary.

Once an intention to revoke has been established, it is necessary to establish whether the intention is absolute or conditional. This is a question of fact and extrinsic evidence is admissible to prove the revocation was only conditional.

If the intention is *absolute*, revocation takes place immediately. If it is *conditional* it does not take place until the condition is fulfilled. Revocation, may for example, be conditional upon the due execution of a new will or codicil.

Where a testator destroys his will with the intention to revoke and intends making a new will, it must be decided whether he intended the revocation of the old will, even if a new and valid will is not executed (absolute intention), or whether he only intended the old will not to take effect on the assumption that a new and valid will does take effect (conditional intention).

If a will has been *lost* or *accidentally destroyed*, probate may be obtained of a copy or reconstruction of the will. However, a court order must first be obtained. The procedure for obtaining such order is set out in Rule 54. The order can be made by a district judge or registrar although they may require that the matter is referred to a judge of the Family Division. The application must be supported by an affidavit to rebut the presumption that the will has been revoked by destruction and, in the case of a reconstruction of a will, evidence on affidavit as to the accuracy of the reconstruction. The district judge or registrar may require additional evidence and may direct that notice be given to persons who would be prejudiced by the application.

Note

1 It is good practice where a testator wishes to revoke their will by destruction, to ensure that the entire will is completely destroyed.

2 It is desirable when revoking a will to remove all doubt as to whether it was intended to be revoked by not only destroying the earlier will, but also including an express revocation clause in the new will.

3 Revocation of a will by destruction does not revoke any codicil to that will, although it may make the codicil difficult to give effect to if worded in such a way as to need to be read in conjunction with the will.

6.7.5   **Alteration of wills and codicils**

The position is governed by s.21.

Alterations made before execution

Any alteration made before the execution of the will is valid – provided it is final rather than deliberative. However, except where the alteration fills in a blank space, there is a rebuttable presumption that alterations have been made *after* execution of the will or any subsequent codicil. Extrinsic evidence, eg. from the person drafting the will or from a witness, or intrinsic evidence is available to rebut the presumption.

Where the alteration fills in a blank space, the presumption is that the alteration was made *before* execution.

Example

After a testator's death, a will is found as follows:

'~~£1000~~ to Robert Redfern.'

The £1000 was in fact crossed through before the will was executed and the witnesses can testify to this.

Even though the alteration was made before the execution of the will, it is presumed to have been made after execution. Affidavit evidence of the witnesses is, however, admissible to rebut the presumption and establish that the alteration was made before execution. The will is therefore admissible to probate as it stands and the legacy to Robert Redfern will not take effect.

Alterations made after execution

If the alteration is made after execution of the will, s.21 provides that it will be valid if duly executed by the formalities required for the execution of the will.

To avoid the need for an affidavit of alteration under Rule 16, alterations made before execution should be duly executed because the normal presumption is that they were made after execution. The formalities are satisfied if the testator and witnesses place their initials in the margin next to the alteration.

When an unattested alteration is made after the execution of the will and the original wording is 'apparent', the will is admitted to probate with the original wording, ignoring the alteration. 'Apparent' for this purpose means that the original words can be deciphered by an expert by 'natural means', eg. holding up the paper to the light or with the aid of a magnifying glass.

Example _____

After a testator's death, a clause in his will is found as follows:

'~~£1000~~ to Robert Redfern.'

The alteration is presumed to have been made after execution of the will. The will is admissible to probate with a legacy of £1000 to Robert Redfern taking effect. _____

If an unattested alteration made after the execution of the will makes any part of the will not 'apparent', probate of the will must be granted with a blank space. No physical interference is permitted or extrinsic evidence admissible to reveal the original words, except where:

- The testator had no intention to revoke *that part of the will*, ie. the words were obliterated by accident or mistake.

  In this case extrinsic evidence, eg. from copies of the will, drafts, infra-red photographs or removal of paper stuck over the words, is admissible to reveal the original words.

- The doctrine of *conditional revocation* applies.

  This most commonly occurs where the intention was that the original wording should only be revoked if the substituted wording is admissible to probate. If the substituted wording is made after execution of the will and not itself executed, then it will not be admissible to probate. 'Extrinsic evidence' is then admissible to reveal the original wording.

Example

A testator's will is found to read as follows:

    2000
'£▓▓▓ to Robert Redfern.'

The original sum is 'not apparent' but as another sum has been substituted it is likely that the doctrine of conditional revocation will apply. Extrinsic evidence will therefore be admissible to determine the original sum which has been obliterated.

6.8   Revival and republication of wills or codicils

A testator may revive a will or codicil or any part thereof which has been revoked provided that it has not been destroyed. Section 22 provides that a will or codicil which has been revoked in whole or in part may only be revived by:

- Its re-execution with proper formalities; or
- A duly executed codicil showing an intention to revive it.

Note

As the section provides that these are the only two methods of revival, a will which has been revoked by a later will cannot be revived by revocation of the later will. Section 34 provides that a revived will is deemed to have been made and executed at the time of its revival.

'Republication' of a will or codicil means basically confirming it. The difference between revival and republication is that the former revives a revoked will or codicil whereas the latter confirms an unrevoked will or codicil. However, the effects of republication are largely the same as those of revival.

6.9   Review of wills

A solicitor should try to prepare a will which provides for all reasonably foreseeable possible circumstances. However, a solicitor will need to specifically draw the client's attention to the need to keep their will under review, particularly in the light of marriage or divorce, but also, possibly, in the light of the enactment of unforeseen tax provisions.

Self-assessment questions

1   True or false?

(a) The will must be signed by the testator in the presence of at least two witnesses.

(b) The testator must sign the will at the foot or the end, and the witnesses must sign directly underneath the testator's signature.

(c) Only the testator need be present at the time when a witness is signing or acknowledging their signature.

(d) A minor can be a witness to the testator's signature.

(e) A spouse of the testator cannot be a witness.

2 What is an attestation clause and why is such a clause desirable?

3 What advice would you give to a client about the execution of their will, assuming that you were not going to be present at the time of execution?

4 What procedures would you adopt in the *execution of a will* if, although personally satisfied that the testator had sufficient mental capacity to make and execute a will, you thought there was a risk that the testator's capacity may be challenged on their death?

5 What is a privileged will and what form may such a will take?

6 What must be established in order to incorporate a document into a will by reference?

7 In what circumstances may it be appropriate to execute a codicil?

8 Your client wishes to make a will. He tells you he is to marry Felicity Jones next month. What advice would you give him?

9 You are advising Sarah Fidelity generally on the breakdown of her marriage. You drafted a will for her a year ago in which she was to leave a substantial part of her estate to her husband Jack. What advice would you give her concerning her will in the light of the breakdown of the marriage?

10 Simon made his first will in December 1980 and in June 1992 he made a new will. Both wills contained a standard clause revoking all previous wills. Each will appointed Trevor executor and they were deposited with him for safe keeping.

In March 1993, Simon wrote to Trevor requesting him to destroy the 1992 will, adding in his letter 'Please make sure you retain my will made in 1980'.

By mistake, Trevor burnt both wills. Simon died last month. Trevor comes to your office to enquire:

(a) Whether either or both wills can be admitted to probate; and

(b) Assuming both or one of the wills can be admitted to probate, what special arrangements regarding admission to probate will be required?

11 Fiona made the following alterations to the typescript of her will:

(a) Before executing the will, she altered a legacy to Keith of £100 to £150 by crossing out the £100 and replacing it by £150.

(b) Before executing the will, she filled in a blank space in a legacy to Sandra with the sum of £2,000.

(c) After the executing the will, she altered a legacy of £300 to Tom by crossing it out and substituting £450.

(d) After executing the will, she completely obliterated the sum of £2,000 in a legacy to the Cancer Research Fund and substituted the sum of £1,000.

Advise Fiona as to the effect of the alterations.

Answer guidance to self-assessment questions

1 (a) False. The testator may acknowledge his signature in the presence of the witnesses. The will may be signed by some other person in the testator's presence and under his direction (*see* 6.1).

(b) False. Although it is desirable that the testator signs at the foot or end of the will and the witnesses place their signatures underneath, this is not a requirement. From the position of the testator's signature it must appear that he intended by his signature to give effect to the will. The witnesses' signatures may be anywhere on the will although the position must be such so as to show an intention to 'attest' (*see* 6.1).

(c) True (*see* 6.1.5).

(d) True. A minor can be a witness to the testator's signature but a very young person is not desirable as they may lack capacity (*see* 6.1.4).

(e) False. A spouse of a testator can be a witness but is likely to be an undesirable choice of witness. If the spouse who is a witness takes a benefit under the will, although the will is valid, the spouse will not be able to claim their gift by reason of s.15, Wills Act 1837 (*see* 6.1.4).

2 *See* 6.2.

3 If the solicitor is not going to be present at the time of the

execution of the will, a letter should accompany the will giving detailed instructions as to precisely how it should be executed. The following points should be made in the letter:

- The client should sign the will at the bottom in the place marked X (by the solicitor before sending) in the presence of two witnesses.

- The testator should sign his usual signature in ink and sign before the witnesses sign.

- The witnesses should then both sign in the presence of the testator in the places marked X (by the solicitor before sending). The witnesses should place their addresses under their signatures.

- The witnesses should not be beneficiaries or the spouses of beneficiaries. They should be witnesses who are easily traceable and preferably persons who are significantly younger than the testator. Minors should not be witnesses.

4   If the will is to be signed on behalf of the testator the solicitor should include a suitably amended attestation clause.

If the will is to be executed in hospital, witnesses should be taken there by the solicitor.

Wherever the will is to be executed, the solicitor should, if possible, get a doctor to examine the client at the time of execution and to provide a statement of the testator's mental capacity at that time. Also, if willing and able to do so, the doctor should be a witness to the will (*see* 6.2–3).

5   *See* 6.5.

6   *See* 6.4.

7   *See* 6.6.

8   Advise the client that if he executes a will prior to his marriage to Felicity Jones, the will will automatically be revoked upon his marriage, unless it is drafted in such a way that it is expressed to be made in contemplation of marriage to Felicity Jones. Thus, the client could either wait until after the celebration of the marriage before executing the will to be drawn up or, alternatively, it should be expressly made to be in contemplation of the marriage (*see* 6.7.2).

9   Advise Sarah that the breakdown of her marriage, and in particular any separation agreement that may be made with her husband, will not alter the effects of her will. If she no longer wishes all/any of her estate to pass to her husband it may be appropriate to draw up a new will at this stage. However, if divorce is imminent, once the divorce has been decreed any gift to her husband will lapse, as will

an appointment of her husband as executor, although the rest of the will remains intact. However, it may still be appropriate to draft a new will if the distribution of the estate is to be different (*see* 6.7.3).

10(a) *Will made in December 1980.*

This is not admissible to probate as it was revoked by the will made in June 1992. Even if the latter will is revoked (*see* below), an earlier will cannot be revived by the revocation of the later will which revoked the earlier will (*see* 6.7.6).

Will made in June 1992.

This is unlikely to have been effectively revoked. Although the will has been actually destroyed by Simon, for revocation by destruction it is necessary to show:

- An intention to revoke (probably present);
- Actual destruction in the presence of the testator and under his direction (not satisfied): *see* 6.7.4. Therefore, unless there is 'duly executed writing, declaring an intention to revoke' within s.20, Wills Act 1837 – which would require Simon's letter to have been signed by him and witnessed (*see* 6.7.1) – there is no effective revocation.

When a will is missing at the date of death, there is a presumption that it has been revoked provided it was last in the possession of the testator. As Trevor has custody of the will, the presumption will not apply.

(b) A copy or reconstruction of the will of June 1992 will be admissible to probate if an order can be obtained from a district judge or registrar. Under Rule 54, Non-contentious Probate Rules 1987, an affidavit will be necessary, setting out the grounds of the application and, if a reconstruction of a will is to be presented, an affidavit as to the accuracy of the reconstruction.

11 *See* 6.7.5

(a) An alteration made before the execution of the will is valid and the will is, therefore, admissible to probate with the altered sum. However, unless an alteration made before execution fills in a blank space, it is presumed to have been made after execution and therefore to be invalid, unless duly executed. Consequently, affidavit evidence will be needed from the witnesses or other suitable persons under Rule 16, Non-contentious Probate Rules 1987 and the will, in altered form, will only be admissible to probate if the presumption of alteration after execution can be rebutted by such evidence. Otherwise the original sum will stand.

(b) *See* (a) – as the alteration fills in a blank space, it is presumed to have been made before execution and the will is admissible to probate with the sum of £2,000.

(c) Alterations made after the execution of the will, unless duly executed, are invalid. As the alteration is apparent (by crossing out), the will is admissible to probate with the original sum of £300.

(d) The alteration is made after execution and not duly executed. It is therefore invalid. As the original sum has been totally obliterated, the alteration is non-apparent. The general rule is that it is not possible to tamper with the will to provide evidence of what is under the obliteration, and extrinsic evidence is not admissible. Consequently, under the general rule the will is admissible to probate with a blank space. However, as there has been a substitution, the doctrine of conditional revocation applies and extrinsic evidence is admissible. Probate is therefore obtained with the original sum of £2,000.

Chapter 7

Intestacy

Introduction   7.1

When a person dies without leaving a valid will, the question of who is to share the assets of their estate is determined by the rules of intestacy. Equally, where a person leaves a valid will(s) but fails to dispose of all their estate under the will(s), what is not disposed of by will, passes in accordance with the rules of intestacy.

Part IV of the Administration of Estates Act 1925, as amended, lays down who is entitled to the deceased's estate after payment of debts and expenses, and in what proportions they are so entitled.

If relatives or dependants consider that the rules of intestacy do not make reasonable financial provision for them, they may make a claim under the Inheritance (Provision for Family and Dependants) Act 1975, and rules of intestacy may be varied by the court (*see* Chapter 14).

The rules of intestacy only apply to property which is capable of being left by will. They do not therefore apply to joint property which passes by survivorship, nominations, life policies written in trust, or to the subject matter of a *donatio mortis causa*.

Apart from a spouse, the rules of intestacy only benefit people who have a direct blood link with the deceased. It follows that they do *not* benefit unmarried partners, parents-in-law and stepchildren. If a deceased wishes such persons to benefit from their estates, they must make a will.

Thus, the aims of this chapter are to:

- Provide an understanding of how property is distributed on intestacy; and

- Re-enforce the advantages of making a will by highlighting the problems which may arise out of dying intestate.

Note

All references are to the Administration of Estates Act 1925 unless otherwise stated.

Avoiding partial intestacy   7.2

Persons are said to have died totally intestate where none

of their estate is effectively disposed of by will, and partially intestate where a valid will only disposes of part of their estate. Broadly, the same rules apply whether the deceased dies totally or partially intestate but there are some significant differences which we explain below (*see* 7.3.1 and 7.5.2).

A partial intestacy may occur in one or two ways:

- The will fails to dispose of the whole of the estate because there is no residuary gift; or
- A residuary gift is included but it fails in whole or in part, because, for example, the beneficiaries under the residuary gift predecease the testator causing the gift to lapse.

It is obviously desirable to draft a will so as to avoid a partial intestacy. Consequently it is important to:

- Be sure to include a residuary gift; and
- Include a substitutional gift in the residuary gift to avoid the problem of lapse (*see* Chapter 4, 4.9).

7.3   Statutory trust for sale

Section 33 provides that on intestacy the personal representatives hold all the deceased's estate upon trust for sale.

Note

The personal representatives have a power to postpone sale for as long as they think fit.

There are, however, two qualifications to the duty to sell:

- Personal representatives shall not sell reversionary interests before they fall into possession, unless there is a 'special reason for selling'; and
- Personal chattels must not be sold unless required for administrative purposes as there are no other assets , or there is a 'special reason' for selling.

From the fund produced by sale, the personal representatives must pay the funeral, testamentary and administration expenses, debts and other liabilities of the deceased.

In the case of *partial intestacy*, they must also pay the legacies (if any) left by the deceased in the will. What remains is 'the residuary estate of the intestate' and it is this that is shared among the beneficiaries in accordance with their entitlement under Part IV of the Act.

7.3.1   Partial intestacy

The statutory trust for sale imposed by s.33 applies to total and partial intestacy. However, where the property undisposed of by the will is held on express trust for sale, this trust prevails over the statutory trust for sale. Conversely, where the property undisposed of in the will is not subject to a trust for sale, the statutory trust for sale applies, provided that there is *a contrary intention in the will.

It follows that it is possible for the will to create an express trust for sale in respect of part of the property and for their to be a statutory trust for sale in respect of another part.

Note

It is important to know whether an express trust for sale or the statutory trust for sale is operating as the terms of the former may differ. For example it may remove the power to postpone sale.

The surviving spouse   7.4

For the purposes of the rules of intestacy, a divorced spouse has no rights in the deceased's estate (in the case of deaths occurring on or after 1 January 1970). Neither has a judicially separated spouse. The Matrimonial Causes Act 1973, s.18(2) treats such a spouse as being dead so long as the separation is still continuing.

If a client consults you about a divorce or judicial separation, you should enquire whether the client has made a will and, if they have not, advise the client that their property will pass to their surviving spouse if they should die intestate before the date of the decree of judicial separation or of the decree absolute on divorce.

Note

An existing will may require reviewing in the light of the divorce/judicial separation.

A spouse's exact entitlement under the rules of intestacy depends on the closeness of any other surviving relatives of the intestate. One of three situations will apply:

- Intestate leaves spouse and issue.
- Intestate leaves spouse and parent(s) or brother(s) and sister(s) (or their issue) surviving but no issue.
- Intestate leaves spouse but neither issue nor parents nor brothers and sisters of the whole blood or their issue.

Intestate leaves spouse and issue   7.4.1

Where the intestate leaves a spouse and issue the estate is divided between the spouse and issue.

Spouse

The spouse takes:

- The deceased's 'personal chattels' absolutely;
- A 'statutory legacy' of £125,000 free of tax and costs, together with interest of 6% per annum from the date of death to the date of payment;
- A *life* interest in *one-half* of the residue of the estate – so long as there is something left in the estate after taking the personal chattels and the statutory legacy.

'Personal chattels' are defined by s.55(1)(x) as 'carriages, horses, stable furniture and effects (not used for business purposes), motor cars and accessories (not used for business purposes), garden effects, domestic animals, plate, plated articles, linen, china, glass, books, pictures, prints, furniture, jewellery, articles of household or personal use or ornament, musical and scientific instruments and apparatus, wines, liquors and consumable stores, but do not include any chattels used at the death of the intestate for business purposes nor money or securities for money'.

Note _____

The assets must *not* be used for business purposes. The phrase 'articles of personal use' was held in *Re Chaplin* (1950) to include a 60-foot motor yacht, and in *Re Crispin's Will Trust* (1975) a collection of watches.

Issue

The issue take:

- The remainder in one-half of the estate subject to the surviving spouse's life interest;
- The other half of the estate absolutely on the 'statutory trusts' (*see* 7.5.1).

7.4.2   **Intestate leaves spouse and parent(s) or brother(s) and sister(s) (or their issue) surviving but no issue**

Where the intestate leaves no issue, but does leave a parent or brother or sister of the whole blood or their issue, the surviving spouse takes:

- 'Personal chattels' absolutely (*see* 7.4.1);
- A statutory legacy of £200,000 free of tax and costs, together with interest of 6% from the date of death to the date of payment;
- *Half* of any residue *absolutely*.

The other half of the residue goes to the parent or parents in equal shares absolutely or, if none, to the brother(s) and sister(s) of the whole blood or their issue on the statutory trust (*see* 7.5.1 and 7.7).

Intestate leaves spouse but neither issue nor parents nor brothers and sisters of the whole blood or their issue

Here the surviving spouse will take the residuary estate which is held on the statutory trust absolutely.

Special rights of the surviving spouse

The surviving spouse is given two special rights of election in order to try to provide greater security for the spouse in the operation of the rules of intestacy:

- The right to redeem the life interest for a lump sum out of the capital; and
- The right to acquire the matrimonial home.

Right to redeem the life interest

Where a surviving spouse is only entitled to a life interest in half of the residue because issue have also been left by the intestate, the surviving spouse can elect to take a lump sum of the capital instead of receiving the income from the trust for sale arising under the life interest.

The election must be made within *12 months of the grant of representation* (unless the court exercises it discretion to extend this time limit): s.47A(5) as amended. It can be exercised by giving notice in writing to the personal representatives: s.47A(6), or, if the surviving spouse is the sole personal representative, by giving notice in writing to the Senior Registrar of the Family Division of the High Court: s.47A(7).

The capital value of the life interest is calculated by reference to published tables which take into account the age of the surviving spouse and the prevailing yield on medium-term Government Stocks: s.47A(3)(a) and (b); Intestate Succession (Interest and Capitalisation) Order 1977 (No 1491). However, where the surviving spouse and issue are all *sui juris*, the life interest may be valued by agreement between the spouse and issue, without the need to observe the statutory provisions.

Note

For the purposes of inheritance tax, no 'transfer of value' is made where the surviving spouse elects to redeem the life interest. However, it will mean that less of the intestate's estate will be treated as passing to the surviving spouse, and less of the estate will attract the spouse exemption and, consequently, more inheritance tax may be payable. This is because, even though the surviving spouse has only a life interest, s/he is treated as owning capital and interest for inheritance tax purposes. Therefore, the whole is spouse exempt. Where the life interest is capitalised, however, the spouse exemption will apply to the surviving spouse's share of the capital, but inheritance tax will be payable on the remainder.

The right to acquire the matrimonial home

The Intestates' Estates Act 1952, Schedule 2 contains provisions designed to make it easier for a surviving spouse to acquire the matrimonial home (or the deceased's share therein).

The term 'matrimonial home' is widely defined to apply to a 'dwelling house' in which the surviving spouse was resident at the intestate's death. It does not require that the intestate was also resident at the date of death. It applies to freehold or leasehold interests of the intestate (except where the lease has less than two years to run) and on total or partial intestacy.

Note

If the surviving spouse is a joint tenant of the matrimonial home, the property will not form part of the intestate's estate and the surviving spouse will take by survivorship.

The surviving spouse has the right to require the personal representatives to appropriate the matrimonial home in total or partial satisfaction of an absolute and/or capitalised interest in the estate.

Where the value of the matrimonial home exceed the value of the spouse's entitlement on intestacy, the PRs can still be required to appropriate it, but the spouse will have to pay 'equality money' to make up the deficit: Schedule 2, para. 5(2).

The date of valuation of the matrimonial home is the *date of appropriation* not the date of death: *Re Collins* (1975). Thus, if property prices are rising at the time of the intestate's death, the surviving spouse should be advised to decide quickly on whether to exercise the right of appropriation.

The right *must* be exercised within *12 months of the grant of representation* (unless the court exercises its discretion to extend the period) by notice in writing to the personal representatives. If the surviving spouse is a personal representative along with other(s), notice must be given to the other(s).

The personal representatives must not sell the matrimonial home before the expiration of the 12 months without the written consent of the surviving spouse, unless it is necessary for the purposes of administration due to lack of other assets.

The Schedule provides that where a spouse is one of two or more personal representatives, the rule that a trustee should not purchase trust property does not prevent the purchase of a dwelling house from the estate. The Schedule says nothing about the position where the surviving spouse is the sole personal representative. It is therefore advisable to either:

- Appoint another personal representative; or
- Obtain the consent of all the other beneficiaries to the estate (only possible if they are *sui juris*); or
- Obtain the consent of the court.

There are *four* situations where the consent of the court is in any case *required* before the surviving spouse can exercise the right to appropriate the matrimonial home. These are where the dwelling house:

- Forms part of a building the whole of which is comprised in the residuary estate; or
- Is held with agricultural land which is so comprised; or
- Was at the intestate's death partly or wholly used as a hotel or lodging house; or
- Was at the intestate's death partly used for non-domestic purposes.

Where one of these four situations applies, the court may only give its consent if it is satisfied that the exercise of the right by the surviving spouse is not likely to diminish the value of the other assets in the residuary estate or make them more difficult to dispose of.

Note

Section 41 gives the personal representatives a general *power* to appropriate assets of an estate in certain circumstances, including on intestacy where the next of kin consent. The court's consent is *never* required.

Where an application to the court is required to give consent before the right of appropriation can be exercised by the surviving spouse, ie. in one of the four situations outlined above, or where the right cannot be exercised for some other reason, a surviving spouse may ask the personal representatives to exercise their *power* under s.41 by appropriating the matrimonial home. There is, however, no right to insist that the personal representatives make the appropriation as they merely have a power, not a duty, to appropriate.

The statutory power of appropriation cannot be relied upon where the value of the asset to be appropriated exceeds the beneficiary's interest in the estate.

7.4.5   Hotchpot

Section 49(1)(aa) provides that where there is a partial intestacy a surviving spouse who acquires any beneficial interest under the deceased's will must bring the benefits into account against the *statutory legacy*.

Note

This does not apply to a specific gift of personal chattels.

Particularly note the following:

- On intestacy (total or partial), a surviving spouse will never be required to bring into account *inter vivos* advancements made to them by the deceased (compare hotchpotch and issue, *see* 7.5.2); and

- Benefits under the will need only be brought into account against the surviving spouse's *statutory legacy*, the spouses right to personal chattels or to a share in the residue of the estate are unaffected.

7.4.6   Commorientes and intestacy

In order to become entitled, on intestacy, the intestate's spouse must survive the intestate. It is immaterial that the spouse only survives the intestate for a very short time.

Where two or more persons die in circumstances rendering it uncertain which of them survived the other, s.184 of the Law of Property Act 1925 provides for a general statutory presumption that the parties died in order of seniority, ie. the younger being deemed to have survived the older (*see* Chapter 13, 13.5.1). The section applies both on intestacy and where the deceased dies leaving a valid will.

However, there is a special rule where the elder of the spouses dies intestate. The Intestates' Estates Act 1952, s.1(4) amends s.184 of the Law of Property Act 1925 to provide that, when administering the estate of the elder spouse only, the younger spouse is presumed to have predeceased. Section 184 applies in the ordinary way when administering the estate of the younger spouse.

Example

If a husband (aged 45) and his wife (aged 43) both die intestate in circumstances rendering it uncertain which of them survived the other, neither of them take on the intestacy of the other.

Under s.1(4) of the Intestates Estates Act 1952 the husband as the older spouse is presumed to have survived his wife, and therefore his estate passes to his next-of-kin on the assumption that his wife is dead. His wife, being younger, is presumed to have survived her husband under s.184 of the Law of Property Act 1925 so that her estate passes to her next of kin on the assumption that her husband is dead.

The rights of issue on intestacy 7.5

The issue of the deceased are the next category of next of kin of the intestate to benefit from the estate after any surviving spouse.

You have seen (7.4 above) that where the intestate leaves a surviving spouse, the issue take one-half of the residuary estate absolutely and the other half of the residuary estate subject to the surviving spouse's life interest. If there is no surviving spouse the issue take the whole of the residuary estate.

Statutory trusts 7.5.1

Where issue are entitled on intestacy, they take the appropriate share of the estate on the 'statutory trusts' set out in s.47. Under this section, the property must be divided in equal shares among such of the children of the intestate who are alive or *en ventre sa mere* at the date of the intestate's death and who either attain the age of 18 or marry under that age.

Where a child predeceases the intestate but leaves issue living at the date of death of the intestate, those grandchildren or their issue take *per stirpes* the share which their parent would have taken provided that they reach 18 or marry under that age.

Note that in order to be a beneficiary under the statutory trust, issue (whether children grandchildren or great grandchildren) must:

● Firstly be alive or *en ventre sa mere* at the intestate's death; and then

● Either attain the age of 18 or marry under that age.

If the issue in question are alive or *en ventre sa mere* at the intestate's death but do not attain 18 years or marry under that age, their share in the estate is distributed as if the beneficiary had never been alive.

Example 1 ————————————————————————

Angela had three children, Benedict, Catherine and Duncan, of whom Benedict and Catherine survive her. Duncan predeceased her, leaving two children, Evan and Fanny, who survive Angela. The residuary estate of £30,000 will in these circumstances be divided:

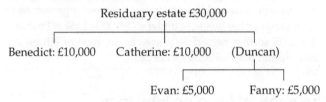

If, however, Catherine, although alive at the death of Angela, dies before attaining the age of 18 or marrying under that age, her share of £10,000 (on the assumption she has no children) is divided accordingly:

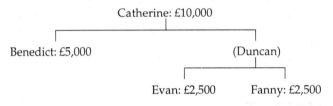

Where a child predeceases the intestate but leaves issue living at the date of the intestate's death, the issue take contingent on attaining 18 years or marriage under that age the share of the residuary estate which their *parent* would have taken, ie. *per stirpes.*

Thus, in Example 1 above, note that the residuary estate has not been split equally in four ways between Benedict, Catherine, Evan and Fanny, but equally three ways, Evan and Fanny taking the deceased Duncan's share which is then divided equally between the two of them.

A minor who marries thereby attains a vested interest but, while minors can give a valid receipt to the personal representatives for income, they cannot give a valid receipt for capital. Consequently, the personal representatives will wish to protect themselves from liability by retaining the capital as bare trustees for the minor until the minor attains 18 years.

As persons who fail to reach the age of 18 or marry earlier are treated as if they had never been alive, this means that property may pass to someone who at the moment of the intestate's death appeared not to be entitled, as in Example 2 below

Example 2 _____

Gregory died intestate, survived by his wife Harriet, their two children Ian and James, and his mother Kitty. Ian and James are aged 9 and 10 respectively at Gregory's death.

On these facts, and assuming Gregory's estate is large enough, Harriet will receive:

● The personal chattels; and

● The statutory legacy of £125,000; and

● A life interest in one half of the residue.

The remainder, subject to the life interest, along with the other half of the residue absolutely will be held on the statutory trusts for Ian and James in equal shares contingent upon their attaining 18 years or marriage under that age.

If either of Ian or James dies unmarried before reaching 18 years, their share will be held for the other on the statutory trusts.

If *both* die unmarried before reaching 18 years, the estate will be distributed as if they had never existed. Thus Harriet's statutory legacy will be increased to £200,000 and the residue of the estate will be divided equally between Harriet and Gregory's mother Kitty, each taking their share absolutely (*see* 7.4.2).

Hotchpot   7.5.2

Sections 47(1)(iii) and 49(1)(a) provide for two hotchpot provisions based on the assumption that parents will want to treat their children equally.

Section 47(1)(iii)

On a total or partial intestacy *inter vivos* advancements to a child of the deceased must be brought into account by the child when assessing the child's entitlement on intestacy unless the intestate showed a contrary intention.

An 'advancement' is a payment of money or transfer of property made with the aim of establishing a child in life or making permanent provision for the child. There is a presumption that a large sum paid at one time is an advancement whereas a small sum is not (large or small being considered both in the abstract and by reference to the size of the estate of the intestate).

A payment made on the marriage of the child is automatically considered to be an advancement, irrespective of the purpose for which it was paid or its size.

Particularly note that:

● The provision applies to both total and partial intestacy.

● The provision only applies if there is no 'contrary intention on the part of the intestate expressed or appearing from the circumstances of the case: s.47(1).

- The test as to what constitutes an advancement is subjective and the onus of proving a contrary intention lies with the party who asserts it: *Hardy v Shaw* (1976).
- The advancement is valued at the date of death.

  This may be significant if an asset, eg. shares, as opposed to cash is given by way of advancement as the asset may have substantially increased or decreased in value by the date of the intestate's death.
- The advancement reduces the child's share under the intestacy by the value of the advancement. However, if the benefit to be brought into account is larger than the child's share, there is no obligation to refund it to the estate.
- The provision only applies to a *child* of the intestate and not to remoter issue. However, if the child predeceases the intestate leaving issue who takes *per stirpes*, the share of the issue will be reduced by the value of the advancement (*see* Example 3 below).

When bringing an advancement into account the following steps must be followed:

Step 1 Calculate the 'notional estate', ie. undisposed of property plus the value of the advancement(s) at death.

Step 2 Divide the 'notional estate' between the children (or issue of a deceased child).

Step 3 Deduct the amount of the advancement(s) from the share of the child or children to whom the advancements have been made.

Step 4 Distribute the 'residuary estate' accordingly.

Example 3

Linda dies intestate leaving undisposed residue of £20,000. She is survived by three adult children: Michael, Nigel and Oliver. Her fourth child Penelope predeceased her leaving an only son Quentin, also an adult, who survived Linda. Linda made advancements to the value of £2,000 to Michael and £2,000 to Penelope:

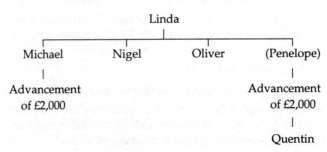

Calculation of entitlement:

Step 1 The 'notional estate' is £24,000 (£20,000 and £2,000 to Michael and £2,000 to Penelope).

Step 2 The estate is to be divided into one quarter shares, ie. £6,000.

Step 3 The shares of Michael and Quentin (taking *per stirpes* the share of Penelope) are reduced by £2,000 each.

Step 4 The undisposed property is divided:

Michael	£4,000
Nigel	£6,000
Oliver	£6,000
Quentin	£4,000
	£20,000 (the original figure of residue)

Section 49(1)(a)

On a partial intestacy, gifts by will to the deceased's issue must be brought into account unless a contrary intention of the deceased is expressed or appears from the circumstances of the case.

Unfortunately the section was badly drafted and it is unclear whether the term 'issue' means children *and* remoter issue so that any member of the family belonging to a certain branch must bring into account everything which has been acquired under the will by that branch. However, this was the view taken at first instance in *Re Young* (1951) and followed in two subsequent first instance decisions – *Re Morton* (1956) and *Re Grover's Will Trust* (1971). The effect of this interpretation is illustrated in Example 4.

Example 4 _____

Robert dies partially intestate leaving three children Sam, Tessa and Una and one grandchild Veronica. By will Robert left £3,000 to his son Sam and £2,000 to his granddaughter Veronica, the child of Una. His undisposed of property is £10,000.

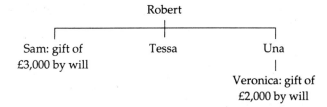

The entitlements on partial intestacy are calculated on the four steps outlined with reference to Section 47(1)(iii) above:

Step 1 The 'notional estate' is £15,000 (£10,000 and £3,000 to

Sam, and £2,000 to Veronica).

Step 2 Each child of Robert is entitled to a one-third share, ie. £5,000.

Step 3 As Sam has already received £3,000, his share is reduced by that amount and, as Veronica has received £2,000, Una's share is reduced by this amount; this is the effect of *Re Young*.

Step 4 The undisposed of property is therefore divided:

Sam	£2,000
Tessa	£5,000
Una	£3,000
	£10,000 (original undisposed of estate)

7.6   Intestacy, adopted, legitimated and illegitimate children

7.6.1   Adopted children

For the purpose of entitlement under the rules of intestacy, an adopted child is deemed related to the adoptive parents and not the natural parents: Adoption Act 1976, s.39(1) and (2)).

An adopted child cannot therefore claim on the intestacy of a natural parent but takes on the intestacy of the adopting parents or adoptive grandparents, brothers or sisters etc. Likewise if the adopted child dies intestate, the child's adoptive parents will be entitled as if the child was their natural legitimate child.

7.6.2   Legitimated children

Legitimated children are deemed to have been born legitimate and can therefore take on intestacy in the same way as any legitimate child: Legitimacy Act 1976, ss.5(1)–(4) and 10(1).

7.6.3   Illegitimate children

In the case of deaths occurring after 4 April 1988, when identifying family relationships for the purpose of the intestacy rules, no distinction is drawn between a child whose parents are or were married to each other and a child whose parents are or were not (Family Law Reform Act 1987).

Where a child is born outside marriage, it may be especially difficult for personal representatives to find the father of the child (entitled on the child's intestacy) if the parents of the child had no continuing relationship. Thus, to facilitate the administration of the intestate's estate, s.18(2), Family Law Reform Act 1987 assists the administration of estates by providing that where the parents of a child are not married to each other at the child's date of birth, it is presumed that the father of the child, or any person claiming through the father, is dead.

This means that, in the absence of evidence to the contrary, the personal representatives may distribute the estate on the basis that no such persons are alive.

Note

As to steps personal representatives should take generally to protect themselves from liability for incorrect distribution of an estate due to ignorance of the existence or whereabouts of persons who may be entitled (*see* 13.4).

The rights of others   7.7

Where there is a surviving spouse   7.7.1

You have already seen that where there is a surviving spouse, subject to the rights of that surviving spouse, the estate of an intestate passes:

- To issue on the statutory trusts; but, if none,
- To parents (equally if both alive); but, if none,
- To brothers and sisters of the whole blood on the statutory trusts.

Where there is no surviving spouse   7.7.2

If there is no surviving spouse or relative as above, the estate of the intestate passes:

- To brothers and sisters of the half blood on the statutory trusts; but, if none,
- To grandparents (equally if more than one); but, if none,
- To uncles and aunts of the whole blood on the statutory trusts; but, if none,
- To the Crown, Duchy of Lancaster or Duke of Cornwall (as *bona vacantia*).

Section 46(1)(vi) gives the Crown, the Duchy of Lancaster and the Duke of Cornwall (as appropriate) discretion to make provision for dependants of the intestate whether they are related to the deceased or not and for other persons for whom the intestate might reasonably have been expected to make provision.

Points to note   7.7.3

- Each category must be considered in the order listed above and only if there is no one in a particular category is it necessary to proceed to the next category.

- The *spouse* of a person within any of the categories has no claim, as there is no blood relationship (necessary for the intestacy rules).
- Relatives who take on the statutory trusts, ie. brothers and sisters of the whole and half blood, and aunts and uncles of the whole and half blood, take on the same basis as issue as set out in 7.5.1. Thus, the relative in question must be alive at the intestate's death and attain 18 years of age or marry earlier and if they have predeceased the intestate they may be replaced *per stirpes* by their own issue who attain the age of 18 or marry earlier.
- There are no hotchpot provisions for relatives other than spouse and issue.

Self-assessment questions

1 Distinguish between the statutory trust for sale, which arises on intestacy, and the statutory trusts.

2 William died intestate leaving: a widow Edna; two children, Frances (aged 26) and George (aged 16); and a grandson Peter (aged 12) by his daughter Henrietta, who predeceased William. William's estate is worth approximately £200,000. How will it be distributed?

3 Nigel died intestate, leaving a widow, Molly and two children. Nigel was the sole owner of the matrimonial home (valued at £150,000). Nigel's estate is valued at approximately £300,000. Molly does not want the matrimonial home to be sold as she wishes to continue to live there with the two children. Advise Molly.

4 Susan died partially intestate leaving a widower Tom and two children, Paul and Mary. Susan gave £20,000 to Tom a year before she died and £3,000 to Paul when he got married. In addition, she left by will her personal chattels and £150,000 to Tom, £2,000 to Paul and £1,000 to Mary. The undisposed of property is £20,000. How will this be distributed?

Answer guidance to self-assessment questions

1 The statutory trust for sale refers to the trust of the whole of the intestate's estate which arises by virtue of s.33 on a total intestacy (and in some cases also operates on a partial intestacy) by which the personal representatives have a general duty to sell the assets of the estate but a power to postpone sale (*see* 7.3).

In contrast, 'the statutory trusts' refers to the terms on

which certain categories of relatives of the intestate, eg. issue, are entitled on intestacy. The entitlement is contingent upon the attaining of the age of 18 or marriage under that age (*see* 7.5.1).

2   William's widow Edna will take:

- William's personal chattels as defined by s.55(1)(x) absolutely.
- The statutory legacy of £125,000 free of tax and costs plus interest of 6% per annum from the date of death to the date of payment.
- A life interest in one-half of the residue. The other half of the residue along with the interest in remainder, subject of Edna's life interest, will be held for William's issue as follows:

  – Frances takes a one-third vested interest;

  – George takes one third contingent on attaining 18 or marriage before;

  – Peter takes *per stirpes* the share of William's deceased daughter, Henrietta, contingent on attaining 18 or marriage before.

3   As Nigel has left a spouse and issue, Molly will be entitled, under the rules of intestacy, to Nigel's personal chattels, a statutory legacy of £125,000 (plus interest) and a life interest in one-half of the residue of the estate. The matrimonial home is worth half of the value of the estate. The residue of the estate can at best be worth £175,000, Molly taking a life interest in one-half.

As a surviving spouse, Molly has the right to require the personal representatives to appropriate the matrimonial home in satisfaction of her statutory legacy and/or capitalised life interest (*see* 7.4.4).

Depending on the value of her life interest, this may or may not be sufficient to raise the £150,000 for the matrimonial home. If it is not sufficient, Molly may supply 'equality money' from her own assets to make up the difference.

4   This situation raises the issue of hotchpot (*see* generally 7.4.5 and 7.5.2). As a surviving spouse, Tom does not have to bring into account *inter vivos* advancements to him. However, he does have to bring into account benefits received under his wife's will other than personal chattels. These are brought into account against the statutory legacy only and reduce his statutory legacy to nothing. Thus, on the partial intestacy of Susan, Tom merely takes a life interest in half the residue, ie. in £10,000.

The remaining £10,000 plus the remainder subject to the

life interest of Tom is held for Susan's issue – Paul and Mary – on the statutory trusts. However, Paul has to bring into account the £3,000 *inter vivos* advancement (on his marriage) and the £2,000 received under the will, and Mary has to bring into account £1,000 received under the will.

To calculate Paul and Mary's entitlement:

- The notional estate is £10,000 (the sum available for immediate distribution) + £3,000 (advancements) + £3,000 (gifts by will) = £16,000.
- Paul and Mary are entitled a half-share each, ie. £8,000.
- Paul's share is reduced by £5,000 (£3,000 + £2,000) and Mary's share is reduced by £1,000.

Paul receives £3,000

Mary receives £7,000

£10,000

Chapter 8

Administration of estates: the first steps/entitlement to a grant

Introduction   8.1

This chapter explains:

- The first steps you need to take following the death of a person, whether you (or your firm) is personal representative (PR) of the deceased or whether you are acting on behalf of the deceased's personal representatives (PRs); and

- Who is entitled to a grant to administer the estate of a deceased person, why the grant is needed, its source and its effects.

Chapter 10 considers the *process* of obtaining a grant.

Immediate actions upon death   8.2

Acting as personal representative compared to   8.2.1
acting for personal representatives

When you are involved after the death of a person, it will either be as PR of the deceased or as a member of a firm acting for the PRs of the deceased.

Where you (or your firm) is appointed executor you will have all the powers and duties of a PR (*see* Chapter 11). Where you (or your firm) is acting for the deceased's PRs your duties will involve:

- Taking the practical steps necessary for the *administration of the estate*, on behalf of the PRs, eg. preparing necessary papers for obtaining a grant, collecting the assets of the estate, paying debts etc, and distribution the estate having prepared the estate's accounts.

- Advising the PRs on the *aspects of the law of succession and revenue law* affecting the administration of the estate.

Note _____

When acting for the deceased's PRs, bear the following professional conduct points in mind.

1   Even if the deceased was your client upon death, the PRs of the deceased are now your client.

2   Although you owe professional duties to the PRs as your client, you must consider the beneficiaries under the estate, as well as any member of the family of the deceased who is not a beneficiary, with whom you may have to deal during the course of administration of the estate. But in the event of a dispute over the administration of the estate, you must be wary of conflicts of interest which may arise from advising the beneficiaries or family.

When acting on behalf of the PRs, it is important that you should consult them regularly and keep them fully informed of actions you have taken on their behalf.

8.2.2   Immediate action after receiving instructions

Where you are called upon to act for PRs, you will need to look into the following matters quickly:

- The will;
- Instructions concerning burial/cremation;
- Securing the deceased's property;
- Death certificate;
- Financial support;
- A meeting with the PRs.

Will
Ascertain whether the deceased made a will and, if so, establish the whereabouts of the original, eg. bank, solicitor's strong room etc. Obtain it and give copies of the will to the PRs.

Once the will has been obtained you may have to consider issues as to its validity, eg. whether the testator lacked capacity and whether the formalities have been complied with, and whether affidavit evidence is going to be required to obtain a grant of representation (*see* Chapter 10, para. 10.7).

Instructions concerning burial/cremation etc
Where the deceased left a will, look immediately to see whether they left instructions for the disposal of their body or for it to be donated for medical research etc (*see* Chapter 4, para. 4.2.6). As any such instructions are not legally binding, you must discuss them with the deceased's family and the PRs.

Secure the deceased's property
If, for example, the deceased lived alone and the deceased's belongings therefore remain in a now empty house, documents and any valuable assets should be removed for safe-keeping.

Death certificate

Obtain copies of the deceased's death certificate from the Registrar of Deaths.

Financial support

Ensure that the deceased's immediate family and other beneficiaries under the will are not left in financial difficulties until they receive entitlement from the deceased's estate. If necessary help them to obtain borrowing facilities.

Insurance

You should obtain details of insurances, eg. house and motor, and take steps to either obtain fresh cover in the name of the PRs or at least to have the PRs' interest noted on the policy. In the case of motor insurance, you should ensure that appropriate family members are covered to drive.

Preliminary meeting with the personal representatives

It is a good idea to arrange an early meeting with PRs to discuss how any IHT due on death will be paid. It is normally possible to anticipate whether IHT will be payable and it is important to sort out which funds are to be used for payment as early as possible. This is because the normal rule is that IHT due on death will be payable before a grant of representation can be obtained (*see* Chapter 9, para. 9.9 and Chapter 10, para. 2.4). Make arrangements at the meeting to obtain funds to pay IHT so that there are no delays in obtaining a grant.

Collecting information   8.2.3

In the early stages of administration, you will need to collect considerable information concerning:

- The deceased, the deceased's immediate family and any dependants;
- The proposed PRs and those with an interest in the estate;
- The various assets and liabilities of the estate.

Most firms have detailed checklist to assist you to elicit the relevant information.

Source and purpose of a grant   8.3

A grant of representation is an order of the High Court. The Family Division of the High Court has exclusive jurisdiction to make grants in England and Wales: s.1(4), Administration of Justice Act 1970.

8.3.1   Types of grant

There are three basic types of grant of representation:

- A grant of probate (*see* 8.5);
- A grant of administration with the will annexed (*see* 8.6);
- A grant of simple administration (*see* 8.7).

8.3.2   Purpose of a grant

The purpose of a grant is two-fold. First, it establishes either the validity of the deceased's will or that the deceased has died intestate. Second, it establishes the authority of the PRs.

8.3.3   Probate jurisdiction

Territorial limits

A grant of representation can normally only be made by the English courts if either the deceased died leaving property in England and Wales or the deceased appointed an executor in England and Wales.

Non-contentious and contentious probate

Probate business is divided into non-contentious (also called probate in common form) and contentious probate (also called probate in solemn form).

Non-contentious business is dealt with by the Family Division of the High Court, while *contentious* probate is within the jurisdiction of the Chancery Division, although the County Court has concurrent jurisdiction to deal with contentious business where the value of the estate of the deceased does not exceed £30,000.

Probate is said to be *contentious* where there is a *dispute* about:

- What document(s) should be admitted to probate, eg. validity of a will or whether it has been effectively revoked; or
- Who is entitled to a grant; or
- Whether a grant should be revoked.

Non-contentious probate may well involve a hearing before a district judge or registrar on some issue, eg. to decide who should take a grant where more than four persons are entitled in the same degree to a grant (four being the maximum number of PRs in respect of the same property). Only if the issue to be decided upon by the district judge or registrar develops into a dispute will the proceedings become contentious. Contentious probate business, usually, has its first stage in non-contentious proceedings. A person wishing to dispute a will or the appointment of a PR may issue a caveat (*see* Chapter 10, para. 10.8).

Non-contentious probate is conducted in accordance with the Non-Contentious Probate Rules (NCPR) 1987. These rules give registrars wide powers in relation to many matters, including the issue of grants.

The procedure for obtaining probate in solemn form is entirely different from that for obtaining probate in common form. It involves the issue of a writ or summons in either the Chancery Division or the County Court. (Knowledge of the procedure is beyond the scope of this course.)

Capacity to take a grant 8.4

We noted in Chapter 4 that any person may be appointed an executor but not everyone will be able to take a grant of representation. Neither a minor nor a mentally disordered person may take out a grant of representation of any sort, but a grant for their 'use or benefit' may be taken out in some circumstances (*see* 8.10.3). In other cases where a person may be unsuitable for one reason or another, eg. a bankrupt, a criminal, an alien resident abroad, the court has discretion to pass over the person entitled and make a grant to some other person entitled (*see* 8.9).

Grants of probate 8.5

A grant of probate will normally only be obtainable by the executor(s) of a valid will, whether expressly or impliedly appointed. However, there are two circumstances where persons other than those appointed may obtain a grant of probate:

- Where the court appoints *a substitute for a PR*: s.50(1)(a), Administration of Justice Act 1985. The court has wide powers to appoint a substitute PR in place of all or any of the existing PRs. If the existing PR is an executor, the substitute becomes an executor.

- Where a valid will only appoints someone to *nominate an executor*. The person nominated may then obtain a grant of probate.

Note _____

1 Section 22, Administration of Estates Act 1925 provides that trustees of settled land of which the deceased was a life tenant, and which remains settled land after the deceased's death, are deemed appointed executors in respect of the settled land alone. However, Rule 29, NCPR 1987, as amended provides that they act as administrators not executors.

2   The fact that the testator died partially intestate does not affect the availability of a grant of probate.

8.5.1   Numbers of executors

Maximum

Probate will not be issued to more than four persons in respect of the same property: s.114(1), Supreme Court Act 1981. Power will be reserved to any others (if they have not renounced) so that they can take out a grant if a vacancy occurs. Section 114(1) allows probate to be granted to four executors in respect of one part of the deceased's estate, and a further four in respect of the remainder of the estate. If a dispute arises as to which of more than four persons are to take a grant, it can be resolved by a hearing before a district judge or registrar: r.27(6), NCPR 1987.

Minimum

Probate may be granted to one executor whether or not a minority or a life interest arises under the deceased's will or an intestacy. (Where such interests arise and there is a grant of administration, at least two PRs are normally required.) However, the court does have discretion to appoint an additional PR to act with a sole executor but the power is rarely exercised: s.114(4), Supreme Court Act 1981.

8.5.2   Chain of representation

Section 7, Administration of Estates Act 1925 provides for automatic transmission of the office of executor on death through proving executors.

The section applies where, after obtaining a grant of probate, a sole surviving executor dies leaving a will which appoints an executor and their executor accepts office. On taking out a grant of probate in respect of the original executor's estate, they automatically become the executor by representation of the original testator. Thus, a grant to administer the original estate is not needed.

Example

Eric is the sole surviving executor of Tom. After obtaining a grant of probate of Tom's will Eric dies. Eric leaves a valid will by which he appoints Fred to be his executor. Fred obtains probate of Eric's will. Fred will be the executor of Eric and by representation the executor of Tom without the need for a further grant in respect of Tom's will.

Note that in this example:

● Fred cannot accept office as executor of Eric and renounce office in respect of Tom. If he is unwilling to act as executor by representation for Tom, he must renounce probate of Eric's will.

- The last executor in an unbroken chain of representation is the executor of all preceding testators. Therefore, continuing the above example, if Fred dies, leaving a valid will appointing George his executor and George obtains probate of Fred's will, George will be the executor by representation of both Eric and Tom.

The chain of representation does *not* operate where:

- The executor who dies is *not the sole or last surviving executor* – in this case, the surviving executors continue to administer the estate;
- The *chain is broken*. This will occur if the sole or last surviving executor dies:

  – before obtaining a grant of probate of the original will; and/or

  – intestate; or

  – leaving a valid will, but not appointing an executor; or

  – leaving a valid will which appoints an executor, but for one reason or another the executor does not obtain a grant of probate of the will of the sole or last surviving executor.

The chain is not broken by a temporary grant of administration: s.7(3).

Example _____

X, a sole or last surviving executor, dies leaving a valid will appointing Y his executor. However, Y is a minor when X dies and so a grant *durante minore aetate* (*see* 8.10.3) is made to Z while Y is a minor. However, once Y obtains majority, Y automatically becomes executor of the original testator's estate.

If the chain of representation is broken and the sole or last surviving executor has not completed the administration of the testator's estate, a grant *de bonis non administratis* will be required to complete the administration (*see* 8.11.1). The persons entitled to such a grant are set out in r.20, NCPR 1987 (*see* 8.6.1).

Effects of a grant of probate   8.5.3

The effects of a grant of probate are twofold:

- Confirmation of the executor's authority; and
- Proof of the terms and proper execution of the will.

Confirmation of the executor's authority

An executor derives authority from the will and may there-fore deal with the estate of the deceased before taking out a grant of probate. In practice, however, a grant of probate will be necessary to *prove* to others that the executor has authority to deal with the estate. Thus, a grant of probate, merely *confirms* the authority of the executor.

As executors have authority (from the will) to deal with the estate they can before grant:

- Exercise all the powers of a PR to administer the de-ceased's estate, eg. they may sell assets;

Note

In some cases a grant may be needed as proof of the executor's title to complete the sale, eg. sales of land, some sales of stocks and shares (although Stock Exchange rules allow shares to be sold subject to the production of a grant in the future).

- Perform their duties, eg. collect in and distribute the assets of the estate;
- Sue or be sued, although a judgment can normally only be entered in the executor's favour after obtaining a grant as the court will require proof of the executor's title.

Proof of the terms and execution of the will

A grant of probate is conclusive evidence as to the terms of the will it is granted in relation to and that the will has been properly executed. The will can only then be made ineffec-tive if the grant of probate is revoked (*see* 8.12).

8.5.4   **Power reserved**

Where a will appoints more than one executor they do not all have to take a grant of probate. Those who do not take the grant have two options. They may renounce their rights (*see* 8.8) or they may have power reserved to them to take out a grant at a later date.

Where power is to be reserved for other executors to take out a grant at a later date, the executor(s) applying for the grant of probate must give notice of the application to the non-proving executors and the oath for executors will normally need to state that notice has been served: r.27(1), NCPR 1987.

An exception to the requirement of giving notice occurs where the persons to whom power is reserved are the proving executor's partners in a firm of solicitors and the partners are not named in the will: r.27(1A).

Executor de son tort   8.5.5

The term *executor de son tort* literally means an executor as
a result of his own wrong. An *executor de son tort* is any
person who without authority deals with the deceased's
estate as if they were executor or administrator.

> *Note*
>
> Acts of charity or humanity, eg. arranging the deceased's funeral
> or protecting the deceased's property by moving it to a safe
> place, are insufficient to make a person *an executor de son tort*.

An *executor de son tort* has *no rights* in respect of the deceased's estate but is liable to the creditors and beneficiaries
of the estate as if they were an executor to the extent that the
assets of the estate have come into their hands: s.28, Administration of Estates Act 1925. Their liability extends to liability for inheritance tax in respect of such property. Liability
ceases as soon as the *executor de son tort* hands over the assets
of the estate to the lawful executor or administrator.

Grants of administration with the will annexed   8.6

A grant of administration with the will annexed (also called a
grant *cum testamento annexo*) is made where the deceased dies
leaving a valid will but one of the following situations occurs:

- The will does not appoint an executor;

- The executor appointed predeceases the testator;

- The executor appointed validly renounces probate;

- The executor appointed has been cited (*see* Chapter 10,
  para. 10.9) but has not taken out a grant of probate;

- In some cases of incomplete administration (*see* 8.11).

Persons entitled to a grant   8.6.1

The persons entitled to a grant of administration with the
will annexed are set out in r.20, NCPR 1987. Persons who
come earlier in the list set out in r.20, take preference to those
who come later.

When applying for a grant, any person persons falling
within category 2 or below must explain on the oath form
(to be completed in order to obtain a grant – *see* Chapter 10,
para. 10.3) why there is no applicant in a prior category. This
is called 'clearing off'.

The list of those entitled to a grant under r.20 follows the
order of entitlement to property under the will and is as
follows.

1   Any *residuary legatee or devisee* holding on trust for any person, ie. if the residuary estate is subject to a trust, the trustees of the residue.

2   Any *other residuary legatee or devisee* (including one for life) or, where the residue is not wholly disposed of by the will, *any person entitled to share in the undisposed of residue* under the rules of intestacy.

Example

Mary leaves her residuary estate to Tom and Tim on trust for Bob for life with remainder to Charles and Diana in equal shares. Charles predeceased Mary and Mary's husband is entitled on her intestacy. Tom and Tim would have prior entitlement to a grant under 1 above, but Bob (as a beneficiary with a life interest), and Diana (as a beneficiary entitled in remainder), and Mary's husband (entitled on intestacy) would all be equally entitled under this category.

(Note that residuary beneficiary with a vested interest is preferred to a residuary beneficiary with only a contingent interest.)

3   The *PR* of any residuary legatee or devisee (but not one for life, or one holding in trust for any other person) or of any person entitled to share in the residue not disposed of by the will.

Example

Continuing the example above, if Diana died soon after Mary's death, Diana's PR would be entitled in this category as would Mary's husband.

Note that Bob's PR would not be entitled as Bob has only a life interest. Neither would the PRs of Tom and Tim who are holding on trust.

4   Any *other legatee or devisee* (including one for life or one holding on trust for any other person) or a *creditor* of the deceased.

This category covers all beneficiaries under the will, other than residuary beneficiaries, including persons holding on trust for another. However, a legatee or devisee with a vested interest is preferred to one with only a contingent interest.

5   The *PR of any other legatee or devisee* (but not one for life or holding on trust for any other person) or of any *creditor* of the deceased.

Example

If a specific legatee survives the testator but dies before taking a grant, their PR will be entitled to a grant under this category.

Note

1 If a beneficiary *predeceases* the testator the doctrine of lapse will normally operate and they will lose their benefit under the will (*see* Chapter 13, para. 13. 5.1). Consequently their PR will have no entitlement to act as administrator under this category.

2 A PR of a trustee or a person with only a life interest falling within this category will not be entitled.

Rules 27(4) and 27(6), NCPR 1987 provide that where two or more persons are entitled in the same degree, ie. they come within the same category, a grant may be made to any of them without notice being given to the others and that disputes between such persons entitled in the same degree are to be decided by a district judge or registrar.

Unless the registrar otherwise directs, as between persons entitled in the same degree administration must be granted to:

- A living person in preference to the PRs of a deceased person; and
- A person of full age in preference to the guardian of a minor: r.27(5), NCPR 1987.

Numbers   8.6.2

Maximum
In applying r.20, NCPR 1987, a grant can only be made to a maximum of four. Where more than four persons are entitled to a grant of administration with the will annexed and there is a dispute amongst such persons as to who is to take the grant, the dispute is resolved by a hearing before a district judge or registrar: r.27(6) NCPR 1987.

Minimum
The minimum number of administrators where a grant of administration with the will annexed is made is generally one. However, where there is a minor beneficiary or a *life interest* in the estate, the grant must be made to not less than two individuals: s.114(2), Supreme Court Act 1981.

Note

Where two administrators are necessary they may be persons who have different entitlements to a grant, eg. one may fall within the first category in r.20, and the other within the second (*see* 8.6.1).

8.6.3 **Effects of a grant of administration with the will annexed**

Proof of content and execution of the will

As with a grant of probate, a grant of administration with the will annexed is conclusive evidence as to the terms of the will and that the will has been duly executed.

Confers authority on administrator

Unlike a grant of probate, which merely confirms the authority of an executor, a grant of administration with the will annexed *confers authority* on the administrator and vests the deceased's property in the administrator. (For the position of the administrator between the death of the testator and the obtaining of the grant of administration with the will annexed – *see* 8.7.3.)

8.7   Grants of simple administration

A grant of simple administration will normally be made where the deceased dies totally intestate. However, where the deceased made a valid will which appoints an executor able and willing to act, but which does not effectively dispose of any of their property, a grant of probate may be made. Similarly, if the will is valid but does not appoint an executor, or no executor is able and willing to act, and neither does the will effectively dispose of any of the deceased's property, a grant of administration with the will annexed may be made.

8.7.1 **Persons entitled to a grant of simple administration**

The order of priority of persons entitled to a grant of simple administration is set down in r.22, NCPR 1987.

The order follows the order of entitlement to an estate on intestacy and requires the person seeking the grant to have a beneficial interest in the estate. Thus, in order to ascertain the person(s) who are entitled to a grant of simple administration you must first apply the rules of intestacy (*see* Chapter 7).

Each category set down in r.22 is listed in priority. An applicant in category 2 or below must therefore explain on the oath form (to be completed in order to obtain a grant – *see* Chapter 10, para. 10.3) why nobody in a prior category is applying for a grant; a process known as 'clearing off'.

Under r.22 the order of priority is:

1 The surviving *spouse*;

2 The *children* of the deceased and the issue of any deceased child who died before the deceased;

3   The *parents* of the deceased;

4   *Brothers and sisters* of the whole blood and the issue of any deceased brother or sister who died before the deceased;

5   *Brothers and sisters of the half blood* and the issue of any deceased brother or sister of the half blood who died before the deceased;

6   *Grandparents* of the deceased;

7   *Uncles and aunts* of the whole blood and the issue of any deceased uncle or aunt of the whole blood who died before the deceased;

8   *Uncles and aunts of the half blood* and the issue of any deceased uncle or aunt of the half blood who died before the deceased.

Subject to the general preference of a living person over a PR of a deceased person (r.27(5), NCPR 1987), the PR of any persons falling within the categories above, has the same right to a grant as the person they represent: r.22(4).

Example _____

X dies intestate leaving four adult children – A, B, C and D – but no spouse. D dies before taking out a grant. This means that D's PR is entitled to a grant in respect of X's estate.

Note _____

1   Relatives falling within categories 2–8 above are to be preferred to the PR of a spouse who is entitled to the whole of the estate ascertained at the time of the application for a grant.

2   A person of full age is preferred to the guardian of a minor where persons are entitled in the same degree applies: r.27(5).

If no-one in the above categories 1–8 has a beneficial interest in the estate, then a grant may be issued to:

9   The Treasury Solicitor claiming *bona vacantia* on behalf of the Crown: r.22(2); or

10 If all prior persons have been 'cleared off' a *creditor* of the deceased or a PR of a creditor or any person who may have a beneficial interest in the event of an accretion to the estate.

An accretion will occur, for example, where, under the rules of intestacy, the estate is so small that it is taken wholly by the spouse. However, in the event of an increase in the size of the estate, others, eg. issue or parents of the deceased, would acquire a beneficial interest in it. Provided the spouse has been cleared off, the issue or parents, as the case may be, are entitled to a grant.

Note

A person applying for a grant of simple administration apart from the Treasury Solicitor or a creditor must have a beneficial interest in the estate by virtue of the rules of intestacy (or will have one if there is an accretion to the estate).

8.7.2 Numbers

Maximum

A grant of simple administration can be made to a maximum of four persons: s.114(1), Supreme Court Act 1981. If more than four persons are entitled in the same degree and a dispute arises as to which persons are to take a grant, it is resolved by a hearing before a district judge or registrar: r.27(6), NCPR 1987.

Minimum

The minimum number of administrators is generally one unless there is a minor beneficiary or a life interest in the estate where the appointment must normally be made to a trust corporation (with or without an individual) or to not less than two individuals: s.114(2), Supreme Court Act 1981. The court has, however, discretion to appoint a sole administrator where there is a minority or life interest and if it appears to the court 'to be expedient in all the circumstances': s.114(2), Supreme Court Act 1981.

8.7.3 Effects of a grant of simple administration

Proof of intestacy

A grant of simple administration is conclusive evidence that the deceased died wholly intestate and without leaving a valid will.

Confers authority on administrator

Unlike a grant of probate, which merely confirms authority, a grant of simple administration is similar to a grant of administration with the will annexed in that it *confers* authority on the administrator and *vests the deceased's property* in the administrator.

Prior to a grant of administration (whether simple administration or with the will annexed) the deceased's estate vests in the President of the Family Division of the High Court: s.9, Administration of Estates Act 1925. The President has no duties to perform in respect of the property vested in him by s.9, but if the deceased's property includes a leasehold interest, notice to quit on the premises may be served by the landlord upon the President.

As an administrator has no authority in relation to the deceased's estate prior to a grant, the doctrine of 'relation back' has been adopted by the courts to protect the deceased's estate from harm between the date of death and the date of grant. It allows an administrator to sue in respect of wrongs to the deceased's estate between death and grant. Apart from this, the authority of an administrator from the grant is without retrospective effect.

Renunciation   8.8

Executors   8.8.1

It is possible for a person who has been appointed an executor to renounce their entitlement to a grant of probate provided that they have not *intermeddled* with the estate and no grant has been made in their favour.

Intermeddling occurs where a potential executor does an act in relation to the testator's property which indicates an intention to take upon the executorship. Examples of such acts include:

- Taking possession of the testator's goods;
- Receiving or releasing debts due to the testator; and
- Writing to request payment of money due upon an insurance policy on the testator's life.

The performance of acts of charity, humanity or necessity (as with an *executor de son tort – see* 8.5.5), do not deprive an executor of their right to renounce.

Administrators   8.8.2

A person entitled to either a grant of administration with the will annexed or to a grant of simple administration may renounce their entitlement up until a grant has been made in their favour. This is so even if they have intermeddled with the estate.

Renunciation is made in writing, signed by the person entitled to the grant, and filed at the probate registry. The most convenient way to renounce is for the person who takes the grant to submit a written statement of renunciation along with the papers required for a grant.

Note _____

1   Once a renunciation has been made it may only be retracted on the order of a district judge or registrar (r.37(3), NCPR 1987) and such order will only be made if it can be shown to be for the benefit of the estate or the beneficiaries or creditors of the estate.

2   If an executor renounces probate this does not operate as a renunciation of any right they may have to a *grant of administration* under rr.20 or 22 NCPR. It is therefore necessary to renounce such right also: r.37(11), NCPR 1987. In contrast, a renunciation of right to a grant of administration in one capacity operates to renounce all rights to a grant of administration.

8.9   Passing over

Under s.116, Supreme Court Act 1981, the High Court has a discretionary power to pass over a person entitled to a grant if it appears to be necessary or expedient to appoint as administrator some person other than the person entitled to take the grant. No exact rules can be laid down as to when the power will be exercised but a common circumstance is where the PR is *unsuitable* for the position either in general or in the circumstances of the case, eg. where the person entitled to the grant is a convicted criminal in prison, or is resident abroad, or is missing.

8.10   Limited grants

A grant may not give authority to (or in the case of a grant of probate, confirm the authority of) a PR to act in respect of the whole estate for all purposes. In this case the grant is said to be limited.

A grant may be either limited as to *property*, or *purpose* or in *time*.

8.10.1   Limited as to property

A grant may be limited to part of the property comprised in the estate, either because the property is settled land or because the testator considers it requires administration by experts, eg. an art collection. In the latter case the grant is described as a grant *save and except* if the general executor, ie. the executor of the rest of the estate, takes the grant before the grant limited to the specified property. If the limited grant is taken before the grant to the general executor in respect of the rest of the estate it is known as a grant *caeterorum* – but there is no practical difference between the two types of grant.

Where the estate includes settled land and the settlement continues after the death of the tenant for life, a grant limited to settled land is required to vest the legal title in the trustees of the settlement rather than the tenant for life's general PRs.

Note

No special PRs are needed:

- Where after the death of the tenant for life, the settlement comes to an end; or
- Where a settlement is *created* by will, in which case the general PRs vest the property in the first tenant for life.

Limited as to purpose   8.10.2

There are three types of grant which are in some way limited as to purpose:

- Grant *pendente lite*;
- Grant *ad litem*;
- Grant *ad colligenda bona*.

Grant *pendente lite*

Literally, this is a grant pending litigation. It is made where there is a probate action in relation to an estate and it allows an administrator appointed by the court to administer the estate until the action is concluded. It does not usually give authority to distribute the estate.

Grant *ad litem*

A grant *ad litem*, ie. limited to an action, is made to enable proceedings to be commenced or continued on behalf of, or against an estate. It is only a power to represent the estate in proceedings. Any person interested in the litigation may apply *ex parte* for a grant to a district judge or registrar.

Grant *ad colligenda bona*

A grant *ad colligenda bona* is made for the purpose of preserving the assets of an estate until a general grant is made. It is made when urgent action is needed and the person entitled to a general grant is not yet in a position apply for it, eg. the appointed executor is abroad. The grant is usually limited to collecting in the estate and doing acts necessary for its preservation. There are no special rules as to who may apply for the grant.

Limited as to time   8.10.3

A grant may be limited as to time either where the grant is taken on behalf of a minor or where it is taken on behalf of a person suffering from mental incapacity.

Grants *durante aetate minore*

A grant *durante aetate minore* occurs where the executor(s) of a will, or the person(s) entitled to be administrators under rr.20 or 22, NCPR 1987, are *all* minors.

The grant is made to someone else until the minor(s) become 18 and it expires automatically when the minor entitled becomes 18, unless another time limit is fixed, eg. until the minor takes out a grant.

The persons entitled to such a grant under r.32, NCPR 1987 (as amended by the NCPR 1991) are:

- A parent of the minor who has or is deemed to have parental responsibility under the Children Act 1989 or a *guardian* appointed under that act;

- An *appointed guardian* – a person appointed by a district judge or registrar under r.32(2) because either no person qualifies under the category above or the registrar has passed over (*see* 8.9) any such person;

- Where two administrators are required (*see* 8.6.2 and 8.7.2) but there is *only one person competent and willing to take out a grant* under either of the above, that person may nominate a second administrator to act with them.

Mental incapacity

Where an executor or administrator is mentally incapacitated and other persons are equally entitled to a grant, a grant will normally be made to an executor or administrator not suffering from any disability with power reserved for the incapacitated executor or administrator to take out a grant on their disability ceasing. However, where the only, or all the executors or administrators entitled to a grant are mentally incapacitated, a grant will normally be made to another person for the 'use or benefit' of the mentally incapacitated person. Exceptionally the court may pass over the mentally incapacitated person.

If a grant is to be made for the 'use and benefit' of the mentally incapacitated executor or administrator, the order of priority of entitlement to a grant is, unless a district judge or registrar acting under r.35 directs otherwise, to the:

- Person authorised by the Court of Protection to apply for a grant;

- Lawful attorney of the incapable person acting under a registered enduring power of attorney, where no person has been so authorised by the Court of Protection;

- Person entitled to the residuary estate of the deceased where there is no such attorney entitled to act, or if the attorney renounces administration for the use and benefit of the incapable person.

Note _____

Unless a district judge or registrar otherwise directs, no grant shall be made under this rule unless all persons entitled in the same degree as the incapable person have been cleared off.

Incomplete administration 8.11

Depending on the circumstances, either a grant *de bonis non administratis*, a *cessate grant* or a grant of double probate may be made at some time after the original grant has been made but before the administration of the estate is complete.

Grant *de bonis non administratis* 8.11.1

When made

Three requirements must be satisfied before such a grant is made:

- A previous grant must have been made with respect to the deceased's estate; and
- The administration of the estate must be incomplete; and
- There is no remaining PR. This may be because of the death of a sole or last surviving PR – so long as in the case of an executor, the chain of representation has been broken (*see* 8.5.2) or because a previous grant has been revoked (*see* 8.12).

To whom made

The rules of priority which govern applications for original grants apply equally to applications for a grant *de bonis non*. Thus, r.20, NCPR 1987 applies to an application for administration *de bonis non* with the will annexed (*see* 8.6.1) and r.22 to an application for simple administration *de bonis non* (*see* 8.7.1).

Cessate grants 8.11.2

A *cessate* grant is made when the original grant was limited as to time and that period of time has expired, provided that the administration of the estate is still incomplete.

The most common occurrence of such a grant is where a grant of administration has been made for the use and benefit of a minor (*see* 8.10.3). When a minor reaches 18, the limited grant to their guardian automatically comes to an end and the minor is entitled to apply for a *cessate* grant.

A *cessate* grant may be a grant of probate, administration with the will annexed, or simple administration, depending upon the circumstances of the application. For example, where the previous grant had been for the use and benefit of a minor because a·minor had been appointed executor of a will, the *cessate* grant will be a grant of probate. Alternatively, if the minor is entitled on intestacy under r.22, the *cessate* grant will be one of simple administration.

8.11.3 Double probate

Double probate is made to an *executor* applying for a grant after a grant of *probate* has been made to another executor. (There is no such thing as a grant of *double administration*.)

A grant of double probate arises in three circumstances:

- Where an executor, not wishing to take out a grant immediately, has power reserved to take out a grant later (*see* 8.5.4); or

- Where *one of a number* of executors is a minor at the time of the original grant. Such a person may apply for double probate on reaching 18 as power is automatically reserved to them; or

Note _____

Where a will appoints a minor as the only executor a *cessate* grant of probate (*see* 8.11.2) will be made to the minor on reaching majority.

_____

- Where an executor has been prevented from taking a grant purely because of the restriction on the number of executors to a maximum of four. Such an executor may later apply for a grant of double probate if a vacancy occurs, eg. one of the proving executors dies.

8.12 Revocation of grants

A grant may be revoked where:

- A subsequent will (or codicil) is discovered, or where it is found that the will appointing the executor to whom a grant has been made is invalid or has been revoked;

- A PR becomes mentally or physically incapacitated or where they disappear or wish to retire;

- Where it is discovered that the grant ought not to have been made to the person to whom it was made because, for example, a person who was previously thought to have predeceased the deceased turns up and has a prior claim to a grant.

Self-assessment questions

1 Distinguish between an executor and an administrator. How does the position of an executor differ from that of an administrator before grant?

2   Angela died in 1988 having by her will appointed Bertie and Chris her executors. Bertie renounced probate but Chris proved the will. Chris died in 1991 leaving a will by which he appointed David his executor. The administration of Angela's estate is incomplete. By whom can the administration of Angela's estate be completed?

3   Simon died leaving a valid will which appoints no executors. His will leaves legacies of £10,000 to each of his children. The residuary of the estate is to pass to his wife Mary absolutely if she survives him by 28 days. Mary survives Simon by two months and dies leaving a will appointing James and John her executors. Who is entitled to a grant in respect of Simon's will?

4   Liza dies intestate leaving an estate worth approximately £200,000 plus personal chattels, a spouse (Richard) and two children, Jane (aged 21) and Paul (aged 12). Who is entitled to a grant to administer her estate?

5   Alfred died recently. His will named his daughter Michelle as executor and trustee. Michelle is aged 15. Explain to Alfred's widow who is entitled to take out a grant in respect of the will and the effect and duration of any grant that may be made now or in the future.

How would the position differ, if at all, if Alfred's will appointed Michelle and her sister Sandra (aged 21) executors and trustees?

Answer guidance to self-assessment questions

1   An *executor* is someone appointed by a will to administer an estate. An *administrator* is someone appointed by the court to administer an estate. This may be because the deceased has died intestate, where a grant of simple administration is made, or because the executor(s) appointed by a valid will are, for one reason or another, unable or unwilling to act. In this case the grant is one of administration with the will annexed.

The basic way in which an executor's position differs from that of an administrator before a grant has been obtained is that, as an executor derives authority to act from the will and the grant merely confirms the executor's authority, an executor has power to administer the estate of the deceased immediately upon death. In contrast, the power of an administrator derives from the grant itself. Thus, subject to exceptions, an administrator has no power to act in relation to the estate before a grant has been obtained.

2   As Bertie has renounced probate he will not be able to take out a grant. David will be able to complete the administration of Angela's estate provided he takes out a grant in respect of Chris' estate (chain of representation, *see* 8.5.2). If David does not take out a grant with respect to Chris' estate for one reason or another, a grant *de bonis non administratis* will need to be obtained (*see* 8.10.1). The order of priority of entitled to a grant will be governed by r.20, NCPR .

3   As Simon has left a valid will which does not appoint executors, a grant of administration with the will annexed will be required. Rule 20, NCPR 1987 governs the order of priority of entitlement to a grant (*see* 8.6.1). Under this rule James and John, as PRs of a residuary beneficiary, will be entitled to a grant. If they do not wish to act, then any of Simon's children as specific legatees, may act.

4   As Liza's estate is worth £200,000 her surviving spouse will take the personal chattels, a legacy of £75,000 and a life interest in half the residue. The remainder of the residue, with one half subject to Richard's life interest, will be divided between Liza's issue and, in the case of Paul who is 12, held on the statutory trusts (*see* Chapter 7).

As there is a life interest, two administrators will be required.

The order of priority of entitlement to a grant follows the order of entitlement on intestacy. Thus, Richard is first entitled to a grant as surviving spouse, and Jane and Paul are next entitled as issue having a beneficial interest in the estate. However, as Paul is a minor he does not have capacity to take out a grant. The grant will therefore be made to Richard and Jane.

5   As the only executor is a minor a grant *durante aetate minore* will be required (*see* 8.9.3). The grant will automatically expire when Michelle reaches 18 unless the grant specifies otherwise.

The persons entitled to a grant *durante aetate minore* are set out in r.32, NCPR 1987 (as amended). Here Alfred's widow as parent of Michelle will be entitled to the grant. When Michelle reaches 18 she can apply for a cessate grant (see 8.10.2). In her case, the *cessate* grant will be a grant of probate.

Chapter 9

Tax on death

Introduction

9.1

This chapter deals with tax liability on death. Income tax (*see* 9.11) and capital gains tax (*see* 9.12) are dealt with in outline while the most important tax on death, inheritance tax, is dealt with fully (*see* 9.2–10).

Chapter 2 provided you with an introduction to the general principles of inheritance tax (IHT) with the main aim at that point of enabling you to appreciate the IHT considerations in advising clients who ask you to prepare a will. We explained that when a person dies they are treated for IHT purposes as having made a transfer of value immediately before their death, the value transferred being the value of their estate immediately before death. Building on Chapter 2, the aim of this chapter is to look very specifically at how IHT is calculated on death, and on whom the liability for, and the burden of, IHT falls on death.

Note

All section numbers in this chapter refer to the Inheritance Tax Act 1984 (IHTA) unless otherwise stated.

Calculating IHT on death

9.2

In calculating IHT due on death you have to take the following distinct steps:

- *Step 1* Identify the deceased's estate (*see* 9.3).
- *Step 2* Value the deceased's estate (*see* 9.4).
- *Step 3* Consider whether any exemptions (*see* 9.5) or reliefs (*see* 9.6) apply.
- *Step 4* Calculate the tax (*see* 9.7).

Identifying the deceased's estate

9.3

A person's 'estate' is the aggregate of all the property to which they are beneficially entitled before death with the exception of 'excluded property' (*see* Chapter 2, para. 2.4.11).

For the purpose of calculating IHT on death, in addition to property passing under the deceased's will and/or the rules of intestacy, the deceased's estate includes:

- Any property held by the deceased as a *joint tenant*

immediately before death. (This will pass by survivorship to the surviving joint tenant(s).)

- *Nominated* property (*see* Chapter 3, para. 3.4.3).
- Property the subject matter of a *donatio mortis causa* (*see* Chapter 3, para. 3.4.4).
- *Property subject to a reservation*, ie. property which the deceased gave away during their lifetime but either did not transfer possession and enjoyment of the property to the donee or the donee did not have possession and enjoyment to the exclusion of the donor.

Example

Michael transferred the legal title to the family home to his son Tim more than seven years before he died. Michael, however, continued to live in the family home until his death.

Note

The Finance Act 1986 introduced the concept of 'property subject to a reservation' to prevent people from avoiding tax by giving property away more than seven years before their death but continuing to use and enjoy that property.

- Certain *trust property*. We have explained (*see* Chapter 2, paras. 2.6.2–3) that where a person is beneficially entitled to an interest in possession in settled property, they are treated as being beneficially entitled to the property in which the interest subsists.

As a person must be *beneficially* entitled to the property immediately before death, you must remember that the following do not form part of the deceased's estate for IHT purposes:

- A *life insurance policy written in trust* for a named beneficiary (*see* Chapter 3, para. 3.4.2). and
- A discretionary lump sum payment made from a pension fund to a person nominated by the deceased (*see* Chapter 3, para. 3.4.3).

9.4 Valuation of the estate

9.4.1 The value of the estate

The value of the estate for IHT purposes is the net amount after deducting debts and other liabilities. To calculate the net estate, you must value the various assets of the estate (*see* 9.4.2–8) and then deduct from this sum the debts and other liabilities.

9.4.2 General rules for valuing assets

As a general principle, in calculating the loss to the donor's estate, the value of the property for IHT purposes is the price which the property might reasonably be expected to fetch if sold on the open market at the date of the transfer: s.160.

For transfers on death this means the value which the property might reasonably be expected to fetch on the open market if sold immediately before the deceased's death.

However, the basic valuation principle is modified for transfers on death by s.171. This provides that 'changes in the value of [the] estate which have occurred by reason of the death ... shall be taken into account as if they had occurred before the death'. This effectively means that where the deceased's death causes the value of an asset in the estate to either increase or decrease in value, the change in value should be taken into account.

Example

A situation which may lead to a *decrease* in the market value of assets is where the deceased is managing director and a majority shareholder in a private company.

A common example of an *increase* in the market value of an asset is a life assurance policy on the deceased's life not written in trust and therefore forming part of the deceased's estate. (The surrender value of a policy, which would be the value of the policy immediately before the deceased's death, would be much less than the maturity value on death.)

In paragraphs 9.4.3–8 we apply the basic valuation principles to particular types of assets and circumstances with any modification to the basic rules which may apply.

Quoted shares 9.4.3

'Quoted shares' are shares quoted on a recognised Stock Exchange or dealt with on the Unlisted Securities Market: s.272. Quoted shares are valued by taking the lower of the two prices on the Stock Exchange Daily Official List for the day of death (or the last or nearest trading day before death) and adding one-quarter of the difference between the lower and higher prices quoted.

Example

The Daily List shows 202p/206p. The value of each share will be 203p.

Unquoted shares 9.4.4

The valuation of unquoted shares is a complex matter but basically they are valued according to the normal market value principle (*see* 9.4.2). This will take into account factors such as the dividend record of the company, the retained earnings, the profitability of the company and the value of assets owned by the company. As the valuation of un-quoted shares is not as straightforward as quoted shares, negotiations may be required with the valuation division of the Inland Revenue in order to reach an agreed valuation.

9.4.5   Land

Where land is held by the deceased in co-ownership (whether as a joint tenant or as a tenant in common), the deceased's interest in the land is normally valued by taking the value of the whole property and dividing it by the number of shares, although a reduction of 10% to 15% is normally allowed to reflect the difficulty of selling such an interest on the open market.

As with unquoted shares, the valuation of land may be difficult and result in negotiations with the district valuer to agree a value for IHT purposes.

9.4.6   Related property

Some assets are worth more when owned in conjunction with other assets. The related property rules are designed to prevent advantage being taken of 'asset splitting' so that husband and wife own separate assets, the total of which value is less than the value of the whole.

Example

If a husband and wife each own less than 50% of shares in a company but taken *together* they own a majority shareholding, their individual shares valued together as part of a majority shareholding will be worth more than their individual shareholdings taken in isolation.

There is a possibility that in such circumstances as owner-ship of shares, spouses may use the spouse exemption (*see* Chapter 2, para. 2.4.1). to avoid IHT by splitting ownership between themselves. In order to prevent this, s.161(2) pro-vides that on a transfer of related property the transferred property and the property related are to be valued as one asset. Tax is then paid on the proportion of the total which is transferred.

Example

Harry owns 30% of the shares in a private company and his spouse Wilma owns 40%. Harry dies. His estate will not be taxed on the value of a 30% holding in the company, but on ³⁄₇ of a 70% shareholding. As a 70% shareholding gives control, a valuation on this basis is likely to be greater than on a 30% shareholding.

All property owned by spouses is related but in most cases the value will not be affected by the related ownership. Common types of property where the valuation *is* likely to be greater as a result of the related property principle are:

- Adjoining land;
- Collections of chattels, eg. a pair of silver candlesticks or a set of chairs;
- Shares in private companies.

Commorientes   9.4.7

Where two or more persons die in circumstances where it is uncertain who died first, the deaths are deemed to have occurred in order of seniority for the purpose of *succession* of property (*see* Chapter 13, para. 13.5.1): s.184, Law of Property Act 1925. However, for IHT purposes each person is assumed to have died at the same instance: s.4(2).

Example

1   Faustus and his son Marlon are killed in a plane crash. It is uncertain which of Faustus and Marlon died first. By his will Faustus leaves all his property to Marlon and Marlon leaves all his property to his wife Angelique.

For *succession purposes* Faustus being the elder, is presumed to have died first, and Faustus' property passes to Marlon. Marlon's property, including that which has been left to him by Faustus, then passes to his wife Angelique. As Faustus and Marlon are deemed to die at the same instant for *IHT purposes*, when calculating the IHT on Marlon's estate it is deemed *not* to include the property received from his father Faustus.

2   Henry (aged 42) and Ann (aged 36) are spouses. The order of their deaths is uncertain. Henry dies leaving all his property to Ann and Ann leaves all her property to Tom, Dick and Zebidee.

For *succession purposes* Ann is deemed to survive Henry, and so Henry's estate passes to Ann, and then Ann's estate (including Henry's estate) passes to Tom, Dick Zebidee. For *IHT purposes* when Henry's property passes to Ann it is spouse exempt. When calculating the IHT on Ann's estate, the property received from Henry's estate is not included. This is obviously very advantageous from the tax point of view but you don't plan to die in circumstances where the order of death is uncertain!

9.4.8   **Deductions**

Liabilities owed by the deceased at the time of death are deductible for IHT purposes provided that they were incurred for consideration in money or money's worth or were imposed by law, eg. Council Tax, provided there is no right to reimbursement: s.162. Reasonable funeral expenses may also be deducted: s.172.

9.5   Exemptions

9.5.1   **General points**

The various exemptions which operate in relation to IHT are outlined in Chapter 2 (*see* Chapter 2, paras. 2.4.1–9). In relation to payment of IHT on death you must note two things about the exemptions:

- The following do *not* apply on death:
  - annual exemption
  - small gifts exemption
  - normal expenditure out of income
  - gifts in consideration of marriage
  - family maintenance.
- The exemptions depend upon the identity of the beneficiary, so it is important to look at the beneficiary of the particular gift to decide whether IHT is payable.

9.5.2   **Partially exempt transfers**

In some cases a transfer on death may be partly taxable and partly exempt because part only of the estate passes to an exempt beneficiary such as a spouse or a charity. In these circumstances s.38 sets out how the IHT is to be calculated and how the burden of IHT falls.

The effect of the section can lead to very complicated calculations depending on the division of the non-exempt parts to the exempt parts of the estate. The application of s.38 to particular situations is beyond the scope of the LPC but the example below illustrates its operation in relation to the situation where specific gifts are made to non-exempt beneficiaries, eg. the testator's children, and the residue is exempt because, for example, it is left to the testator's spouse. The position depends on whether or not the specific gifts bear their own tax.

Example

1   *Specific gifts are made 'subject to tax'.*

Where specific gifts are made subject to tax there is no difficulty. Herbert leaves a legacy of £200,000 to his daughter Davina, with the residue to his wife Wanda. He has made no lifetime transfers and his estate is worth £400,000. As the gift to Davina exceeds the nil-rate band and Davina is a non-exempt beneficiary, IHT will be payable. The residue is exempt (spouse exemption). If the gift is made 'subject to tax' you calculate the tax on the gift (£200,000).

£150,000 @ 0%	Nil
£50,000 @ 40%	£20,000

Davina therefore receives £180,000 (£200,000 – £20,000).

2   *Specific gifts do not bear their own tax.*

Here the non-exempt specific gifts are in effect given as 'net gifts', ie. tax paid. Thus, when calculating the IHT payable out of the residue, the 'net gifts' have to be grossed up. Put another way, to find the value transferred you have to calculate the sum which after deduction of IHT would leave £200,000.

Facts as above, except the 'specific gift to Davina does not bear its own tax'

Gross-up specific gifts	£
150,000 [1]	150,000
50,000 grossed up at 40% (50,000 × $\frac{100}{60}$)	83,333
Gross gift	233,333

[1] Nil rate band – not taxable so no grossing up is required.

Calculate the IHT on death on the (grossed up) gift.

150,000 @ 0%	—
83,333 @ 40%	33,333

Davina receives the £200,000 legacy in full. IHT on the gift has to come out of the residue so Wanda receives:

£200,000 – £33,333	166,667

A method of checking your calculation is to add the non-exempt estate, the exempt estate and the IHT together; this cannot exceed the original value of the estate, in this example £400,000.

Note _____

Compare the amount of IHT payable in the two examples above. In drafting a will you must advise the client that if, in these circumstances, a specific gift is made free of tax, the IHT payable may be much higher than if the specific legacy is given 'subject to tax'.

Reliefs   9.6

A relief does not completely exempt given property from

IHT liability but operates to reduce the value transferred by a transfer. The various reliefs available in relation to liability for IHT were fully explained in Chapter 2, paras. 2.4.1-4). They are:

- Quick succession relief;
- Agricultural relief;
- Business property relief;
- Relief on growing timber.

9.7 Calculating the IHT payable

Having identified the deceased's estate (Step 1), valued the estate (Step 2), applied any exemption or reliefs (Step 3), you are now in the position to calculate the tax payable. To do this you must apply the correct rate of tax and take into account the principle of cumulation (*see* Chapter 2, paras. 2.3.1-2).

The rates of tax applicable on death are:

- First 150,000 at 0%;
- Balance of the estate at 40%.

Because of the principle of cumulation the PRs must ascertain whether the deceased made any transfers of value in the seven years before they died. These may be either:

- Immediately chargeable transfers, eg. a gift on discretionary trust; or
- Potentially exempt transfers. These transfers become chargeable as a result of the transferor's death within seven years.

The value transferred by such transfers must be aggregated with the death estate.

Note

There are additional exemptions available on lifetime gifts falling within the above categories and you must take these into account when calculating the value transferred in order to aggregate the sum with the death estate.

Example

Tessa died leaving by will legacies (payable free of tax) of £20,000 to each of her four children, and the residue 'subject to payment of funeral, testamentary and administration expenses, debts and other liabilities ...' to her husband Harry absolutely.

At her death Tessa's assets and liabilities were:

Assets	£
Half share in the matrimonial home held as a joint tenant with Harry	150,000
Ordinary shares in ABC plc	55,000
Current account at Barclays Bank plc	500
Y insurance company policy written in trust for her four children	25,000
Personal chattels	3,000
Liabilities	
Income tax due	500
Personal loan from Barclay's Bank plc	2,000
Funeral expenses	1,000

Six years before her death Tessa made a gift of £10,000 to her son Robert at the time of his marriage and two years before she died she made gifts of £10,000 to each of her 10 grandchildren.

Step 1: Identify estate

Half share in matrimonial home	150,000
Shares	55,000
Current account	500
Personal chattels	3,000
	208,500

Note: As the insurance policy is written in trust it is not an asset of Tessa's estate.

Step 2: Value estate

Assets valued for the purpose of the example (as per figures given).

Assets of estate	208,500
Less total of liabilities	3,500
	205,000

Step 3: Apply exemptions and reliefs

Residue	205,000
Less: legacies @ 20,000 × four children	(80,000)
(Balance to spouse)	125,000

Step 4: Calculate tax liability

Gift to Robert on marriage	10,000	
Annual exemption year preceding marriage	(3,000)	
Annual exemption year of marriage	(3,000)	
Marriage exemption	(5,000)	Nil

Gift to grandchildren 10 × 10,000	100,000
Annual exemption last year	(3,000)
Annual exemption this year	(3,000) 94,000 [1]
Nil-rate band applicable to Tessa's estate on death	150,000
Less: Cumulative total	94,000
	56,000

Tax on Tessa's estate: must fall on the legacies

66,000 [2]	66,000
14,000 grossed up @ 40% (14,000 × $^{100}\!/_{60}$)	23,333
Gross value of gifts	89,333

[1] Cumulative total

[2] Balance of nil rate band – not taxable so no grossing up is required.

Tax =

66,000 @ 0%	—
23,333 @ 40%	9,333

Residue to Harry is free of tax but subject to IHT payable on legacies, ie.

125,000 – 9,333	115,667

9.8   The burden of IHT

The burden of IHT is a question of which beneficiaries of the estate are going to bear the burden of any IHT payable on death.

Where the deceased dies leaving a will there may be an express direction in the will as to whether or not a particular gift bears its own tax. If there are no such directions, statutory rules operate.

To understand how the burden of IHT is allocated between the beneficiaries, property which is free estate and which vests in the PRs (*see* 9.8.1) and property which is free estate which does not vest in the PRs (*see* 9.8.2) must be distinguished. If the property is trust property the trustees of the settlement are liable for the IHT (*see* 9.9). The question of the burden of IHT on the beneficiaries under the general estate does not arise as the burden falls on the trust fund.

9.8.1   Property which vests in the personal representatives

If a gift is made by will and the testator expressly provides that a particular gift(s) are or are not to bear the burden of IHT, the testator's wishes prevail. So, for example, if the will provides that a particular legacy is to be paid 'free of tax', then IHT will be a testamentary expense paid from the property available for payment of debts of the estate (*see* Chapter 12, para. 12.4). Conversely, if the will provides that a particular legacy is to be paid 'subject to tax', then the legacy will be paid 'net' of tax according to the 'estate rate' (*see* 9.8.3).

Note

Although the testator's express wishes normally prevail, a direction in a will that an *exempt share of residue* is to bear the IHT attributable to a *non-exempt share of residue* will be disregarded: s.41.

In the absence of an express provision in a will governing the burden of IHT, s.221 applies. This provides that IHT payable on death is to be treated as part of the general testamentary and administration expenses of the estate in so far as it is attributable to free estate which vests in the deceased's PRs.

This means that it is paid from property available for payment of debts of the estate, which is primarily any undisposed of property or residue (*see* Chapter 12, para. 12.4). However, it is normal to provide in a will that the residue of the estate is subject to the payment of debts, funeral, testamentary and administrative expenses (*see* Chapter 4, para. 4.8.2).

Property which does not vest in the personal representatives

9.8.2

Property which is free estate and which does not vest in the deceased's PRs amounts to property which passes outside any will or the rules of intestacy, but for which the PRs are liable to pay the IHT, specifically:

- The deceased's share in joint property;
- The subject matter of a *donatio mortis causa*; or
- A statutory nomination.

In these circumstances the PRs are, subject to a contrary intention in a will, entitled to recover the tax from the person in whom the property is vested: s.211(3).

Example

Arnie and Bernie (brothers) held freehold land as joint tenants. Arnie dies. Bernie takes Arnie's share and becomes sole owner by survivorship. Arnie's PRs can recover IHT attributable to the land from Bernie.

9.8.3   Apportioning the burden of IHT

Where the burden of inheritance tax is to be divided between different beneficiaries or between the PRs and, say, the trustees of trust property included in the estate for IHT purposes, IHT must be apportioned among the various assets comprised in the estate according to their value. This may be done by calculating the average rate of tax on the estate as a percentage, ie. the estate rate:

$$\frac{\text{Total tax}}{\text{Value of estate}} \times 100$$

This is necessary because the nil rate band reduces the 40% rate to a lower average rate.

Where the deceased's nil rate band has been completely used up by lifetime transfers, the estate rate will be 40%. However, in other cases, rather than calculating the estate rate as a percentage, it is easier to allocate a proportionate part of the total inheritance tax to each beneficiary by dividing the item of property by the total value of the estate:

$$\text{Total tax} \times \frac{\text{Beneficiary's share of estate}}{\text{Total estate}}$$

Example

X dies without having made any *inter vivos* transfers. His will leaves a house to Y (valued at £200,000) and which is expressly provided to be subject to tax, and the residue of his estate (valued at £300,000 net) to Z.

Step 1: Calculate the IHT payable

Band (£)	Rate (%)	Tax (£)
0–150,000	Nil	Nil
150–500,000	40	140,000

$$\frac{\text{Y's share}}{\text{of burden}} \text{ (total tax) } 140,000 \times \frac{200,000 \text{ (Y's share)}}{500,000 \text{ (total estate)}} = 56,000$$

$$\frac{\text{Z's share}}{\text{of burden}} \text{ (total tax) } 140,000 \times \frac{300,000 \text{ (Z's share)}}{500,000 \text{ (total estate)}} = 84,000$$

9.9   Liability for IHT on death

9.9.1   Liability to the Revenue for inheritance tax on death

Section 200(1), Inheritance Tax Act 1984 sets out the categories of persons who are accountable to the Revenue for the inheritance tax due on death. The section will be considered in order to ascertain the extent of the PR's liability.

We are *not* here concerned with which beneficiary actually bears the burden of the inheritance tax but with who is accountable to the Revenue for the tax. The burden of the inheritance tax was discussed in para. 9.8. The extent to which the PRs are liable for the inheritance tax on death must be understood in order to be able to complete correctly the Inland Revenue Account (*see* Chapter 10).

Liability of the personal representatives   9.9.2

The PRs are liable for the inheritance tax on any *free estate* of the deceased. This does not therefore include trust property (subject to what is said below about settled land) but it does for this purpose include gifts made by:

- *Donatio mortis causa;*
- Nominated property; and
- Joint property of the deceased, whether held by the deceased as a joint tenant or tenant in common.

Even though such property may not vest in the PRs, they are liable to the Revenue for the inheritance tax, although s.211(3), Inheritance Tax Act 1984 gives them the right to obtain reimbursement from the person in whom such property does vest.

In addition, the PRs are liable for the tax attributable to any land which was subject to a strict settlement within the Settled Land Act 1925 immediately before the deceased's death *which devolves upon them*. You must therefore understand when the property subject to a strict settlement devolves upon the PRs.

Where a strict settlement continues after the death of the deceased the land devolves on the trustees of the settlement: s.22, Administration of Estates Act 1925. In consequence it is the trustees of the settlement who are liable to the Revenue for the inheritance tax attributable to the estate. The deceased's PRs will only be liable if:

- The settlement comes to an end with the death of the deceased; or
- The land is not settled prior to the deceased's death but becomes settled under the deceased's will.

Example

Land is held by way of a strict settlement for David for life, then to Chris for life, with remainder to Edwina in fee simple.

On David's death the settled land will devolve on the trustees of the settlement who will be liable to pay the inheritance tax, but on the death of Chris, as the settlement will come to an end, the land will devolve on the PRs of Chris who will be liable to pay the inheritance tax.

9.9.3 Liability of trustees

Subject to what we have said about settled land (*see* above), trustees are liable to the Revenue for inheritance tax attributable to trust property.

9.9.4 Liability for additional tax on lifetime gifts

Additional tax may become payable:

- Where the transferor does within seven years of a potentially exempt transfer (*see* Chapter 2, para. 2.2.2);
- Where the transferor dies within seven years of a chargeable transfer.

The PRs *may* become liable for this tax and for this reason should be careful not to completely distribute the estate until they are satisfied that the tax has been paid, otherwise they will be personally liable to the Revenue.

The *transferee* is primarily liable, but the deceased's *PR* become liable if the tax remains unpaid for 12 months after the end of the month of death. However, the PRs' liability is limited to the extent of the deceased's assets which they *actually received* or which they would have received but for their own neglect or default.

9.9.5 Gifts with reservation

Where a gift is made with reservation of benefit, the *donee* of the gift is primarily liable for the IHT attributable to the property. However, if the tax remains unpaid for 12 months after the end of the month of death the deceased's *PRs* become liable but only to the extent of the deceased's assets which they have *actually received* or which they would have received but for their own neglect or default.

9.10 Time for payment of inheritance tax

9.10.1 General position

Normally, the PRs will have to pay any inheritance tax due before they can obtain a grant of representation (*see* Chapter 10, para. 10.2.4). This is because a grant of representation cannot be obtained before delivery of the Inland Revenue Account, and PRs must on delivery of the Inland Revenue Account pay all IHT for which they are liable (other than IHT on instalment option property – *see* 9.10.2).

However, as a general rule, on a transfer on death, or on a lifetime transfer where tax or extra tax is payable because of the death of the transferor, the inheritance tax becomes payable (due) *six months after the end of the month in which the death occurred*. Where tax is paid after this date interest is chargeable on it. The rate of interest is set down by statutory instrument and is currently 8%.

Instalment option

In the case of certain types of property an instalment option is available and inheritance tax need not therefore be paid within six months after the end of the month in which the death occurred (*see* 9.10.1).

If the instalment option is to be taken up by the PRs they must give notice to this effect in the completion of the relevant Inland Revenue Account (*see* Chapter 10, para. 10.4).

Method of payment

Where the instalment option is taken the tax is payable in *10 equal annual instalments*. The first instalment is due six months after the end of the month in which the death occurred, ie. on the date on which all the tax would be due if the instalment option were not taken.

Even where the instalment option is taken, the taxpayer may decide to pay all remaining instalments at any time within the 10-year period. All the outstanding instalments *must* be paid where the asset is sold.

Practical considerations

Where the instalment option is taken in respect of non-agricultural land which is not comprised in a business, interest is payable on the whole of the outstanding tax and it is added to each instalment. Consequently, in deciding whether or not to opt for the instalment option in relation to land falling within this category, you must consider whether the inheritance tax can practically be raised immediately in order to avoid the payment of interest. In the case of all other types of instalment option property, interest is only payable if an instalment of tax is overdue.

Inheritance tax has to be paid on non-instalment option property and instalment option property where the instalment option has not been exercised in order to obtain a grant of representation. As it is often difficult to raise the inheritance tax before grant (*see* Chapter 10, para. 10.5), it is common for PRs to elect to pay by instalments initially even though they intend to pay off the outstanding sum in one lump sum later on.

Qualifying property

The instalment option applies to the following types of

property in the case of transfers on death:

- Freehold and leasehold land, ie. any land;
- Shares and securities in a company giving the deceased control of the company immediately before death;
- Unquoted shares or securities in a company in which the deceased did not have control, but where the Revenue is satisfied that the payment of tax in one sum would cause undue hardship;
- Unquoted shares or securities which did not give the deceased a controlling interest but where at least 20% of the tax payable on the estate is attributable to those shares and any other instalment option property;
- Unquoted shares which did not give the deceased control, but which were worth at least £20,000 at the time of the transferor's death and *either* they represent at least 10% (by nominal value) of all the shares in the company *or* they are ordinary shares and are at least 10% (by nominal value) of all the ordinary shares in the company;
- A business or an interest in a business including a profession or vocation.

Note

'Unquoted shares' means shares not quoted on a recognised stock exchange although shares are still regarded as unquoted for this purpose if they are quoted on the USM: Finance (No 2) Act 1992.

9.11   Income tax

The general principles of income tax are covered in the Pervasives Companion. Here we are specifically concerned with income tax in the context of:

- The period up to deceased's death; and
- In the administration period.

9.11.1   Income of the deceased

Any liability of the deceased to income tax must be paid by the PRs. It is regarded as a debt owing at death and as such is deductible in calculating the net estate for IHT purposes. Conversely, if a refund of income tax paid is obtained, it is regarded as an asset which increases the size of the estate for IHT purposes.

It is the responsibility of the deceased's PRs immediately following death to make a return to the Inland Revenue of the income (and capital gains – *see* 9.12) of the deceased for the period commencing on 6 April before the deceased's death and ending with the date of death.

The pre-death tax return should be submitted as soon as possible after death because it may take some time to ascertain how much income tax is due/to be refunded and this will affect the calculation of IHT liability. However, to avoid delay in obtaining a grant of representation (which can only generally be obtained once an Inland Revenue Account has been submitted and the IHT due has been paid), the PRs are permitted to estimate the income tax liability of the deceased when completing the Inland Revenue Account. At a later stage a corrective account is submitted when the sum of tax due has been agreed with the Inland Revenue (*see* Chapter 13).

In submitting the pre-death income tax return, note that:

- Calculation of the deceased's income tax is done in the usual way by deducting any charges on income payable before death together with any reliefs or allowances. However, a *full year's* personal reliefs and allowances can be claimed, regardless of the date of death.

- Only income received or due before death is included in the return. Income receivable after death is income of the estate and is dealt with separately.

Income arising after death 9.11.2

Different rules apply to income received by the estate during the period of administration. The administration period commences the day after the date of death and continues until the complete administration of the estate: s.695, Income and Corporation Taxes Act 1988. For the purpose of income tax, the administration is regarded as complete on the date when the residue is ascertained for distribution.

For each income tax year (or part) during the administration period the PRs must submit a return to the Inland Revenue of the income they have received from the deceased's estate.

Calculation of personal representatives' liability
PRs cannot claim any of the reliefs available to individuals, neither can they pay tax at the lower rate available to individuals. However, they can claim relief for interest paid on a loan to pay IHT.

Note _____

Relief for interest paid on IHT can only be deducted for one year and is claimable only insofar as the loan is for tax on *personalty* vesting in the PRs: s.364, Income and Corporation Taxes Act 1988.

PRs pay basic rate tax on the taxable income of the estate whatever the amount and type of income, higher rate is never payable. There is a special rate (20%) for tax payable on dividends received by the PRs, although in most cases the PRs will have no income tax to pay on dividends received as basic rate tax has already been deducted at source.

Note

Where the PRs have obtained a loan to pay IHT and as such are entitled to relief for interest paid, if they have no income tax to pay because if has been deducted at source, they can seek a refund from the Inland Revenue.

9.12   Capital gains tax

Apart from in very limited circumstances where property is settled, the death of an individual does not give rise to capital gains tax (CGT) liability. This is because death is not a 'disposal' for CGT purposes: s.62(1)(a), Taxation of Chargeable Gains Act 1992. However, CGT needs to be considered by PRs in connection with:

- Disposals made by the deceased up until death; and
- Disposals made by the PRs during the administration period.

(The general principles of CGT are covered in the *Pervasives* Companion.)

9.12.1   Disposals made by the deceased up until death

Any liability of the deceased for CGT must be paid by the PRs and as with income tax is a debt owing by the deceased which may be deducted when calculating IHT due on death. Conversely, as with income tax refunds, an overpayment of CGT will be regarded as an asset of the estate, increasing its size for IHT purposes.

As with income tax, immediately following the deceased's death the PRs must submit to the Inland Revenue a return of the capital gains (if any) of the deceased for the period commencing on 6 April before the death and ending with the date of death. Because of the effect on the calculation of IHT liability on death of the deceased's CGT liability, the pre-death return should be submitted by the PRs as soon as possible after the deceased's death and if necessary an estimate figure for CGT liability included in the Inland Revenue Account (*see* 9.11.1 as for income tax).

Disposals made by the personal representatives during the administration

Although there is no disposal of assets for CGT purposes on death, in the course of the administration of the estate the PRs may need to sell assets in order to pay debts and other liabilities. If they do so, they will be liable to CGT on any gains made after the deduction of any losses they have incurred on disposals.

Calculation of CGT on disposals by personal representatives

PRs pay CGT at a rate equivalent to the basic rate of income tax. The indexation allowance is available to them in precisely the same way that it is available to individuals.

In addition to the usual deductions for incidental selling expenses, PRs can deduct a proportion of the cost of valuing the estate for probate purposes. The Inland Revenue publishes a scale of permitted deductions (SP 7/81) but more than the amounts stated can be claimed where it can be shown that the actual loss is greater.

PRs' rights to claim *exemptions and reliefs* are limited in the following ways:

- The annual exemption is only available for the tax year of death, and the two following tax years;

- The only or main residence exemption does not apply to PRs, although if before and after death a residence has been used as their only, or main, residence by individuals who are entitled under a will or the rules of intestacy to the whole or substantially the whole of the proceeds of sale of the house either absolutely or for life, the exemption can be claimed (Inland Revenue Concession D5).

CGT and related tax considerations as to which assets should be sold if necessary for administration purposes are considered in Chapter 12, para. 12.6.3.

Self-assessment questions

1   Will the following assets be regarded as part of the deceased's estate for IHT purposes?

(a) A half share in a house held by the deceased as a joint tenant.

(b) A valuable antique chair given by means of a *donatio mortis causa*.

(c) A life insurance policy written in trust for the deceased's children.

(d) A painting given to the deceased's nephew by deed of gift 10 years before he died, but which remained hanging in the deceased's house up until the date of his death.

(e) A discretionary lump sum payment made to the deceased's brother from a pension fund at the nomination of the deceased.

2   The deceased who died on a Sunday held 500 shares in XYZ plc, a quoted company. The Stock Exchange Daily List for the Friday before he died showed 102p/106p for XYZ plc and Monday following his death it showed 106p/110p. How will the shares in XYZ plc be valued for IHT purposes?

3   Harvey who died recently held 30% of the shares in QRS Ltd and his wife, Wendy, held at the time of his death 40% of the shares in QRS Ltd. How, if at all, will this affect the valuation of Harvey's shareholding in QRS Ltd for IHT purposes?

4   Sandra and her daughter, Tessa, die in a car crash. It is not known who died first. By will Sandra left all her estate to Tessa and Tessa by her will left all her estate to her partner, Victor, to whom she is not married. How will IHT on (a) Sandra's and (b) Tessa's estate be calculated?

5   List the IHT exemptions which do *not* apply to transfers on death.

6   Harvey died recently leaving a will which provides that the residue of his estate was to be paid to his wife subject to payment of all his 'funeral, testamentary and administration expenses, debts and other liabilities'. At his death he held a one-third share in a freehold house as a joint tenant with his brothers, Ian and John. On whom will the burden of IHT with respect to Harvey's share in the freehold house fall?

7   Explain whether the PRs of Peter are liable to the Revenue for any inheritance tax attributable to the following assets of Peter.

(a) A half share in a house which has passed to Peter's brother by right of survivorship.

(b) A Rolls Royce which has passed to Peter's friend, Miranda, by means of a *donatio mortis causa*.

(c) Settled land, of which Peter was the tenant for life, which upon Peter's death passes to his brother Richard in fee simple.

(d) Shares given by Peter to his sister, Sophie, three years before he died.

8 Distinguish between the responsibility of PRs to, on the one hand, pay income tax on income from the deceased and, on the other, to pay income tax on income after the deceased's date of death.

9 Broadly, in what circumstances may PRs be liable for CGT?

Answer guidance to self-assessment questions

1 *See* 9.3 generally.

(a) Yes.

(b) Yes.

(c) No.

(d) Yes (gift subject to a reservation).

(e) No.

2 *See* 9.4 generally.

The shares will each be valued at 107p. Monday is the nearest trading day to Sunday and 107p is quarter up on the difference between the lower and higher price quoted.

3 The shares held by Harvey and Wendy are related property (*see* 9.4.7). Together Harvey and Wendy have a majority shareholding. Shares valued as part of a majority shareholding are likely to be worth more than Harvey's 30% shareholding taken on its own.

4 *See* 9.4.7 generally.

As the order of Sandra and Tessa's death is uncertain, Sandra, the elder is presumed to have predeceased Tessa. Her estate will pass to Tessa, and assuming Sandra's nil rate band is used up, tax will be payable. However, when calculating the IHT on Tessa's estate, it is deemed not to include the property she received from Sandra's estate. IHT will be calculated on Tessa's estate not including the property received from Sandra.

5 *See* 9.5 generally.

• Annual exemption;

• Small gifts exemption;

• Normal expenditure out of income;

• Gifts in consideration of marriage;

• Family maintenance.

6 *See* 9.8.2 generally.

Ian and John, who take Harvey's share by survivorship.

7   *See* Chapter 10.3.1 generally.

(a) Yes.

(b) Yes.

(c) Yes, as the settlement has come to an end on the death of Peter.

(d) Sophie is primarily liable and the PRs only become liable for any tax remaining unpaid 12 months after the end of the month in which the death of Peter occurred (*see* 9.9.4).

8   *See* 9.11.1 and 9.11.2.

9   *See* 9.12 generally.

They are liable for CGT in connection with:

• Disposals made by the deceased up until death; and

• Disposals made by themselves when they sell assets in the course of administration of the estate.

Chapter 10

Obtaining a grant

Introduction 10.1

Chapter 8 was concerned with who is entitled to a grant to administer an estate in particular circumstances and the purpose and effect of such grants. Chapter 10 is concerned with the practical steps to be taken in order to obtain a grant of representation.

It is important to appreciate that a personal representative (PR) may obtain a grant of representation and proceed to administer an estate without the assistance of a solicitor. However, we are concerned with the procedure to be adopted by a solicitor who is either a PR or acting for a PR and where probate is to be obtained in common form.

What do you need to obtain a grant? 10.2

You must (as appropriate to the circumstances of the application) send or deliver the following to the Principal Registry or one of the district registries or sub-registries or designated local probate office (whichever you select):

- The will(s) (and codicil(s)), if any, duly marked;
- The appropriate oath;
- Probate fees;
- The Inland Revenue Account and cheque or money order for any inheritance tax due;
- Affidavit evidence (if necessary).

The will(s) (and codicil(s)), if any, duly marked 10.2.1

The will should be marked by the executors (or administrators) and by the solicitor before whom the supporting oath is sworn/affirmed (*see* 10.2.2).

If the original will has been lost or destroyed it may be possible for an order for the proof of a copy or reconstruction to be obtained. The procedure for obtaining such an order is set out in the Non-Contentious Probate Rules 1987, rule 54. The application must be supported by such evidence on affidavit as the applicant can adduce as to:

- The existence of the will after the testator's death. If there is no evidence of the existence of the will after the testator's death, evidence must be brought of any other facts on which the applicant relies to rebut the presumption that the will has been revoked by destruction (*see* Chapter 6, para. 6.7.4).

- In the case of a reconstructed will, the accuracy of the reconstruction.

- In the case of an oral will, the contents of the will.

Normally, a photographic copy of the will is attached to the grant of representation by the registry, but the applicant's solicitor will be required to provide a typewritten engrossment of the will where:

- It is unsuitable for photographic reproduction; or

- The will contains inadmissible material, eg. alterations, irrelevant and/or offensive material.

In these cases the registrar has discretion to allow a facsimile copy produced by photography as an alternative to an engrossment.

Where a will is totally or partly written in pencil a copy of the will with all the words written in pencil underlined in red ink must be lodged with the will.

As it is necessary to lodge the original will with the application for a grant of representation it is important that the solicitor ascertains as soon as possible after death that the will is admissible to probate. The solicitor should check that the will:

- Is the deceased's last will;

- Has not been revoked (*see* Chapter 6, para. 6.7);

- Has been properly executed (*see* Chapter 6, paras. 6.1–3).

If the solicitor anticipates that the registrar may require affidavit evidence because the validity of the will in all respects is not certain (*see* 10.7), eg. because the will does not contain an attestation clause or because the will is in a damaged condition, the solicitor should at this point obtain the necessary affidavit evidence, rather than waiting for the registrar to ask for it on submission of the application for grant, which will cause delay.

10.2.2   The appropriate oath

This must be sworn or affirmed by the PR before an independent solicitor (*see* 10.3).

10.2.3   Probate fees

The scale of fees is based on the value of the net estate passing under the grant.

The Inland Revenue Account and cheque or money order for any inheritance tax due

10.2.4

An Inland Revenue Account will be required unless the estate is 'excepted'. This is so even though no inheritance tax may be payable on death (*see* 10.5).

On delivery of the Inland Revenue Account, the PRs must pay all the IHT for which they are liable (other than IHT on instalment option property (*see* Chapter 9, para. 9.10.2).

Note

PRs must in any event deliver an Inland Revenue Account within 12 months of the end of the month of death, otherwise they become liable to penalties.

The Inland Revenue Account is completed on a standard printed form and is sent by post together with any inheritance tax (and interest thereon – *see* Chapter 9, para. 9.10.1) payable to the Central Accounting Office at Worthing. Cheques should be crossed and made payable to the Inland Revenue. The receipted account is returned to the solicitor who then delivers it to the registry/probate office along with the other relevant papers.

At an early stage the solicitor should obtain details of the deceased's property and debts in order to be able to begin to evaluate the size of the deceased's estate in order to ascertain whether IHT will be payable on death, and if so the likely amount of liability.

Where a solicitor is acting for the PRs they should ask the PRs for building society passbooks, details of bank accounts, and share certificates. They should also write to the relevant body holding any of the deceased's assets to obtain exact valuations. You may need to produce the death certificate as evidence of death in order to obtain the information.

It is also advisable at an early stage, so as to avoid delay, to instruct stockbrokers and other valuers (where necessary) to value the deceased's assets to enable you to complete the Inland Revenue Account.

Affidavit evidence (if necessary)

10.2.5

Where, for example, alterations have been made to the will or the will contains no attestation clause, affidavit evidence will be required (*see* 10.7). Such affidavit evidence should be delivered to the registry/probate office along with the other relevant papers.

You are not required to lodge the deceased's death certificate with the application for the grant, as confirmation of death is contained in the relevant oath sworn by the deceased's PR. However, you can obtain copies of the deceased's death certificate from the Registrar of Deaths to send to holders of the deceased's assets to get details of the assets.

10.3 Oath forms

The various different types of grant of representation were explained in Chapter 8. In order to obtain a grant of representation the application must be supported by the appropriate form of oath. This section explains which oath form the intending PRs should complete and how it should be completed.

The purpose behind requiring PRs to complete the appropriate oath form is:

- To provide information about the deceased;
- To explain the basis on which the application for a grant is made;
- For the intending PRs to swear that they will administer the estate according to the law.

There are three main types of oaths:

- Oaths for executors (*see* 10.3.7);
- Oaths for administrators with the will annexed (*see* 10.3.8);
- Oaths for administrators (*see* 10.3.9).

Paragraphs 10.3–5 deal with points about completing oath forms, common to all types of oaths either all, or more than one of the oath forms.

Note

If a mistake of law or a typographical error is made on the face of an oath the probate registry will issue a 'stop notice'. This prevents the application from proceeding until the mistake has been rectified. This may require the oath to be resworn by the PRs. Not only will this cause delay but it will probably create a bad impression on the client. You should therefore take special care to ensure that:

- The correct oath form is selected; and
- The form is properly completed.

10.3.1 Swearing the oath

Whatever type of oath is submitted to the probate registry, the PRs must either swear or *affirm* the truth of the information given in it. If an applicant wishes to affirm, the words 'make oath and say' (which appear twice on each form) should be deleted and replaced by the words 'do solemnly and sincerely affirm'. Also the words 'sworn by' in the jurat at the end of each form should be deleted and replaced by the words 'affirmed by'.

Whether the oath is sworn or affirmed this must be done before a commissioner for oaths or a solicitor holding a current practising certificate, who in either case, is not connected with the firm of solicitors acting for the PRs. An applicant who swears the oath will be required to hold the New Testament or Bible while saying 'I swear by Almighty God etc', whereas an applicant who merely affirms is required to say 'I do solemnly sincerely and truly declare and affirm etc'.

The place and date of swearing must be given precisely, eg. it is not sufficient just to name the town.

Solicitor's name and address   10.3.2

The name and address of the extracting solicitor should be put in the top right hand corner of the oath in the space provided. This ensures that any queries concerning the oath are sent to the extracting solicitor and not to the intending PRs.

It is important to add the solicitor's reference in the space provided as this will then be included in the grant when it is returned by the probate registry. This is useful for third parties who may wish to make contact with the solicitor acting for the PRs.

The Registry   10.3.3

The reference on the oath forms (*see* 10.3.7–9) to the High Court is because the probate registry is part of the High Court. An application can be made in *any* registry, it does not have to be the principal registry or the district registry in the area where the deceased died.

Details about the deceased   10.3.4

Name
The deceased's true and full name should be given in the appropriate place on the oath form. The deceased's true name is the name in which their birth was registered, or in the case of a married or divorced woman who adopted her husband's name, the surname of the woman's husband. However, the true name of a person may have been altered by deed poll or by habit and repute. A name is only regarded as altered by habit and repute if a person has abandoned their former name for all purposes for a long period of time.

If the deceased held assets in a name(s) other than their true name, the other name(s) must also be given. If the deceased simply used another name, but their will was not in this name nor were any of their assets recorded in this name, the name should not be included in the oath. An explanation justifying the inclusion of the name should be given at the end of the oath immediately before the jurat.

Example

The deceased's true name Cederic Reginald Blacklin Boot. However the deceased usually referred to himself as Reginald Boot and executed his will in this name. The oath should read:

IN the Estate of Cederic Reginald Blacklin Boot otherwise known as Reginald Boot ...

At the foot by the jurat the following should be inserted:

The deceased's true name was Cederic Reginald Blacklin Boot, however he was also known as Reginald Boot and he made and duly executed his will in this name.

Address

The deceased's usual residential address at the time of death should be given. If the usual residential address of the deceased at the time of death differs from the address in the will, the address at the date of death should be followed by the words 'formerly of' and the address in the will.

Date of death

The date of death as it appears in the certificate of death and the deceased's age at death must be inserted.

Domicile of the deceased

If the deceased died domiciled in England or Wales this should be recorded as 'England and Wales' as England and Wales are one jurisdiction.

10.3.5　　**Settled land**

Each of the oath forms (*see* 10.3.7–9) contain a paragraph relating to settled land, settled before the death of the deceased and continuing as settled land after the deceased's death. If there is no such settled land (normally the case) the paragraph is left as it is printed. If there is settled land the word 'no' must be deleted. Furthermore, usually where there is settled land on the death of the tenant for life, the property vests in the trustees of the settlement and not the deceased's PRs. The trustees of the settlement are special person representatives taking out a grant limited to the settled land. If this is the case then the general PRs must qualify the paragraph concerning the PRs' undertakings by inserting in the appropriate spaces the words 'save and except settled land'. If the deceased's general PRs are the trustees of the settlement the paragraph should be completed by inserting the words 'including settled land'.

Example

Land is held by way of strict settlement on trust for Angela for life, then to Brenda for life, with remainder to Caroline. The trustees of the settlement are Damian and Ernest. Angela has just died. Her PRs are Frank and Gertrude. The oath for executors will be completed in the following way by Frank and Gertrude with regard to the settled land:

... and that we will (i) collect, get in and administer according to the law the real and personal estate *save and except* settled land of the said deceased; (ii) when required to do so by the court, exhibit on oath in the court a full inventory of the said estate *save and except settled land* ...

If Damian and Ernest were Angela's PRs then in the places where the words 'save and except settled land' appear, the words 'including settled land' should appear.

Gross and net estate   10.3.6

Each of the oath forms (*see* 10.3.7–9) require the PRs to swear or affirm as to the gross and net values of the property *which vests in them*, ie. it is not concerned with property which does not pass under the grant, joint property for example. The relevant paragraph contains two alternatives one of which must be deleted.

1 'the gross estate passing under the grant does not exceed £... and the net estate does not exceed £... *and this is not a case where Inland Revenue Account is required to be delivered.'*

This paragraph should only be completed if an Inland Revenue Account is not required to be completed by the PRs. This will only be the case if the estate is an 'excepted estate' (*see* Chapter 10, para. 10.5.2). When completing paragraph (i) it is not necessary to swear to the exact gross and net values of the estate. The gross estate should be sworn to as not exceeding £125,000 and the net estate as not exceeding one of the figures on which fixed probate fees are payable, ie. £125,000, £100,000, £70,000, £40,000, £25,000 or £10,000, as appropriate. The net estate is used to calculate the level of probate fees. (*See* the example on the next page.)

2 'the gross estate passing under the grant amounts to £... *and the net estate £... .*

If the estate is not an 'excepted estate' so that an Inland Revenue Account must be completed this paragraph should

---

Example

Paul's estate

Assets	£
Personal chattels	3,000
Cash	1,000
½ share in family house held as tenant in common	60,000
	64,000

Debts	£
Mortgage debt	10,000

Paul's PRs should swear that the gross estate does not exceed £125,000 and the net estate does not exceed £70,000.

---

be completed and paragraph (i) (above) deleted. When completing paragraph (ii) the precise gross and net estate passing under the grant must be stated. These figures for the gross and net estate passing under the grant are the figures which will appear in the probate summary of the relevant Inland Revenue Account (either IHT 200 or 201) when completed (*see* para. 10.5.5).

10.3.7   Oath for executors

The following points relate specifically to the oath to be sworn or affirmed by executors, points general to all types of oaths having been dealt with in paragraphs 10.3.1–6.

Information about the executors

After the paragraph containing the deceased's name, the full names and addresses of the *proving* executors should be set out. The paragraph should commence 'I' or 'We' depending on whether there is more than one executor. The order of names should normally be the same as that given in the will. However, as the order of names given in the oath is repeated in the grant of representation and correspondence is generally addressed to the first named PR, where a solicitor or other professional person is to act as PR, it is common for that person's name to be given first in the oath.

True name

The true names of the intending PRs should be given. As one of the purposes behind the oath is to explain the basis of the applicant's right to a grant, if a PR's true name is not stated in the will, this requires explanation. If the discrepancy is slight, eg. the will refers to the executor as Jim Smith and his true name is James Smith, then it is sufficient to say 'James Smith in the will called Jim Smith'. In other circumstances the discrepancy should be fully explained, eg. the executrix changed her name:

- By deed poll (date);
- By habit and repute and had completely abandoned her former name;
- On marriage.

Address
Unless the executor is acting in a professional capacity, when a business address only may be given, an intending executor's full, private and permanent address should be given.

Specific paragraphs
'Make Oath and say that [I/we] believe the paper writing now produced ...' The paragraph commencing has two purposes:

- It makes the oath binding on the deponents; and
- It identifies the document(s) to be admitted to probate. The words 'now produced to and marked by [me/us] refer' to the requirement that the will and any codicil(s) thereto must at the time the oath is sworn or affirmed be produced by the proving executor(s) to the independent solicitor.

The will (and codicil(s)) are exhibited to (incorporated into) the oath. They are 'marked by' the proving executor(s) by each executor signing the will. The signatures should be placed away from the text of the will, if possible, either along the top of it or in the margin.

If the original will is not available the word 'original' in this paragraph should be deleted. If the original will is lost or destroyed, the oath should refer to the true last will and testament as contained in a copy thereof or reconstruction or other form it may take.

'And I/we further make oath and say that notice of this application has been given to ...' The Non-Contentious Probate Rules 1987, rule 27 require notice of intention to make an application for a grant of probate must be given by the proving executor(s) to all non-proving executors to whom power is being reserved.

That such notice has been given is stated on the oath, placing the name of the executor(s) to whom power has been reserved. The district judge or registrar can dispense with the need to give notice if satisfied that it is impracticable for the proving executors to do so, eg. because an executor is missing, or because it would result in unreasonable delay/expense. Application for such dispensation

Oath for Executors

IN THE HIGH COURT OF JUSTICE Extracting Solicitor..........................

FAMILY DIVISION   Address ....

THE DISTRICT PROBATE REGISTRY AT

(1) Insert name. If alias required, insert "otherwise | giving other name|." See (20).

(2) Delete as appropriate.

(3) Give full name, address and occupation, or, if none, description. For female deponents, add "Mrs.", "Miss", "Ms." as appropriate.

IN the Estate of (^{1})

deceased.

I/We (^{2}) (^{3})

(4) If appropriate, substitute "do solemnly and sincerely affirm".

(5) Add "with|insert no. | Codicil(s) thereto", as appropriate.

make oath and say. (^{4})   that
I/we (^{2}) believe the paper writing   now produced to and marked by me/us (^{2})
to contain the true and original last Will and Testament (^{5})

of (^{1})

of

formerly of

(6) If exact age not known, give best estimate.

(7) Where there are separate units of domicil in the country, specify the particular state, province, etc.

(8) Delete if not appropriate.

(9) Settled land may be included in the grant if the executors are also the special executors for that purpose. In this case, identify the settlement.

(10) Insert relationship only if needed to establish entitlement.

Power reserved to

deceased.

who died on the   day of   19 ,
aged   years (^{6}) domiciled in (^{7})
and that to the best of my/our (^{2}) knowledge, information and belief there was |no| (^{8})
land vested in the said deceased which was settled previously to h   death (and
not by h   Will (^{5})   )
and which remained settled land notwithstanding h   death (^{9})

And I/we (^{2}) further make oath and say (^{4})
that I am/we are (^{2}) (^{10}) (^{11})

the other Executor(s)

(11) Describe, e.g. "the sole", "the surviving" "one of the", "two of the". Where power reserved to non-proving executor(s), complete note in margin above, giving names. (See (19)).

(12) If there is settled land which is to be included, insert "including settled land". If the settled land is not to be included insert "save and except settled land". Do not insert anything if there is no settled land.

Execut   named in the said

and that I/we (^{2}) will (i) collect, get in and administer according to law the real and personal
estate (^{12})
of the said deceased; (ii) when required to do so by the court, exhibit in the court a full
inventory of the said estate (^{12})
and render an account thereof to the court: and (iii) when required to do so by the High
Court, deliver up to that court the grant of probate.

(continued overleaf)

(13) Delete words in square brackets if an Inland Revenue Account *not* required.

(14) Delete words in square brackets if an Inland Revenue Account *is* required.

(15) If Inland Revenue Account *not* required, insert for deaths up to 31.3.83 "£25,000", deaths thereafter up to 31.3.87 "£40,000", deaths thereafter up to 31.3.89 "£70,000", deaths thereafter up to 31.3.90 "£100,000", deaths thereafter up to 31.3.91 "£115,000", deaths thereafter "£125,000".

(16) If Inland Revenue Accounts *not* required, insert "£10,000", "£25,000", "£40,000", "£70,000", "£100,000", or "£200,000", as appropriate.

(17) If Inland Revenue Account *is* required, show exact figure.

(18) Delete words in square brackets if Inland Revenue Account *is* required.

(19) Delete if power not reserved. If notice not given, add "save........" and identify. Give reasons in separate covering letter.

(20) If alias required, state true name and reason for alias.

To the best of my/our (²) knowledge, information and belief the gross estate passing under the grant |amounts to| (¹³) |does not exceed| (¹⁴) £   (¹⁵) (¹⁷) and the net estate |amounts to| (¹³) |does not exceed| (¹⁴) £   (¹⁶) (¹⁷) |and that this is not a case in which an Inland Revenue Account is required to be delivered| (¹⁸).

(¹⁹) And I/we further make oath and say (⁴)
that notice of this application has been given to the executor(s) to whom power is to be reserved.

(²⁰)

Sworn by   the above-named
Deponent

at

this   day of

Before me,

A Commissioner for Oaths/Solicitor.

should be made by letter.

'And [I/we] further make Oath and say that [I/we] [am/ are] ...' Here the executor must explain their right to apply for the grant. If all of the executors named in the will are applying for a grant they should say:

'... we are the two [or other appropriate number] executors named in the said will.'

If only some of the living executors are applying for a grant they should say:

'[I am] We are two of (or other appropriate number) the executors named in the said will.'

If one or more of the executors appointed is dead but all the living executors wish to take out a grant they should say:

'[I am] We are the two (or other appropriate number) surviving executors named in the same will'

If one or more of the executors appointed is dead and not all the living executors wish to take out a grant they should say:

'[I am] We are two (or other appropriate number) of the surviving executors named in the said will.'

Where an executor has died there is no need to provide evidence of their death in making an application for a grant.

10.3.8   Oath for administrators with the will annexed

The oath for administrators with the will annexed is very similar to the oath for executors. Only the two significant points of difference with the oath for executors are discussed in this paragraph. Points common to all oaths including the oath for administrators with the will annexed are discussed in paragraph 10.3.6.

Minority and/or life interest
If a minority and/or life interest arises under the will (or on partial intestacy) it is normally necessary for two administrators with the will annexed to be appointed (*see* Chapter 8, para. 8.6.2). For this reason the oath must state whether a minority and/or life interest arises. If a minority, but no life interest arises the appropriate paragraph should be completed as follows:

'and that *a* minority ~~and~~ *but no* life interest in the estate ...'

... and [I/we] further make Oath and say
At this point in the form the administrators must *clear off* persons in a higher category of entitlement under rule 20 of the Non-Contentious Probate Rules which governs the order of entitlement of administrators with the will annexed (*see* Chapter 8, para. 8.6.1).

In clearing off, it is first necessary to explain why there are no executors, eg. the will did not appoint executors, all the executors renounced, predeceased etc. The oath must then explain why any other person with a prior right is not seeking a grant, eg. death, renunciation, failure to appear to citation (*see* 10.9). It is not necessary to clear off persons who are entitled in the same degree as the applicant.

Example

Carol died leaving a will appointing Daisy as executrix. Daisy predeceased Carol. Edward is entitled under the will to Carol's residuary estate. Edward should swear (in the appropriate place):

'... that Daisy the executrix appointed in this will predeceased the deceased.'

Finally, the oath must state the precise capacity in which the applicant is applying for a grant.

Example

X dies leaving a valid will appointing an executor who predeceases her. The will makes a number of specific gifts including one to Mary, who wishes to apply for a grant. The residue of X's estate is left to Sam who has renounced his right to probate. The oath should say:

'that the executor appointed in the will predeceased the deceased and that the residuary beneficiary of the will has renounced probate, and that I am one of the legatees named in the will ...'

Oath for administrators   10.3.9

Only the points which are unique to the oath for administrators are discussed in this paragraph. Points which apply to all oaths, including the oath for administrators were discussed in paragraph 10.3.6.

died ... Intestate

At this point in the form the applicant must clear off all categories of persons with a prior right under rule 22, Non-Contentious Probate Rules 1987 (*see* Chapter 8, para. 8.7.1). This is done by stating either that the deceased left no one in the prior categories set out in rule 22 or that the deceased did leave such persons but that they have since:

- Renounced their rights; or
- Failed to appear to a citation; or
- Died without taking a grant.

Oath for Administrators with the Will.

IN THE HIGH COURT OF JUSTICE

Extracting Solicitor ....

FAMILY DIVISION

Address ....

THE DISTRICT PROBATE REGISTRY AT

(1) Insert name. If alias required, insert "otherwise [giving other name]". See (20).

IN the Estate of (¹)

deceased.

(2) Delete as appropriate

(3) Give full name, address and occupation, or if none, description. For female deponents, add "Mrs.", "Miss", Ms." as appropriate.

I/We (²) (³)

(4) If appropriate, substitute "do solemnly and sincerely affirm.

(5) Add "with [insert no.] Codicil(s) thereto" as appropriate.

make oath and say, (⁴)   that
I/we (²) believe the paper writing   now produced to and marked by me/us (²)
to contain the true and original last Will and Testament (⁵)

of (¹)

of

formerly of

deceased,

who died on the   day of   19   ,

(6) If exact age not known, give best estimate. .

aged   years (⁶) domiciled in (⁷)

(7) Where there are separate units of domicil in the country, specify the particular state, province, etc.

(8) Delete which alternative is not appropriate.

(9) Delete if not appropriate.

(10) Settled land may be included in the grant. It must be established that every applicant is also entitled to a grant in respect of the settled land. The settlement must be identified.

that [a] [no] (⁸) minority and [a] [no] (⁸) life interest arises in the estate; and that
to the best of my/our(²) knowledge, information and belief there was [no](⁹) land
vested in the said deceased which was settled previously to h   death (and not by
h   Will (⁵)   )
and which remained settled land notwithstanding h   death(¹⁰)

And I/we (²) further make oath and say (⁴)
that (¹¹)

(11) Here clear off prior entitlements. E.g. If residuary legatees/devisees applying. show as appropriate that testator did not appoint any executors or that they predeceased him or survived and have since died without taking probate. or renounced. or failed to take a grant following citation. (In latter instance identify the order authorising grant to citor).

(12) State title to grant. Give relationship to deceased only if needed to establish entitlement.

that I am/we are (²) (¹²)

(continued overleaf)

(13) If there is settled land to be included, insert "including settled land". If the settled land is not to be included, insert "save and except settled land". Do not insert anything if there is no settled land.

(14) Delete words in square brackets if an Inland Revenue Account *not required.*

(15) Delete words in square brackets if an Inland Revenue Account *is required.*

(16) If Inland Revenue Account *not required,* insert for deaths up to 31.3.83 "£25,000", deaths thereafter up to 31.3.87 "£40,000", deaths thereafter up to 31.3.89 "£70,000", deaths thereafter up to 31.3.90 "£100,000", deaths thereafter up to 31.3.91 "£115,000", deaths thereafter "£125,000".

(17) If Inland Revenue Account *not required,* insert "£10,000", "£25,000", "£40,000", "£70,000", "£100,000", or "£200,000", as appropriate.

(18) If Inland Revenue Account *is required,* show exact figure.

(19) Delete words in square brackets if Inland Revenue Account *is required.*

(20) If alias required, state true name and reason for alias.

that I/we(²) will (i) collect, get in and administer according to law the real and personal estate(¹³)   of the said deceased; (ii) when required to do so by the Court, exhibit in the Court a full inventory of the said estate.(¹³)   and render an account thereof to the Court, and (iii) when required to do so by the High Court, deliver up to that Court the grant of letters of administration; that to the best of my/our(²) knowledge, information and belief

the gross estate passing under the grant [amounts to] (¹⁴) [does not exceed] (¹⁵) £   (¹⁶) (¹⁸) and the net estate [amounts to] (¹⁴) [does not exceed] (¹⁵) £   (¹⁷) (¹⁸) [and that this is not a case in which an Inland Revenue Account is required to be delivered] (¹⁹).

(²⁰)

		⎞
Sworn by the above-named		⎟
Deponent		⎟
at		⎬
this day of 19 ,		⎟
Before me,		⎠

A Commissioner for Oaths/Solicitor.

Probate Form OT19D (District Registry)
Published by Stat Plus Group plc, London, SW19 2PU ©
ZF1831   Stat Plus Group plc   Revised July 1991

Oath for Administrators

IN THE HIGH COURT OF JUSTICE
FAMILY DIVISION

Extracting Solicitor . . . .

Address. . . . .

THE DISTRICT PROBATE REGISTRY AT

(1) Insert name. If alias required, insert "otherwise [giving other name]". See (19)

IN the Estate of (¹)

deceased.

(2) Delete as appropriate.
(3) Give full name, address and occupation, or, if none, description. For female deponents, add "Mrs", "Miss", Ms" as appropriate.

I/We (²)(³)

(4) If appropriate, substitute "do solemnly and sincerely affirm".

make oath and say (⁴)
that

of

deceased,

(5) If exact age not known, give best estimate.
(6) Where there are separate units of domicile in the country, specify the particular state, province, etc.
(7) State status of deceased. E.g. "a bachelor", "a spinster", "a widow", etc., as appropriate. Show as necessary how classes with prior entitlement are cleared off, e.g. "without issue, or parent", etc.

died on the   day of   19

aged   years (⁵) domiciled in (⁶)

intestate (⁷)

(8) Delete which alternative is not appropriate.
(9) Delete if not appropriate.
(10) If there was settled land, it may be included in the grant. It must be established that every applicant is also entitled to a grant in respect of the settled land. The settlement must be identified.

or any other person entitled in priority to share in h   estate by virtue of any enactment and that [a] [no] (⁸) minority and [a] [no] (⁸) life interest arises under the intestacy; and that to the best of my/our (²) knowledge, information and belief there was [no] (⁹) land vested in the said deceased which was settled previously to h   death and which remained settled land notwithstanding h   death (¹⁰)

(11) Give applicant's title to grant.

And I/we (²) further make oath and say (⁴)
that I am/we are (²) the (¹¹)

(12) If there is settled land to be included, insert "including settled land". If the settled land is not to be included insert "save and except settled land". Do not insert anything if there is no settled land.

of the said intestate,
that I/we (²) will (i) collect, get in and administer according to law the real and personal estate (¹²)   of the said deceased; (ii) when required to do so by the Court, exhibit in the Court a full inventory of the said estate (¹²)   and render an account thereof to the Court, and (iii) when required to do so by the High Court, deliver up to that Court the grant of letters of administration; that to the best of my/our (²) knowledge, information and belief *(continued overleaf)*

(13) Delete words in square brackets if an Inland Revenue Account *not* required.

(14) Delete words in square brackets if an Inland Revenue Account *is* required.

(15) If Inland Revenue Account *not* required, insert for deaths up to 31.3.83 "£25,000", deaths thereafter up to 31.3.87 "£40,000", deaths thereafter up to 31.3.89 "£70,000", deaths thereafter up to 31.3.90 "£100,000", deaths thereafter up to 31.3.91 "£115,000", deaths thereafter "£125,000".

(16) If Inland Revenue Account *not* required, insert "£10,000", "£25,000", "£40,000", "£70,000", "£100,000", or "£200,000", as appropriate.

(17) If Inland Revenue Account *is* required, show exact figure.

(18) Delete words in square brackets if Inland Revenue Account *is* required.

(19) If alias required, state true name and reason for alias.

the gross estate passing under the grant [amounts to] (^{13}) [does not exceed] (^{14}) £ (^{15}) (^{17}) and the net estate [amounts to] (^{13}) [does not exceed] (^{14}) £ (^{16}) (^{17}) [and that this is not a case in which an Inland Revenue Account is required to be delivered]. (^{18}) (^{19})

Sworn by   the above-named
Deponent

at

this   day of

Before me,

A Commissioner for Oaths/Solicitor.

As a surviving spouse has first claim to a grant if the deceased left no spouse the oath should first say, died intestate 'a single man (woman)' 'a widow(er)' (as appropriate).

Other persons entitled under rule 22 are cleared off by stating that the deceased died *without* 'issue', 'parent', 'brother or sister of the whole blood' etc (as appropriate).

Note

The words on the oath 'or any other person entitled in priority to share in [his/her] estate by virtue of any enactment' make it clear that there are no adopted or legitimated relatives or relatives whose parents were not married, surviving the deceased.

The words must be deleted, however, where there is a surviving spouse and/or issue because such persons would not then rank in priority to the applicant. Apart from these situations, the line should be retained in this oath.

Example

X dies intestate. He has no wife or children and his parents have predeceased him. He is survived by three sisters of the whole blood, one of whom is Moira, who wishes to apply for a grant. The oath should read:

'Intestate a single man without issue or parent or any other person entitled in priority to share in his estate by virtue of any enactment ...'

Minority/life interests

As at least two administrators are needed where there is a minority and/or life interest in the estate, it is necessary to state in the oath whether or not this is the case (*see* further 10.3.8 minority/life interests).

And [I/we] further make Oath and say

Here the applicant is required to show their precise relationship to the deceased and also state whether they are 'the only person entitled to the estate of the deceased' or 'one of the persons entitled to share in the estate of the deceased' or 'a person who may have a beneficial interest in the estate of the said deceased in the event of an accretion thereto'.

A surviving spouse should be described as 'the lawful widow(er)' or 'lawful wife (husband)' as appropriate. An adopted child should be described as the 'lawful adopted child'. However, the word 'lawful' is not needed in describing any other relationship to the deceased.

Example _____

Taking the facts of Example 1 above, Mary should state in the oath:

'And I further make Oath and say that I am the sister of the whole blood of the deceased and one of the persons entitled to share in the estate of the said Intestate ...'

_____

Payment of IHT   10.4

Before a grant of representation can be obtained it is normally necessary to fill in and lodge an Inland Revenue Account (*see* 10.5) and to pay any inheritance tax for which the PRs are liable. In this paragraph it is proposed to examine the extent of the PR's liability for inheritance tax on death (*see* 10.4.1) and the extent to which such tax must be paid on delivery of the Inland Revenue Account (*see* 10.4.2).

Liability to the Revenue for inheritance tax on death   10.4.1

The Inheritance Tax Act 1984 (s.200(1)) sets out the categories of persons who are accountable to the Revenue for the inheritance tax due on death. The section will be examined in order to ascertain the extent of the PR's liability. It is important to understand that we are at this stage not concerned with which beneficiary actually bears the burden of the inheritance tax but who is accountable to the Revenue for the tax. The burden of the inheritance is discussed in Chapter 9, para. 9.8. It is necessary to understand the extent to which the PRs are liable for the inheritance tax on death in order to be able to complete correctly the Inland Revenue Account.

Time for payment of inheritance tax   10.4.2

General position
It has already been explained that as a general rule the PRs will have to pay any inheritance tax due before they can obtain a grant of representation. However, the inheritance tax on a transfer on death or on a lifetime transfer where tax or extra tax is payable because of the transferor's death within seven years, as a general rule, becomes payable (due) *six months after the end of the month in which the death occurred*. Where tax is paid after this date interest is chargeable on it. The rate of interest is set down by statutory instrument and is currently 8%.

Instalment option
In the case of certain types of property, inheritance tax need not be paid within six months after the end of the month in

which the death occurred as an instalment option is available.

If the instalment option is to be taken up by the PRs of the deceased they must give notice to this effect in the completion of the relevant Inland Revenue Account (*see* 10.5).

Where the instalment option is taken the tax is payable in *10 equal annual* instalments. The first instalment is due six months after the end of the month in which the death occurred, ie. on the date on which all the tax would be due if the instalment option were not taken.

Even where the instalment option is taken, the taxpayer may decide to pay all remaining instalments at any time within the 10-year period. All the outstanding instalments *must* be paid where the asset is sold.

Where the instalment option is taken in respect of non-agricultural land which is not comprised in a business, interest is payable on the whole of the outstanding tax, and it is added to each instalment. Consequently, in deciding whether or not to opt for the instalment option in relation to land falling within this category, it will be important to consider whether the inheritance tax can practically be raised immediately in order to avoid the payment of interest. In the case of all other types of instalment option property interest is only payable if an instalment of tax is overdue.

Inheritance tax has to be paid on non-instalment option property and instalment option property where the instalment option has not been exercised, in order to obtain a grant of representation. As it is often difficult to raise the inheritance tax before grant (*see* 10.6) it is common for PRs to elect to pay by instalments initially even though they intend to pay off the outstanding sum in one lump sum later on.

The instalment option applies to the following types of property in the case of transfers on death:

- Freehold and leasehold land;
- Shares and securities in a company giving the deceased control of the company immediately before death;
- Unquoted shares or securities in a company in which the deceased did not have control, but where the Revenue is satisfied that the payment of tax in one sum would cause undue hardship;
- Unquoted shares or securities which did not give the deceased a controlling interest but where at least 20% of the tax payable on death is payable by the person paying the tax on those shares, is either tax on those shares or on those shares and other instalment option property;

- Unquoted shares which did not give the deceased control, but which were worth at least £20,000 at the time of the transferor's death and *either* they represent at least 10% (by nominal value) of all the shares in the company *or* they are ordinary shares and are at least 10% (by nominal value) of all the ordinary shares in the company;
- A business or an interest or a business including a profession or vocation.

Note _____

Unquoted shares means shares not quoted on a recognised stock exchange. However, shares are regarded as unquoted for this purpose even if they are quoted on the USM (Finance (No 2) Act 1992).

Inland Revenue accounts   10.5

It has been explained that before a grant of representation can be obtained it is normally necessary to fill in and lodge an Inland Revenue Account and to pay any inheritance tax for which the PRs are liable (*see* 10.4). This paragraph examines the different forms which may be required and how to complete these forms. Certain estates are 'excepted estates' where no Inland Revenue Account is needed (*see* 10.5.2).

Unless an estate is an 'excepted estate' a standard printed form will need to be filled in by the solicitor acting for the PRs even where no inheritance tax is due on the estate. If tax is to be paid on delivery of the account a cheque is sent with the form.

The form requires the solicitor acting on behalf of the PRs to make a 'self-assessment' of the inheritance tax liability of the PRs. The Inland Revenue check this assessment to determine whether or not it is correct. If it is discovered at a later date that the Inland Revenue Account does not reflect accurately the assets and liabilities of the deceased's estate a corrective account must be filled in within six months of discovery of the mistake.

Where an estate is not an 'excepted estate' so that an Inland Revenue Account has to be prepared, it is necessary to decide which of the standard printed forms is appropriate to the deceased's estate. There are three possibilities IHT Form 200, or IHT Form 201 (*see* 10.5.3) or IHT Form 202 (*see* 10.5.4). The following paragraphs will explain the circumstances in which each form is appropriate and will provide guidance, to further clarify the instructions already given on the forms, as to how each form should be completed.

10.5.1 Time limit for delivery of Inland Revenue accounts

Where an Inland Revenue Account is required it must normally be delivered within 12 months of the end of the month in which the death occurred. In certain exceptional circumstances it may be delivered later. However, it is important to note that inheritance tax becomes payable on transfers on death, six months after the end of the month in which the death occurred. Tax paid after this date has interest chargeable on it, currently at a rate of 8%.

10.5.2 'Excepted estates'

An Inland Revenue Account need not be lodged with the probate registry if the estate is an 'excepted estate'. An 'excepted estate' is broadly a small estate, where the deceased has a nil cumulative total for inheritance tax purposes. *All* the following conditions have to be satisfied before an estate is an 'excepted estate':

● The estate must consists only of property passing within any of the following four categories:

– Under the deceased will

– Under the rules of intestacy

– By nomination of an asset taking effect on death

– By operation of the rule of survivorship in relation to property held as a joint tenant beneficially.

Thus, for example, if the estate includes trust property the estate cannot be an 'excepted estate'. Strictly speaking, if the estate includes property passing by means of a *donatio mortis causa* it does not fall within one of the four categories above but the Revenue will, nevertheless, still normally regard the estate as 'excepted' if it fulfils the other conditions.

and

● The total *gross* value of the property must not exceed £125,000.

Note

For the purpose of determining the value of the estate, where the deceased is a joint owner of property, only the value of the deceased's beneficial interest is taken into account.

and

● Not more than the value of £15,000 must be attributable to property situated outside the UK.

and

● The deceased died domiciled in the UK.

and

- The deceased made no chargeable transfers (or potentially exempt transfers which have become chargeable as a result of the transferor's death within seven years) during their lifetime.

Note

1 An estate cannot be 'excepted' where the deceased gave away property *inter vivos* subject to a reservation and at their death the reservation was still subsisting or if the reservation was released within seven years of the deceased's death.

2 The Inland Revenue can make a demand that an Account be completed, but the demand must be made within 35 days of the date of issue of the grant of representation.

3 If the PRs discover at a later stage that the estate is not an 'excepted estate' they must submit the appropriate Inland Revenue Account within six months of discovery.

IHT Form 202   10.5.3

Broadly speaking, IHT Form 202 is used in the case of comparatively small and straightforward estates where no inheritance tax is payable at the date of death. *All* the following conditions have to be satisfied:

- The estate must consists only of property situated in the UK and pass within any of the four following categories:
  - under the deceased will
  - under the rules of intestacy
  - by nomination
  - by operation of the rule of survivorship in relation to property held as a joint tenant beneficially;

Note

As with 'excepted estates' (*see* 10.5.2) the Revenue will normally allow this form to be used where some of the property passed by means of a *donatio mortis causa*, provided the other conditions are satisfied.

- The total *net* value of the estate after deducting any exemptions and reliefs claimed does not exceed the nil rate band;
- The *gross* value of the estate before deduction of exemptions and reliefs must not exceed twice the inheritance tax threshold;
- The deceased made no chargeable transfers or potentially exempt transfers within seven years of their death.

Note

A transfer of value may have been made within seven years of

Inland
Revenue
Capital Taxes Office

Inland Revenue Account
for Inheritance Tax

This Account is for use only for an original grant where the deceased died on or after 18 March 1986 and was domiciled in the United Kingdom, and

- the whole of the estate is situated in the UK
- the deceased within seven years of the death neither made any lifetime transfers of value chargeable with Inheritance Tax nor had any interest in settled property
- the net estate after exemptions and reliefs does not exceed the Inheritance Tax threshold at the death
- the gross estate before exemptions and reliefs does not exceed twice the Inheritance Tax threshold at death.

If the deceased died before 18 March 1986 or you need any further help or information, contact the Capital Taxes Office where the staff will be pleased to help you.

Before you start to fill in this Account, read the Guidance Notes in booklet IHT 210. The marginal notes on this Account refer to the relevant paragraphs of the booklet. They will help you to fill it in quickly and correctly. If you need more space use a separate sheet of paper showing to which section of the Account it relates.

Insert 'Principal', or the name of the District and 'District'

In the High Court of Justice Family Division (Probate), The ⬚ **Registry**

Solicitor(s) or Agent(s)

Please give your full name and address including postcode, using capital letters, even if the DX code is given

Please give the full name and title of the deceased using CAPITAL letters

In the estate of
Surname

Title and Forenames

All communications concerning Inheritance Tax will be sent to the solicitors or agents unless the executors or administrators request otherwise

DX Code

Show, for example, 9 January 1993 as 09 Jan 1993

Date of birth   **Date of death**

Your reference

Marital Status

Married ⬚   Single ⬚   Divorced ⬚   Widowed ⬚

Surviving relatives

Husband ⬚   Wife ⬚   Child(ren) ⬚   Parent(s) ⬚

You may wish to give the name of the person dealing with this estate

Contact

Domicile

England and Wales ⬚   Scotland ⬚   N. Ireland ⬚

Telephone

Address

Give the last known usual address of the deceased including postcode

Fax

Tax District and reference

Please give the occupation of the deceased

Occupation

If available, please give this information

National Insurance No

Date of Grant (For official use only)

Executors or intending administrators

Give the full names and permanent addresses including postcode of the executors or intending administrators

IHT202(1993)

1

Nominated and Joint Property

You must answer these first two questions

Note 7
If 'Yes', please give full particulars below

Note 8
If 'Yes', also answer the following questions

Did the deceased nominate any Savings Bank Account, Savings Certificates or other assets in favour of any person?

Yes ☐ No ☐

Was the deceased joint owner of any property of any description or did the deceased hold any money on a joint account?

Yes ☐ No ☐

On a separate sheet of paper state for each item of joint property

- the name(s) of the other joint owner(s)
- when the joint ownership began or when the joint account was opened

Note 9

- by whom and from what source the joint property was provided and if it or its purchase price was contributed by more than one of the joint owners, the extent of the contribution made by each

Note 10

- how any income was dealt with and enjoyed

If 'Yes' include the value below

Did any joint property pass by survivorship?

Yes ☐ No ☐

If 'Yes' include the value as part of the Free Estate

Did any joint property pass under the deceased's Will or intestacy?

Yes ☐ No ☐

Nominated and Joint Property

All claims for exemptions or reliefs should be made on Page 4

Particulars of the property	Gross value at date of death

See Note 24 and first paragraph of Note 46 before continuing

Deceased's share of liabilities in respect of the property

Name of creditor	Description of liability	Amount

Carry the net value forward to Page 4 Box A

Net value **A**

Note 13

Free Estate

All claims for exemptions or reliefs should be made on Page 4

All the property of the deceased in respect of which the grant is required

Property without the Instalment Option

	Gross value at date of death
Notes 14, 15 and 16 — Stocks, shares, debentures and other securities, as set out on IHT 40 quoted or listed in the Stock Exchange Daily Official List and others, except those qualifying for the instalment option	
Note 17 — Premium Savings Bonds and National Savings Certificates (including interest)	
Cash and cash at Bank or Savings Bank, a building society, a co-operative or friendly society, including interest to the date of death, as statement attached	
Note 20 — Policies of insurance and bonuses thereon (if any) on the life of the deceased, as statement attached	
Saleable value of policies of insurance and bonuses (if any) on the life of any other person, as statement attached	
Income Tax repayable	
Carried forward	

For Official use only

Property without the Instalment Option - continued

Brought forward

Note 21
Please attach a valuation if one has been obtained

Household and personal goods, including pictures, china, clothes, books, jewellery, stamp, coin and other collections, motor cars, boats etc

Sold, realised gross

Unsold, estimated

Note 22
Please state the name and date of death of the testator or intestate

Interest in an unadministered estate

Other assets not included above or as instalment option property

Carry the total forward to Page 4 Box B

Total | B

Notes 24, 25 and 26

Liabilities at the date of death and funeral expenses

Name of creditor	Description of liability	Amount

Note 27
Carry the total forward to Page 4 Box E

Total | E

Property with the Instalment Option

Gross value at date of death

Note 28   Land and buildings as described on IHT 37 attached

Note 29   Business interests (state nature of business)

- Net value of deceased's interest in business, as statement or balance sheet attached

Note 30
Please give the name of the firm

- Net value of deceased's interest as a partner in the firm of

as statement or balance sheet attached

Note 31   Stocks, shares, debentures and other securities as set out on form IHT 40

- which gave the deceased control of the company

- other unquoted shares or securities

Carry the total forward to Page 4 Box C

Total | C

Note 32

Liabilities

Name of creditor	Description of liability (and property on which charged)	Amount

Carry the total forward to Page 4 Box F

Total | F

For Official use only

3

Probate Summary

Aggregate Gross Value
which in law devolves on and vests in the personal
representatives of the deceased, for and in respect
of which the grant is to be made

B [   ]   Totals

+ C [   ]   = D [   ]

Deduct liabilities

E [   ]

+ F [   ]   = G [   ]

Net estate for Probate purposes D - G = H [   ]

Tax Summary

Nominated and joint property (net)   A [   ]

As box H above   + H [   ]   = J [   ]

Notes 42, 43,
44 and 45

Deduct exemptions and reliefs

Nature	Net value	Amount
[ ]	[ ]	[ ]

= K [   ]

Net estate for tax purposes J - K = L [   ]

Note 55

Declaration

Tick the appropriate box

I/We wish to apply for a   • Grant of Probate   [ ]

                • Grant of Letters of Administration   [ ]

                • Grant of Letters of Administration with Will annexed   [ ]

                • Grant [   ]   [ ]

To the best of my/our knowledge and belief all the statements made and particulars given in this Account and its
accompanying schedules are true and complete.

I/We have made the fullest enquiries that are reasonably practicable in the circumstances to ascertain the value of all
assets, interests, liabilities, etc.

The deceased within 7 years of the death neither made transfers of value chargeable with Inheritance Tax (ie no
transfers of value that were not covered by the IHT exemptions nor any gifts, subject to a reservation to the donor).

The estate at the death did not include any property situate outside the UK.

The deceased did not have an interest in settled property at the death nor had within 7 years of death an
interest in settled property or settled any property.

Notes 56 and 57

I/We understand that the issue of the Grant does not imply acceptance by the Inland Revenue of any of the statements
or values included in this Account.

Warning

An executor or intending
administrator who fails
to make the fullest
enquiries that are
reasonably practicable in
the circumstances may be
liable to penalties.

You may be liable to
penalties or prosecution
if you fail to disclose, in
this Account and in your
answers to the questions
on Page 2 all the property
in respect of which tax
may be payable.

[   ]   Name   [   ]

                    Signature

                    Date

[   ]   Name   [   ]

                    Signature

                    Date

the deceased's death if no inheritance tax was payable because of the availability of exemptions; and

- The deceased made no gifts subject to a reservation within seven years of their death;
- The deceased did not have an interest in settled property at their death;
- The deceased did not have an interest in settled property nor did they settle any property within seven years of their death.

If these conditions are not satisfied and the estate is not an 'excepted estate' either IHT 200 or IHT 201 will have to be completed (*see* 10.5.4).

10.5.4   IHT Form 200 and IHT Form 201

If an estate is not an 'excepted estate' (*see* 10.5.2) and IHT Form 202 cannot be used (*see* 10.5.3) then either IHT Form 200 or IHT Form 201 must be completed. IHT Form 200 is used for the estate of a person who dies domiciled in the United Kingdom whilst IHT Form 201 is used for the estate of a person who dies domiciled outside the United Kingdom. It is beyond the scope of the course for students to be acquainted with the inheritance tax position of the person who dies domiciled outside the UK and thus IHT Form 201 is not considered further.

10.5.5   Guidance for completing IHT Form 200

Guidance as to how IHT Form 200 should be completed can be obtained from the form itself and form IHT 210 'Guidance Notes on Completion of Inland Revenue Accounts'. The following additional points of guidance correspond to the various pages of the form.

Page 1
This is designed to give information to the Inland Revenue about the deceased and the deceased's PRs. In completing the details of executors only the names and addresses of *proving* executors should be included and their names should appear in the order in which they appear in the will. If administrators are to be appointed, their names should appear in the order of entitlement.

Page 2
Page 2 comprises 'Section 1 – Lifetime Gifts or Transfers of Value'. This section is designed to give a complete picture of the deceased's IHT situation at death as chargeable transfers or PETs made by the deceased within seven years of death will affect the IHT payable on death.

Questions are asked about gifts and transfers of value made by the deceased during their lifetime. They are to be answered by ticking the relevant YES/NO box. The information must still be given even though it has already been given to the Inland Revenue during the deceased's lifetime. If the answer to any of the questions is 'YES' full details must be set out on the form.

'**Did the deceased within seven years of death ...**' In answering the three questions which are prefixed by this sentence it is important to remember the following points:

- Lifetime gifts which are subject to the exemptions set out in Note 1, eg. the spouse exemption should not be mentioned. Note 1 does not, however, include all the available exemptions. The following only should not be included:
  - gifts to spouses;
  - gifts within the annual exemption;
  - gifts not exceeding 250 (small gifts exemption).
- Premiums on a policy of life assurance are not included on page 2 if:
  - the proceeds vest in the deceased's PRs (because the policy is *not* written in trust) (*see* Chapter 3, para. 3.4.2); or
  - if the proceeds are payable to or held on trust for the deceased or the deceased's spouse (Note 2 IHT 210).

Thus if a policy of life assurance is written in trust for a person(s) other than the deceased's spouse details should be given of each policy with the amount(s) and date(s) of the premiums paid.

'**Did the deceased at any time on or after 18 March 1986 dispose of any property by way of gift where ... '** This section refers to gifts with reservation (*see* Chapter 9, para. 9.9.5).

Details of *lifetime gifts or transfers of value* All transfers of value made by the deceased during his lifetime should be entered in chronological order deducting any exemptions or reliefs available.

Superannuation benefits Details of any lump sum benefit payable under a pension policy as a result of death should be mentioned here. Additionally, Note 6 requires the 'YES' box to be ticked and details supplied, if the deceased disposed of such benefit, eg. by nomination or declaration of trust, within two years of death.

Page 3: Section 2 – Nominated and Joint Property
Nominated and joint property of the deceased is liable to IHT but the property does not vest in the deceased's PRs.

Inland Revenue Account for Inheritance Tax

This Account is for use only where the deceased died on or after 18 March 1986 and was domiciled in the United Kingdom.

If the deceased died before 18 March 1986 or you need any further help or information, contact the Capital Taxes Office where the staff will be pleased to help you.

Before you start to fill in this Account, read the Guidance Notes in booklet IHT 210. The marginal notes on this Account refer to the relevant paragraphs of the booklet. They will help you to fill it in quickly and correctly. If you need more space use a separate sheet of paper showing to which section of the Account it relates.

Insert 'Principal', or the name of the District and 'District'

In the High Court of Justice Family Division (Probate), The _____ **Registry**

Please give your full name and address including postcode, using capital letters, even if the DX code is given

Solicitor(s) or Agent(s)

In the estate of

Surname

Please give the full name and title of the deceased using CAPITAL letters

Title and Forenames

All communications concerning Inheritance Tax will be sent to the solicitors or agents unless the executors or administrators request otherwise

DX Code

Show, for example, 9 January 1993 as 09 Jan 1993

Date of birth   **Date of death**

Marital Status

Married ☐   Single ☐   Divorced ☐   Widowed ☐

Surviving relatives

Husband ☐   Wife ☐   Children ☐   Parent(s) ☐

Your reference

Domicile

England and Wales ☐   Scotland ☐   N. Ireland ☐

You may wish to give the name of the person dealing with this estate

Contact

Address

Telephone

Give the last known usual address of the deceased including postcode

Fax

Tax District and reference

Please give the occupation of the deceased

Occupation

If available, please give this information

National Insurance No

Date of Grant (For official use only)

Executors or intending administrators

Give the full names and permanent addresses including postcode of the executors or intending administrators

IHT 200(1993)

1

You must answer all the questions in this section

Section 1 - Lifetime gifts or transfers of value

Did the deceased within 7 years of death

	Yes	No
Note 1 — make any gift, settlement, or other transfer of value? (See Note 1 as to the transfers you should not include)	☐	☐
Note 2 — pay any premium on a policy of life assurance not included on Page 4 Section 3A of this form?	☐	☐
Note 3 — cease to be entitled to any beneficial interest in possession in settled property?	☐	☐

Note 4

Did the deceased at any time on or after 18 March 1986 dispose of any property by way of gift where

	Yes	No
possession and enjoyment of the property was not bona fide assumed by the donee?	☐	☐
the property was not enjoyed to the entire exclusion of the deceased?	☐	☐
any benefit was retained by contract or otherwise?	☐	☐

Details of lifetime gifts or transfers of value

Please enter in chronological order details of each lifetime gift or transfer of value. You should deduct any exemptions or reliefs due (See Note 5). Enter the chargeable value showing how you have calculated this

Date of disposition	To whom given (name and address)	Description of asset(s) at date of transfer	Value

Carry the total chargeable value of lifetime transfers to Page 10 Box A unless the property given was subject to a reservation retained by the deceased at the date of death, in which case it should be included in Section 5 on Page 8

Total chargeable value of gifts made within 7 years of death

Show on a schedule details of all gifts made within 7 years of the earliest transfer but do not carry the value of these gifts to Page 10 (See Note 54).

Note 6

Superannuation benefits

	Yes	No
Was any provision, apart from State Pension, made by the deceased, the deceased's employers or otherwise for retirement, pension, or other superannuation benefits?	☐	☐
If 'Yes' were any benefits payable, or dispositions made as described in Note 6?	☐	☐

For Official use only

2

Section 2 - Nominated and Joint Property

You must answer the first two questions in this Section

Note 7
If 'Yes', please give full particulars in Section 2A

Did the deceased nominate any Savings Bank Account, Savings Certificates or other assets in favour of any person?   Yes ☐   No ☐

Note 8

Was the deceased joint owner of any property of any description or did the deceased hold any money on a joint account?   Yes ☐   No ☐

On a separate sheet of paper state for each item of joint property

* the name(s) of the other joint owner(s)

* when the joint ownership began or when the joint account was opened

Note 9

* by whom and from what source the joint property was provided and, if it or its purchase price was contributed by more than one of the joint owners, the extent of the contribution made by each

Note 10

* how any income was dealt with and enjoyed.

If 'Yes' include the value in Section 4A or 4B

Was any joint property situated outside the UK?   Yes ☐   No ☐

If 'Yes' include the value in Section 2A or 2B if the property was situated in the UK

Did any joint property pass by survivorship?   Yes ☐   No ☐

If 'Yes' include the value in Section 3A or 3B if the property was situated in the UK

Did any joint property pass under the deceased's Will or intestacy?   Yes ☐   No ☐

Section 2A - Nominated and Joint Property without the Instalment Option

Particulars of the property   Gross value at date of death

Note 11
All claims for exemptions or reliefs should be made in Section 6 on Page 9

See Note 24 and first paragraph of Note 46 before continuing

Deceased's share of liabilities in respect of the property

Name of creditor	Description of liability	Amount

Carry the net value forward to Page 10 Box 1

Net Value ☐

Section 2B - Joint Property with the Instalment Option

Particulars of the property   Gross value at date of death

All claims for exemptions or reliefs should be made in Section 6 on Page 9

See Note 24 and first paragraph of Note 46 before continuing

Deceased's share of liabilities in respect of the property

Name of creditor	Description of liability	Amount

Carry the net value forward to Page 10 Box 8

Net Value ☐

Note 12

Is tax to be paid by instalments?   Yes ☐   No ☐

For Official use only

Note 13	**Section 3 - Free Estate in the UK**	

All claims for exemptions or reliefs should be made in Section 6 on Page 9

All the property of the deceased in respect of which the grant is required

Section 3A - Property without the Instalment Option

		Value at date of death
Notes 14, 15 and 16	Stocks, shares, debentures and other securities as set out on IHT 40:	
	quoted or listed in the Stock Exchange Daily Official List except so far as included in Section 3B	
	others, except so far as included in Section 3B	
	Uncashed dividends and interest received, dividends declared, and interest accrued due to the date of death in respect of the above investments, as statement attached	
	Premium Savings Bonds	
Note 17	National Savings Certificates including interest to the date of death	
	Bank accounts including interest to the date of death, as statement attached	
	Money with the National Savings Bank, a building society, a co-operative or friendly society, including interest to the date of death, as statement attached	
	Cash (other than cash at banks, etc)	
	Money out on mortgage including interest to the date of death, as statement attached	
Note 18	Debts due to the deceased including interest to the date of death (except book debts included in section 3B) as statement attached	
	Rents including apportionment of rents of the deceased's own real and leasehold property to the date of death	
Note 19	Income arising but not received before the death, from real and personal property in which the deceased had a life or other limited interest	
Please state the source		
		Accrued
		Apportioned
	Any other income, apportioned where necessary, to which the deceased was entitled at the date of death (for example pensions, annuities, director's fees, etc), as statement attached	
Note 20	Policies of insurance and bonuses thereon (if any) on the life of the deceased, as statement attached	
	Saleable value of policies of insurance and bonuses (if any) on the life of any other person, as statement attached	
	Amounts payable under private health insurance schemes	
	Income Tax repayable	
Note 21 *Please attach a valuation if one has been obtained*	Household and personal goods, including pictures, china, clothes, books, jewellery, stamp, coin and other collections, motor cars, boats etc	
	Sold, realised gross	
	Unsold, estimated	
Note 22 *Please state the name and date of death of the testator or intestate*	Interest in an unadministered estate	
	Carried forward	

4

Section 3A - Property without the Instalment Option - continued

Brought forward

For Official use only

Note 23
Please state how the
deceased acquired the
interest and the estimated
value at the date of the
deceased's death

Interest in expectancy

Other personal property as listed below or as statement attached

Carry the total forward to
the Probate Summary on
Page 11 Box L

See Note 24 and first
paragraph of Note 46
before continuing

Note 25

Gross value of property without the Instalment Option

Liabilities at the date of death and funeral expenses

Name of creditor	Description of liability	Amount

Note 26

Funeral expenses

Note 27
Carry the total forward
to the Probate Summary
on Page 11 Box Q

Total liabilities

Carry the net total
forward to Page 10
Box 2

Value of property without the Instalment Option less liabilities

Section 3B - Property with the Instalment Option

All claims for exemptions or reliefs should be made in Section 6 on Page 9

Note 28

Land etc owned by the deceased in the UK (not being settled land) as described on IHT 37 attached

Note 29

Business interests
Net value of deceased's interest in the business(es), as statement or balance sheet attached

Note 30

Net value of deceased's interest as partner in the firm of

Please give the name of the firm

as statement or balance sheet attached

Note 31

Stocks, shares, debentures and other securities, as set out on IHT 40
Shares or securities which gave the deceased control of the company immediately before the death (*Section 228(1)(a) Inheritance Tax Act 1984*)

Unquoted shares or securities with in Section 228(1) (b), (c) or (d) Inheritance Tax Act 1984. (All other unquoted shares or securities should be included in Section 3A)

Carry the total forward to the Probate Summary on Page 11 Box M

Gross value of property with the Instalment Option

See Notes 24, 32 and the first paragraph of Note 46 before continuing

Liabilities charged at the date of the deceased's death on the property included above other than those already reflected in the net value of Business interests

Name of creditor	Description of liability and property on which charged	Amount

Carry this total forward to the Probate Summary on Page 11 Box R

Total liabilities

Carry the net total forward to Page 10 Box 9

Value of property with the Instalment Option less liabilities

	Yes	No

Note 33

Is tax to be paid by instalments?

Value at date of death

For Official use only

6

Section 4 - Foreign Property

Note 34

Section 4A - Property without the Instalment Option

Note 35

Particulars of the property

Value at date of death

All claims for exemptions or reliefs should be made in Section 6 on Page 9

Gross Value

Note 36

Liabilities in respect of the property above or due outside the UK

Name and address of creditor	Description of liability	Amount

Total liabilities

Carry the net total forward to Page 10 Box 3

Value of property without the Instalment Option less liabilities

Section 4B - Property with the Instalment Option

Note 35

Particulars of the property

Value at date of death

All claims for exemptions or reliefs should be made in Section 6 on Page 9

Gross Value

Liabilities in respect of the property above or due outside the UK

Name and address of creditor	Description of liability	Amount

Total liabilities

Carry the net total forward to Page 10 Box 10

Value of property with the Instalment Option less liabilities

	Yes	No
Note 37	Is tax to be paid by instalments?		

7

Note 38

Section 5 - Settled Property and Gifts with Reservation

All other property to which the deceased was beneficially entitled or was treated as beneficially entitled.

You must answer the question opposite

Was the deceased, at the date of death, entitled to a life interest, annuity or other interest in possession in settled property whether as beneficiary under a settlement or otherwise? See Note 39

Yes	No
☐	☐

Note 39

If so, please state below the name(s) of the settlement(s), the trustees and their solicitors.

Note 40
Please note that the value of any property within Section 5 must be included on Page 10 even if you are not liable for the tax on that property.
Enter the value in Box 15 and/or Box 16 unless you are paying tax on delivery, in which case enter it in Box 4 and/or Box 11.

All claims for exemptions or reliefs should be made in Section 6 on Page 9

Section 5A - Property without the Instalment Option

Particulars of the property	Value at date of death

Liabilities in respect of the property above	Amount

Carry the net value forward to Page 10 Box 4

Property on which tax is being paid now on delivery of this Account   Net value

Carry the net value forward to Page 10 Box 15

Property on which tax is not being paid now   Net value

Section 5B - Property with the Instalment Option

Particulars of the property	Value at date of death

All claims for exemptions or reliefs should be made in Section 6 on Page 9.

Liabilities in respect of the property above	Amount

Carry the net value forward to Page 10 Box 11

Property on which tax is being paid now on delivery of this Account   Net value

Carry the net value forward to Page 10 Box 16

Property on which tax is not being paid now   Net value

Note 41   Is tax to be paid by instalments?

Yes	No
☐	☐

For Official use only

8

See Notes 42, 43, 44 and 45

Section 6 - Exemptions, Exclusions and Reliefs against Capital

For Official use only

Property without the Instalment Option on which tax is being paid on delivery of this Account

Property in Sections: 2A, 3A, 4A, and 5A

Description of property and Section of Account in which included	Nature of relief claimed	Net value of property	Amount of relief claimed

Carry this total forward to Page 10 Box 6

Total of reliefs etc

Property with the Instalment Option on which tax is being paid on delivery of this Account

Property in Sections: 2B, 3B, 4B, and 5B

Description of property and Section of Account in which included	Nature of relief claimed	Net value of property	Amount of relief claimed

Carry this total forward to Page 10 Box 13

Total of reliefs etc

Property on which tax is not being paid on delivery of this Account

Property in Sections: 2B, 3B, 4B, 5A and 5B

Description of property and Section of Account in which included	Nature of relief claimed	Net value of property	Amount of relief claimed

Carry this total forward to Page 10 Box 18

Total of reliefs etc

Section 7 - Liabilities within Section 103, Finance Act 1986

If the reply to either question is 'Yes' see Note 46

In the case of any liability for which a deduction has been taken in this Account

                                                   Yes   No

did the consideration for any such debt or incumbrance incurred or created on or after 18 March 1986 consist of property derived from the deceased?

was the consideration given by any person who was at any time entitled to, or amongst whose resources there was at any time, any property derived from the deceased?

Any deduction claimed may be disallowed for Inheritance Tax purposes

Note 47

Calculation of Inheritance Tax

The tax calculated to be due is payable prior to lodging the application for the grant.
The Account will be fully examined after the grant has been issued.

Summary for determining the chargeable estate

You may use the reliefs box to show against which property a particular exemption, exclusion or relief has been taken

Section 1   Total of chargeable transfers from Page 2   A ☐

Part 1.   Property without the Instalment Option

Section	Net Total	Reliefs	Value after Reliefs
Bring forward the totals from Sections 2A, 3A, 4A, 5A and 6
2A	1		
3A	2		
4A	3		
5A	4		
Sub-total	5	6	7

Part 2.   Property with the Instalment Option

Bring forward the totals from Sections 2B, 3B, 4B, 5B and 6

2B	8		
3B	9		
4B	10		
5B	11		
Sub-total	12	13	14

Part 3.   Other Property on which tax is not being paid on this Account

Bring forward the totals from Sections 5A, 5B and 6

5A	15		
5B	16		
Sub-total	17	18	19

	Box 5 + 12 + 17	Box 6 + 13 + 18	Box 7 + 14 + 19
Totals			B

Aggregate chargeable transfers   A + B =   C ☐

Note 48

Calculation of Tax

Tax on C
on first   £ ☐   ☐

Plus
balance of £ ☐   @ ☐ % =   ☐

There will be no tax chargeable on A unless it exceeds the date of death threshold

Total ☐

Less tax on A at death rate

on first   £ ☐   ☐

Plus
balance of £ ☐   @ ☐ % =   ☐

Total ☐

Note 49
Please attach a schedule showing how you have calculated the relief

Less Quick Succession Relief   ☐

Total tax chargeable on B above   •   D ☐

10

Apportionment of tax payable on this Account

Any capital figure multiplied by $\frac{D}{B}$ gives the proportion of tax assessable on the capital

Note 50

From Box 7 opposite

Property without the Instalment Option £ [　　　] x $\frac{D}{B}$ = [　　　]

Note 51
Please attach a schedule showing how you have calculated the relief

   Less reliefs against tax other than Quick Succession Relief [　　　]

Net tax **E** [　　　]

Note 52
Tax becomes due 6 months after the end of the month during which the death occurred. Unpaid tax including tax being paid by instalments carries interest from and including the day after the due date irrespective of the reason for the late payment

Carry this total forward to Box F below

   Add interest on net tax from [19] **to** [19]

   [ ] **years** [ ] **days** @ [ ] **%** = [　　　]

That part of Box 14 opposite on which tax is to be paid now either in full or by instalments

   Total tax and interest on property without the Instalment Option **F** [　　　]

Property with the Instalment Option £ [　　　] x $\frac{D}{B}$ = [　　　]

   Less reliefs against tax other than Quick Succession Relief [　　　]

Net tax **G** [　　　]

   Add interest on net tax from [19] **to** [19]

   [ ] **years** [ ] **days** @ [ ] **%** = [　　　]

Note 33

Include the date the last instalment became due

Instalments [ ] **tenths of net tax** **H** [　　　]

   Add interest on instalments now assessed from [19] **to** [19]

   [ ] **days** @ [ ] **%** = [　　　]

If the due date for the second or subsequent instalment has now passed and interest relief is not appropriate, add here interest on the whole of the net tax on property with the Instalment Option up to the due date of the last instalment

   Add interest on whole of net tax on instalment property from [19] **to** [19]

   [ ] **years** [ ] **days** @ [ ] **%** = [　　　]

Carry this total forward to Box J below

   Total tax and interest on property with the Instalment Option **J** [　　　]

Tax Summary

For official use only

EDP [　　　]

   Total tax and interest – Property without the Instalment Option **F** [　　　]

   Total tax and interest – Property with the Instalment Option **J** [　　　]

Financial Services Office

   Total tax and interest payable now on this Account **K** [　　　]

Signature of Solicitor(s) or agent(s) for the applicant(s)   Date

[　　　] [　　　]

If tax is payable, send the Account for receipting to Inland Revenue Financial Services Office **by post** at Barrington Road Worthing West Sussex BN12 4XH or by DX 90950 Worthing 3 or take it **by hand** to Room G21 West Wing Somerset House Strand London WC2

Probate Summary

Aggregate Gross Value
which in law devolves on and vests in
the personal representatives of the
deceased, for and in respect of which
the grant is to be made.

    Section 3A **L** [　　　]

    Section 3B **M** [　　　]

Only include at N general power property

    Section 5 **N** [　　　]

   Total to be carried to the Probate papers **P** [　　　]

   Deduct

   Section 3A, total of liabilities and funeral expenses **Q** [　　　]

   Section 3B, total of liabilities **R** [　　　]

   Net estate for Probate purposes **S** [　　　]

Declaration

Note 55

I/We wish to apply for a
- Grant of Probate ☐
- Grant of Letters of Administration ☐
- Grant of Letters of Administration with Will annexed ☐

Tick the appropriate box

- Grant of _____ ☐

To the best of my/our knowledge and belief all the statements made and particulars given in this Account and its accompanying schedules are true and complete.

I/We have made the fullest enquiries that are reasonably practicable in the circumstances to ascertain the value of all assets, interests, liabilities etc.
- Where it has been possible to obtain exact values these have been included.
- Where exact values have not been obtained the values included are the best estimates which could be made on the information available, and
  I/We undertake, as soon as the final values are obtained, to deliver a further Account, and to pay any additional tax and interest for which I/we may be liable.

I/We have aggregated on Pages 10 and 11 the value of chargeable gifts and settled property.

So far as the tax on property disclosed in this Account may be paid by instalments, I/we elect to pay or not to pay by instalments as indicated in the Sections, and I/we understand that interest may be payable on unpaid tax in accordance with the statutory rules.

Notes 56 and 57

I/We understand that the issue of the Grant does not imply acceptance by the Inland Revenue of any of the statements made or values included in this Account.

Warning

An executor or intending administrator who fails to make the fullest enquiries that are reasonably practicable in the circumstances may be liable to penalties.

Name

Signature

Date

You may be liable to penalties or prosecution if you fail to disclose, in this Account and in your answers to the questions on Pages 2, 3, 8 and 9, all the property in respect of which tax may be payable.

Name

Signature

Date

Name

Signature

Date

Name

Signature

Date

Section 2 is divided into 2A and 2B. Section 2A deals with property without the instalment option and Section 2B deals with property with the instalment option (*see* Chapter 9, paras. 9.10.1–2). Even where the PRs do not intend to exercise the instalment option, details of property on which the instalment option is available should be entered in Section 2B. It is important to remember to deduct any liabilities attaching to Section 2A property in the liabilities box for Section 2A and any liabilities attaching to Section 2B property, in the liabilities box for Section 2B.

In relation to land, the term 'joint property' refers to co-ownership as joint tenants. It does not include any co-ownership interests of the deceased held as a tenant in common which will fall within Section 3B (page 8).

In stating the gross value at the date of death of joint property only the deceased's 'share', not the whole value, should be entered. Technically, due to the rule of survivor-ship, on death the deceased's share in property held as joint tenants is nil. However, the deceased 'share' immediately before death must be entered, ie. 50% of the total value.

Jointly held *foreign property* is recorded in Section 4 page 7.

The final question on page 3 is whether the tax is to be paid by instalments. In most cases where the instalment option is available it is exercised even if the outstanding instalments are paid off soon after obtaining a grant. This is because it may be difficult to raise the IHT in order to obtain a grant.

Page 4: Section 3A – Free Estate in the UK

This section (continued on page 5) basically deals with property which:

- Is UK property; and
- Vests in the deceased's PRs; and
- Is non-instalment option property.

The details of assets requested (on this and any other page of the form) should be rounded down to the nearest pound sterling, eg. if deceased's cash at date of death was £472.87 this should be shown as £472. Debts recorded, should be rounded up to the nearest pound sterling, eg. a debt of £176.12 should be shown as £177.

Stocks, shares, debentures and other securities It is necessary to take care to ensure you do not include shares etc on which the instalment option is available in this section (*see* Chapter 9, para. 9.10.2).

If the deceased owned a number of holdings of stocks and shares, only the total value should be set out on page 4 but schedule Form IHT 40 should be completed and attached. If a stockbroker has valued the various shareholdings etc the stockbroker's valuation report can simply be annexed in place of Form IHT 40.

Shares etc are valued on the '¼' up basis (*see* Chapter 9, para. 9.4.3).

Income arising, but not received before death ... in which the deceased had a life or other limited interest This amounts to income due to the deceased from property held in a settlement of which the deceased was a beneficiary. In order to ascertain whether to complete the 'accrued' or 'apportioned' box in relation to the income, it will be necessary to establish from the trust instrument whether the Apportionment Act 1870 has been excluded. If it has been excluded any interest or dividend declared on the trust assets, but not actually paid to the deceased *before death*, belongs to the deceased's estate and should be recorded as 'Accrued'. If the Apportionment Act 1870 has not been excluded, income will need to be apportioned between the deceased's estate and the trust on a daily basis (*see* Chapter 4, para. 4.11.4 – *Exclusion of rules of appointment*), the apportioned income being recorded in the 'Apportioned' box.

Policies of insurance and bonuses thereon (if any) on the life of the deceased ... Insurance policies written in trust for a third party should not be included here as they do not form part of the deceased's estate. They should already have been mentioned on page 2 (*see* above).

Page 5: Property without the instalment option

This is a continuation from page 4 of Section 3A. The total from the bottom of page 4 (carried forward) should be placed in the brought forward box on the top of page 5.

Interest in expectancy The details of any reversionary interest, ie. interest in remainder where a prior interest is still subsisting, must be given here, even if it is 'excluded' property as it forms part of the estate for probate purposes. However, if the reversionary interest is excluded property it is deducted as such in Section 6 on page 9.

Other personal property as listed below or as statement attached Items which can appear here include superannuation benefits which are payable in the deceased's estate as of right, rather than at the discretion of the trustees. (If they are only discretionary they do not form part of the death estate – *see* Chapter 9, para. 9.3.)

Liabilities at the date of death and funeral expenses It is vital to remember that the liabilities of the deceased charged on property attracting the instalment option should *not* be stated here. Types of debts which should be included are outstanding liabilities of rates, electricity and gas bills, insurance premiums, income tax due.

Funeral expenses allowable must be 'reasonable'. This is explained in Note 26 (IHT 210) to include the cost of a tombstone or headstone marking the site of the deceased's grave but no other memorial.

Page 6: Section 3B – Property with the instalment option

This is instalment option property which is UK property and vests in the PRs of the deceased. Whether or not the instalment option is going to be exercised such property must be recorded on this page.

For details of instalment option property *see* Chapter 9, para. 9.10.2.

In relation to land held in co-ownership it should be remembered that where the land is held as joint tenants as opposed to tenants in common it shall be recorded on page 3 (Section 2 Nominated and Joint Property).

Where the land is held as tenants in common only the value of the deceased's share should be included. A formal valuation or Form IHT 37 should be annexed.

With regard to the 'net value' of business interests, this is ascertained from the previous three years' balance sheets prepared by the accountant acting for the particular business. These should be annexed to the account.

For *stocks, shares, debentures* etc either a formal valuation (*see* explanation in relation to page 4) or Form IHT 37 should be annexed.

Liabilities charged at the date of the deceased's death ...

Remember:

- Only to include liabilities on instalment option property, eg. mortgage on land falling with Section 3B;
- If the liable is a joint liability, eg. a joint mortgage of the family home, then only the deceased's share, ie. half the value of the liability, should be recorded.

Page 7: Section 4 – Foreign Property

As with the previous sections it is divided into instalment and non-instalment option property, and liabilities relating to instalment option property need to be placed in Section 4B, with other liabilities placed in Section 4A.

Section 4 includes property which is owned by the deceased situated outside the UK, but on which the deceased's

PRs are liable to pay tax, eg. deceased's villa in Spain.

Page 8: Section 5 – Settled Property and Gifts with Reservation

It is once again divided into instalment and non-instalment option property with liabilities relating to instalment option property being placed in Section 5B and other liabilities in Section 5A.

Section 5 should include details of:

- Any trust fund in which the deceased had a right to income immediately before death. The value of the trust fund is the value recorded in 'Value at date of death' box.

Example ───────────────────────────

A fund worth 200,000 is held on trust for Angela for life, with remainder to Bill. At Angela's death 200,000 should be recorded in the 'Value at date of death' box.

───

- Property which was given away by the deceased during their lifetime but in which they reserved a benefit up until the date of death (*see* Chapter 9, para. 9.9.5).

Whether the details of the trust/reservation of benefit are put in the instalment option, or not instalment option box, obviously depends upon the subject matter of the trust or the property in which a benefit has been reserved. If the trust property consists of assets falling within both categories, eg. quoted shares and land, then separate totals must be shown for the part of the fund falling within each category.

Both Section 5A and Section 5B draw a distinction between 'Property on which tax is being paid now on delivery of this Account' and 'Property on which tax is not being paid now'. If the tax is to be paid on the delivery of the Account it is tax payable by the deceased's PRs. Conversely if it is property on which tax is not being paid now the principle liability for IHT (*see* Chapter 9, paras. 9.9.2–3) falls on the donee or the trustees of the settlement and not on the PRs. Normally, in the case of a trust, this property will be 'Property on which tax is not being paid now', and the primary liability will be on the trustees. This is because trust property is only recorded in Section 5 where the settlement has not come to an end. When the settlement has come to an end with the deceased's death, the trust property vests in the deceased's PRs, making them primarily liable for the IHT, and is recorded in Section 1. Thus the only situations in the case of a trust where the PRs should fill in the box opposite 'Property on which tax is being paid now on delivery of the Account' are:

- Where the trustees of the settlement are also the deceased's PRs; and
- Where the trustees of the settlement have given the money to the deceased's PRs to discharge on behalf of the trustees.

Note

Where the box(es) 'Property on which tax is not being paid now' is completed because the PRs are not paying the IHT on the trust property or property subject to a reservation, the property still forms part of the deceased's tax estate. Consequently the total IHT payable as a result of death has to be apportioned between the PRs and trustees and donees falling within Section 5.

Page 9: Sections 6 and 7

Section 6: Exemptions, Exclusions and Reliefs Against Capital All exemptions and reliefs (*see* Chapter 9, paras. 9.5–6) except Quick Succession Relief and Double Taxation Relief (which are claimed on page 10) should be claimed.

The exemptions and reliefs must be claimed against the section of the form in which the asset qualifying for the relief is recorded, eg. if the property is shares which are free estate in the UK (Section 3) and non-instalment option property, the 'Description of property and Section of Account in which included' box must say S.3A shares.

It is important to remember to record the net value of the property against which the exemption or relief is claimed, eg. if it is land worth £200,000 subject to a mortgage of £100,000, the figure of £100,000 should be included.

Section 7: Liabilities Within Section 103, Finance Act 1986 Section 103 does not allow certain debts which in effect have been artificially created for tax avoidance purposes, to be deducted. Section 7 requires the PRs to declare that none of the debts deducted in the account fall within this category. A full understanding of this aspect of the form is not expected of students, as it is in practice rare that the 'YES' box will have to be completed.

Page 10: Calculation of inheritance tax

The object of page 10 is to calculate the total IHT payable as a result of the death and to apportion it between the instalment and non-instalment option property.

As the form is being completed the various totals should be carried forward and recorded on page 10 (or 11 as appropriate), eg. at the bottom of page 3 the form says 'carry the net total forward to Page 10 Box 8'.

The purpose of this part of page 10 is to calculate the total chargeable estate and the rates of IHT. In completing the boxes it is important to appreciate that the column headed 'Reliefs' in fact refers to all exemptions and reliefs claimed on page 9.

Page 11

The purpose behind this page is to apportion the tax between the PRs and other persons liable and also to summarise the IHT position generally (Tax Summary) and the IHT position relating to the death estate (Probate Summary). The Probate Summary sets out the gross and net values of the property vesting in the PRs as a result of death. These two figures are inserted in the oath form which also needs to be completed to obtain a grant of representation (*see* 10.3.6).

Page 12

This page contains the PRs' declaration as to the accuracy of the information given in the Account.

Note the following points about it:

- It is not uncommon for the PRs to be unable to provide a final valuation of all the assets and liabilities of the estate. For example, the amount of income tax repayment due to the deceased may not have been finalised. The value of personal chattels are often estimated. If this is the case then the paragraph commencing 'I/We have made the fullest enquiries ...' should not be deleted. If there are no estimated values etc recorded, the entire paragraph shall be deleted.

- Where the estate includes instalment option property the PRs must make an election as to whether they are going to pay by instalments. It shall be remembered, if they make such an election this does not prevent them from paying the outstanding instalments off early and if electing to pay by instalments does reduce the amount of money to be raised to pay the IHT to obtain the grant.

- The Account need only be signed and dated by the PRs. It does not need to be sworn.

The PRs will be liable to a fine and prosecution if the information contained in the form is incorrect.

Guidance for completing IHT Form 202   10.5.6

Guidance as to how to complete IHT 202 can be obtained from the form itself and from IHT 210 'Guidance Notes on Completion of Inland Revenue Accounts'. The following additional points of guidance correspond to the various pages of the form.

Inland Revenue Account for Inheritance Tax

This Account is for use only for an original grant where the deceased died on or after 18 March 1986 and was domiciled in the United Kingdom, and

- the whole of the estate is situated in the UK
- the deceased within seven years of the death neither made any lifetime transfers of value chargeable with Inheritance Tax nor had any interest in settled property
- the net estate after exemptions and reliefs does not exceed the Inheritance Tax threshold at the death
- the gross estate before exemptions and reliefs does not exceed twice the Inheritance Tax threshold at death.

If the deceased died before 18 March 1986 or you need any further help or information, contact the Capital Taxes Office where the staff will be pleased to help you.

Before you start to fill in this Account, read the Guidance Notes in booklet IHT 210. The marginal notes on this Account refer to the relevant paragraphs of the booklet. They will help you to fill it in quickly and correctly. If you need more space use a separate sheet of paper showing to which section of the Account it relates.

Insert 'Principal', or the name of the District and 'District'

In the High Court of Justice Family Division (Probate), The [   ] **Registry**

Please give your full name and address including postcode, using capital letters, even if the DX code is given

Solicitor(s) or Agent(s)

Please give the full name and title of the deceased using CAPITAL letters

In the estate of
Surname

Title and Forenames

All communications concerning Inheritance Tax will be sent to the solicitors or agents unless the executors or administrators request otherwise

DX Code

Show, for example, 9 January 1993 as 09 Jan 1993

Date of birth   **Date of death**

Marital Status

Married   Single   Divorced   Widowed

Surviving relatives

Husband   Wife   Children(s)   Parent(s)

Your reference

You may wish to give the name of the person dealing with this estate

Contact

Domicile

England and Wales   Scotland   N. Ireland

Address

Telephone

Give the last known usual address of the deceased including postcode

Fax

Tax District and reference

Please give the occupation of the deceased

Occupation

If available, please give this information

National Insurance No

Date of Grant (For official use only)

Executors or intending administrators

Give the full names and permanent addresses including postcode of the executors or intending administrators

IHT202(1993)

1

Nominated and Joint Property

You must answer these first two questions

Note 7
If 'Yes', please give full particulars below

Did the deceased nominate any Savings Bank Account, Savings Certificates or other assets in favour of any person?

Yes ☐ No ☐

Note 8
If 'Yes', also answer the following questions

Was the deceased joint owner of any property of any description or did the deceased hold any money on a joint account?

Yes ☐ No ☐

On a separate sheet of paper state for each item of joint property

* the name(s) of the other joint owner(s)

* when the joint ownership began or when the joint account was opened

Note 9

* by whom and from what source the joint property was provided and if it or its purchase price was contributed by more than one of the joint owners, the extent of the contribution made by each

Note 10

* how any income was dealt with and enjoyed

If 'Yes' include the value below

Did any joint property pass by survivorship?

Yes ☐ No ☐

If 'Yes' include the value as part of the Free Estate

Did any joint property pass under the deceased's Will or intestacy?

Yes ☐ No ☐

For Official use only

Nominated and Joint Property

All claims for exemptions or reliefs should be made on Page 4

Particulars of the property	Gross value at date of death

See Note 24 and first paragraph of Note 46 before continuing

Deceased's share of liabilities in respect of the property

Name of creditor	Description of liability	Amount

Carry the net value forward to Page 4 Box A

Net value **A** ☐

Free Estate

Note 13

All the property of the deceased in respect of which the grant is required

All claims for exemptions or reliefs should be made on Page 4

Property without the Instalment Option

	Gross value at date of death
Notes 14, 15 and 16 Stocks, shares, debentures and other securities, as set out on IHT 40 quoted or listed in the Stock Exchange Daily Official List and others, except those qualifying for the instalment option	
Note 17 Premium Savings Bonds and National Savings Certificates (including interest)	
Cash and cash at Bank or Savings Bank, a building society, a co-operative or friendly society, including interest to the date of death, as statement attached	
Note 20 Policies of insurance and bonuses thereon (if any) on the life of the deceased, as statement attached	
Saleable value of policies of insurance and bonuses (if any) on the life of any other person, as statement attached	
Income Tax repayable	
Carried forward	

Property without the Instalment Option - continued

Brought forward

For Official use only

Note 21
Please attach a valuation if one has been obtained

Household and personal goods, including pictures, china, clothes, books, jewellery, stamp, coin and other collections, motor cars, boats etc

Sold, realised gross

Unsold, estimated

Note 22
Please state the name and date of death of the testator or intestate

Interest in an unadministered estate

Other assets not included above or as instalment option property

Carry the total forward to
Page 4 Box B

Total **B**

Notes 24, 25 and 26

Liabilities at the date of death and funeral expenses

Name of creditor	Description of liability	Amount

Note 27
Carry the total forward to
Page 4 Box E

Total **E**

Property with the Instalment Option

Gross value at date of death

Note 28

Land and buildings as described on IHT 37 attached

Note 29

Business interests (state nature of business)

• Net value of deceased's interest in business, as statement or balance sheet attached

Note 30
Please give the name of the firm

• Net value of deceased's interest as a partner in the firm of

as statement or balance sheet attached

Note 31

Stocks, shares, debentures and other securities as set out on form IHT 40

• which gave the deceased control of the company

• other unquoted shares or securities

Carry the total forward to
Page 4 Box C

Total **C**

Note 32

Liabilities

Name of creditor	Description of liability (and property on which charged)	Amount

Carry the total forward to
Page 4 Box F

Total **F**

Probate Summary

Aggregate Gross Value
which in law devolves on and vests in the personal
representatives of the deceased, for and in respect
of which the grant is to be made

Totals

B
C
D

Deduct liabilities

E
F
G

Net estate for Probate purposes D - G = H

Tax Summary

Nominated and joint property (net) A

As box H above + H = J

Notes 42, 43, 44 and 45

Deduct exemptions and reliefs

Nature	Net value	£	Amount

= K

Net estate for tax purposes J - K = L

Declaration

Note 55

Tick the appropriate box

I/We wish to apply for a • Grant of Probate

• Grant of Letters of Administration

• Grant of Letters of Administration with Will annexed

• Grant

To the best of my/our knowledge and belief all the statements made and particulars given in this Account and its accompanying schedules are true and complete.

I/We have made the fullest enquiries that are reasonably practicable in the circumstances to ascertain the value of all assets, interests, liabilities, etc.

The deceased within 7 years of the death neither made transfers of value chargeable with Inheritance Tax (ie no transfers of value that were not covered by the IHT exemptions nor any gifts, subject to a reservation to the donor).

The estate at the death did not include any property situate outside the UK.

The deceased did not have an interest in settled property at the death nor had within 7 years of death an interest in settled property or settled any property.

Notes 56 and 57

I/We understand that the issue of the Grant does not imply acceptance by the Inland Revenue of any of the statements or values included in this Account.

Warning

An executor or intending administrator who fails to make the fullest enquiries that are reasonably practicable in the circumstances may be liable to penalties.

You may be liable to taxation or prosecution if you fail to disclose, in this Account and in your answers to the questions on Page 2 all the property in respect of which tax may be payable.

	Name	
	Signature	
	Date	

	Name	
	Signature	
	Date	

4

Page 1
See page 1 IHT 200.

Page 2
Nominated and joint property Nominated and joint property does not vest in the deceased's PRs but it does form part of the deceased's estate for IHT purposes. Details of all joint property whether held as joint tenants or tenants in common need to be completed on a separate sheet of paper giving the details requested on the form.

Under the second heading 'Nominated and Joint Property', joint property refers to property held by the deceased as a joint tenant as opposed to a tenant in common. If, for example, the deceased held the family home as a tenant in common with their spouse, the property should be included under the heading 'Free Estate' - Property with the Instalment Option (page 3 of the form). The note beside the question in the first box on page 2 'Did any joint property pass under the deceased's Will or intestacy?', makes this clear.

Note

There is no division between instalment and non-instalment option property in this part of the form as in others.

Where assets were jointly owned the value of the deceased's share and not the whole value should be shown.

Any debts payable out of the nominated property held as joint tenants should be shown and the total of such debts should be deducted to give the net value of joint and nominated property. In the case of joint property it is important only to deduct the amount of the deceased's liability.

Example

H and W hold the family home (worth 200,000) as joint tenants. The home is subject to a mortgage of 50,000 of which H and W are joint mortgagors. H dies. The gross value at date of death of H's share is 100,000. A liability of only 25,000, ie. half the mortgage, can be offset against this.

Free estate Details of free estate must be given partly on page 2 and partly on page 3. This is all property which vests in the PRs at the deceased's death and which passes under the deceased's will or the rules of intestacy. Unlike nominated and joint property, free property is divided into instalment and non-instalment option property.

Property without the instalment option
Stocks, shares, debentures etc See comments for stocks, shares,

debentures etc as made in relation to IHT 200.

Policies of insurance and bonuses thereon See comments for policies of insurance and bonuses thereon made in relation to IHT 200.

The liabilities of the deceased not relating to instalment option property should be recorded along with the funeral expenses.

Property with the instalment option In this section assets which would qualify for the instalment option if there were tax to pay should be recorded, as well as the liabilities relating to those assets. Remember that land held by the deceased as a tenant in common should be recorded on this part of the form.

Page 4

This page consists of three distinct elements, the Probate Summary, the Tax Summary and the Declaration to be made by the PRs of the deceased.

The *Probate Summary* calculates the value of the property vesting in the deceased's PRs. The aggregate gross value (Box D) and the Net estate for probate purposes (Box H) will also appear on the oath sworn by the PRs.

The *Tax Summary* adds the value of the deceased's estate for probate purposes to the value of any Nominated and Joint Property which does not vest in the deceased's PRs and which is not part of the estate for probate purposes. IHT is then calculated on the combined totals. The total chargeable estate (Total L) cannot exceed 150,000 as otherwise tax will be payable and IHT 200 should be used rather than IHT 202.

The *Declaration* need only be signed and dated by the PRs. It does not need to be sworn. The PRs will be liable to a fine and prosecution if the information contained in the form is incorrect.

When the form has been completed and signed it should be sent to the probate registry with the oath etc. As there is no tax to pay it is unnecessary to send it to the Inland Revenue, as is the case with IHT 200.

Raising the IHT   10.6

As the PRs normally have to pay the inheritance tax that is due before they can obtain a grant of representation (*see* Chapter 9, para. 9.10 and 10.2.4), they will have to find ways of raising the money to pay the tax without recourse to assets which require a grant of representation. The various alternatives and their relative merits will be considered in the following paragraphs 10.6.1–5.

10.6.1   Small payments

There is *discretion* to pay up to £5,000 to the persons appearing to be entitled to a grant from any of the following sources:

- Money held in the National Savings Bank, Trustee Savings Bank, Savings Certificates or Premium Bonds (Administration of Estates (Small Payments) Act 1965.

- Money payable on death to a member of a trade union, an industrial or provident society or a friendly society (Administration of Estates (Small Payments) Act 1965).

- Arrears of salary, wages or superannuation on benefits due to employees of government departments (Administration of Estates (Small Payments) Act 1965).

- Pensions due to police, firemen or members of the Army or Air Force (Administration of Estates (Small Payments) Act 1965).

- Money invested in a building society (Schedule 7, para. 1, Building Societies Act 1986).

Note

1   If the sum due to the deceased in respect of a particular source exceeds the £5,000 limit, a grant is needed for the *whole* amount and not just the excess over £5,000.

2   A copy of the death certificate will be needed to obtain payment.

10.6.2   Payments/transfers made direct to the Inland Revenue

Where the deceased held an insurance policy, the proceeds of which were payable to the deceased's estate, the insurance company *may* agree to send the whole of the proceeds, or the sum needed to pay inheritance tax, directly to the Inland Revenue's Capital Taxes Office. Similarly, a building society *may* agree to send funds of the deceased (up to an unlimited figure) directly to the Inland Revenue.

As a general rule, inheritance tax has to be paid by cheque. However, the Revenue has discretion to accept certain assets of the deceased in total or partial satisfaction of the inheritance tax liability on the estate: s.230, Inheritance Tax Act 1984. For assets to be acceptable the Secretary of State must be satisfied that they have significant national scientific, historic or artistic interest and, in the case of land, that it has some kind of amenity value and the public have reasonable access to it.

Sales of assets

10.6.3

The option of selling assets of the estate in order to raise money to pay the inheritance tax is only available to executors and not to administrators. This is because executors derive their authority from the will, whereas administrators only acquire authority from the grant. Even, for an executor, however, it may be difficult to sell assets of the estate before grant as the purchaser may require proof of their title. As to which assets should be sold from the tax point of view, *see* Chapter 12, para. 12.6.

Borrow from a bank

10.6.4

Borrowing the money from a bank is a very common method of raising the cash to pay inheritance tax. The bank may be the deceased's bank or the PR's bank. However, whichever bank is selected, a separate loan account must be opened, rather than simply allowing the deceased's bank account to become overdrawn.

The bank is likely to require an undertaking from the PRs to the effect that they will repay the bank from the assets of the estate which they realise first.

Note

If the PRs have appointed a solicitor to act for them, the bank may require a further undertaking from the solicitor. In this event the solicitor should obtain irrevocable authority from the PRs to give such an undertaking.

The obvious disadvantage of borrowing money from a bank over the other methods so far discussed is that the loan will carry interest. For this reason, quite apart from any undertaking which is given to the bank, it is important to repay the loan as quickly as possible. Furthermore, although for the purpose of calculating income tax liability, the PRs may deduct interest paid on a loan taken out to pay inheritance tax (Income and Corporation Taxes Act 1988 s.364(1)), the interest is only deductible for a period ending in one year from the date when the loan was taken out.

Borrow from a beneficiary

10.6.5

In order to avoid the expense of a bank loan which will reduce the income from the estate available to the beneficiaries, the beneficiaries themselves, if they have funds available, may be willing to lend money for payment of the inheritance tax interest - free. It is not uncommon that a beneficiary has funds available for this purpose from one of the following sources:

- The proceeds of an insurance policy taken out by the deceased and which is payable directly to the beneficiary, eg. a policy taken out under s.11, Married Women's Property Act 1882 (*see* Chapter 3, para. 3.4.2);

- A lump sum paid by the trustees to a beneficiary under a superannuation scheme to which the deceased contributed;

- From assets held jointly by the beneficiary and the deceased especially where the assets are easily realisable, eg. money held in a joint bank or building society account.

10.7　Affidavits

Depending on the circumstances of the cases, in order to obtain a grant of representation affidavit evidence may be required to provide evidence of:

- Due execution of the will;

- Knowledge and approval on the part of the testator;

- The time at which an unattested alteration has been made;

- The condition of a will;

- The date of execution of a will;

- Attempted revocation.

Paragraphs 10.7.1–6 look more closely at the circumstances in which affidavit evidence will be required.

10.7.1　Affidavit of due execution

When required

The Non-Contentious Probate Rules 1987, rule 12(1) provide that an affidavit of due execution is required where:

- The will contains no attestation clause (*see* Chapter 6, para. 6.2); or

- The attestation clause is insufficient; or

- Where it appears to the district judge or registrar that there is some doubt as to the due execution of the will, eg. where the will contains an attestation clause, but the testator has signed the will only on the envelope containing the will.

From whom the evidence should be obtained

Ideally, affidavit evidence should be obtained from one of the witnesses to the will, but if no witness is conveniently available, it can be obtained from anyone who was present when the will was executed. If neither a witness nor any other person present is available to give evidence, under rule 12(2) the district judge/registrar may accept affidavit evidence from any other persons who may be able to provide evidence of due execution in the circumstances. For example, if the issue in doubt is whether the signature is in the testator's handwriting, affidavit evidence from any person who is in a position to know the testator's signature may be accepted.

Note

Where no affidavit evidence of due execution of any sort is available the district judge/registrar may apply the maxim *omnia praesumunter rite ac solemniter esse acta* (*see* Chapter 6, para. 6.2) and admit the will to probate.

Affidavit of knowledge and approval   10.7.2

Before a will is valid, a testator must know and approve the contents of their will (*see* Chapter 1, para. 1.4). In the case of a duly executed will for which the testator has testamentary capacity the knowledge and approval of the testator are generally presumed. There is, however, no such presumption in the case of a blind or illiterate testator, or where the will has been signed on behalf of the testator, or there are suspicious circumstances (*see* Chapter 1, para. 1.4). In any of these circumstances the attestation clause should be adapted (*see Chapter* 1, para. 1.4.1). In the absence of this, the registrar will wish to be satisfied that the testator had knowledge of and approved the contents of the will. Affidavit evidence will normally be required for this purpose.

Affidavit of alteration   10.7.3

Where a will appears to contain an unattested alteration other than the completion of a blank space, the registrar will require evidence to show whether the alteration was present when the will was executed. If the alteration was present at the time of execution the alteration is valid but not if it was made after execution. (There is a rebuttable presumption that an unattested alteration was made after execution of the will – *see* Chapter 6, para. 6.7.5.) The registrar has a useful time-saving power to disregard any alteration which appears to be of no practical importance (rule 14(2)), eg. an alteration to a gift which has lapsed.

Affidavit to establish that a document has been validly incorporated into a will   10.7.4

Where a will contains a reference to another document so as to suggest that the document ought to be incorporated in the will, a registrar will require that the document is produced and may call for affidavit evidence as to the incorporation of the document. (For requirements of incorporation by reference *see* Chapter 6, para. 6.4.)

10.7.5 Affidavit to establish the date of execution

Where there is doubt as to the date on which the will has been executed the registrar may require affidavit evidence to establish the date of execution.

10.7.6 Affidavit of attempted revocation

Where there is any suggestion of attempted revocation of a will by burning, tearing, or otherwise destroying or anything else leading to a presumption of revocation by the testator (*see* Chapter 6, para. 6.7.4), this has to be accounted for to the satisfaction of the district judge or registrar. For this purpose the registrar may require affidavit evidence.

10.8   Caveats

10.8.1 Definition

A caveat is a notice entered at any probate registry to prevent a grant of probate or administration being made without notice first being given to the person who enters the caveat, known as the caveator: Non-Contentious Probate Rules 1987, rule 44.

10.8.2 Purpose

The main purpose of a caveat is to enable a person who is considering opposition to a grant to obtain evidence or legal advice on the matter. It is sometimes a preliminary step to the issue of a writ or citation (*see* 10.9). Where the object of the caveator is not to prevent a grant being issued but merely to have notice of it, it is more appropriate to apply for a standing search to be made (*see* 10.10).

10.8.3 Duration and effect

The effect of a caveat is that no grant can issue after its entry until it is removed or ceases to have effect. It is effective for six months unless the registrar directs otherwise: rule 44(3). An application can be made within the last month of the six month period during which a caveat remains in force for its renewal for a further six months: rule 44(3).

10.8.4 Entry of a caveat

Any person wishing to enter a caveat or a solicitor on their behalf must do so by completing Form 3 in the appropriate book at the registry or by sending by post notice in Form 3. Notice of entry of a caveat in the Principal Registry or in a district registry is immediately given to the Leeds District Probate Registry which maintains the current index of grant applications.

Warning of caveats   10.8.5

When a person applying for a grant finds that it has been stopped by the entry of a caveat, they may issue a warning. This is a notice issued out of the Leeds District Probate Registry warning the caveator to enter an appearance at that Registry within eight days setting out their interest or, if they have no contrary interest but wish to show another reason against the sealing of a grant, to issue and serve a summons for directions: rule 44(6).

Possible responses to issue of a warning   10.8.6

- The caveator takes no steps within the eight days of service of the warning. In this event the application for a grant may proceed and the caveat is removed.

- The caveator withdraws their caveat once a warning has been issued. The person warning is then free to proceed with their application for a grant.

- The caveator, within the eight days of service of the warning, enters an appearance. In this case the caveat remains in force until a district judge or registrar otherwise directs. This may, for example, be until a probate action is commenced, as the commencement of such an action normally prevents a grant from being made.

- The caveator issues and serves a summons for directions within eight days of the service of the warning. On the hearing of the summons the district judge will decide whether the person warning should be passed over.

Citations   10.9

A citation is a document issued by the principal or a district registry whereby the person issuing (the *citor*) calls upon the person cited (the *citee*) to provide a reason why a particular step should not be taken.

There are three types of citation, to:

- Accept or refuse a grant of probate or administration;
- Take probate;
- Propound a will.

10.9.1 To accept or refuse a grant of probate or administration

Where a person who has a prior right to a grant of probate or administration delays or declines to take it, but will not renounce their right, they may be cited to accept or refuse a grant by a person having an inferior right.

10.9.2 To take probate

Where an *executor* has intermeddled with an estate (*see* Chapter 8, para. 8.5.5) and has not taken a grant within six months of the death, they may be cited by any person interested in the estate to show why they should not be ordered to take a grant. A citation cannot be issued until at least six months after the testator's death nor at any time whilst proceedings as to the validity of the will are pending: rule 47(3).

10.9.3 To propound a will

Where a person believes that a will which has not been proved is invalid and they themselves are interested under an earlier will or an intestacy, they may cite the executors and beneficiaries to propound it: rule 48.

> *Note*
>
> Where an executor is doubtful as to the validity of a codicil to a valid will, they should not use the citation procedure but prove the will and then ask the court to pronounce against the codicil in solemn form, making those persons interested under the codicil parties to the action.

10.10 Standing searches

The purpose of a caveat is to enable a person who is considering opposition to a grant to obtain evidence or legal advice on the matter before a grant is made to someone else (*see* 10.8). Where a person merely wishes to know when a grant has been made so as to be able to make a claim against an estate they should not enter a caveat but make a standing search. In most cases such a person could enter a citation (as a creditor is entitled to a grant of administration on clearing off the beneficiaries) but a standing search is more appropriate.

A standing search is made by lodging Form 2 at the Principal or district registry. An office copy of any grant made within the 12 months before or six months after the search will then be given to the applicant. The period of the search can be extended for further six month periods.

Self-assessment questions

1 You have been appointed executor of the will of James Watts and you wish to take out a grant of probate. James Watts' net estate is worth approximately £180,000. What papers will be required in order to obtain the grant of probate?

2 What should you remember about the swearing or affirming of the oath of an executor or administrator?

3 You are acting for John and Mary Price who are executors of the will of their father Christopher Price. You have ascertained that inheritance tax of £45,000 will have to be raised in order to obtain the grant of probate. The only beneficiaries under Christopher's will are his widow, Charlotte and John and Mary themselves. Christopher had £10,000 in a building society account at the date of his death, and had taken out an insurance policy within s.11, Married Women's Property Act 1882, which is written in trust for Charlotte and is worth £25,000.

   Advise John and Mary as to possible ways of raising the money for payment of inheritance tax.

4 You are approached by Norman Blaxland whose father, Cederic, died last week. He shows you a homemade will and tells you he wishes to obtain probate of the will (which appoints him executor). The will dated three weeks ago comprises a single sheet of paper which is slightly torn through Cederic's signature. Norman has no explanation for this. Cederic's signature appears before the final legacy of £200 to a charity. Two witnesses have placed their signatures below that of Cederic. One legacy has been altered by striking with a pen line through the figure 500 and replacing it by 200. The will is in Norman's handwriting and Norman tells you his father was too weak to write at the time. Under the will Norman receives approximately half of his father's estate.

   What problems will there be in admitting the will to probate and how will you attempt to overcome these problems?

5 Distinguish between caveats and citations.

Answer guidance to self-assessment questions

1 (a) James Watts' will duly marked.

(b) Oath for executors completed and sworn.

(c) Probate fees (300).

(d) Inland Revenue Account (whichever is appropriate) together with the cheque or money order for any inheritance tax due.

(*See* generally 10.2)

2 It must be sworn or affirmed by the PR before an *independent* solicitor.

3 (a) Explain to John and Mary that they have power to sell assets of the estate before grant in order to raise the tax but that they may have difficulty in satisfying a purchaser of their title without a grant.

(b) Explain that it should be possible to obtain a bank loan to pay the tax, but that this method of raising the tax has the obvious disadvantage of the need to pay interest. Therefore other methods of raising the money should be considered first.

(c) Suggest approaching Charlotte Price for a loan to the estate out of the proceeds of the insurance policy taken out under s.11, Married Women's Property Act 1882 which is written in trust for her. This does not form part of Christopher's estate and the trustees of the policy will, if they have not already, pay the proceeds directly to her.

(d) The 10,000 in the building society does not fall within the 'small payments' category (*see* 10.6.1). Up to 5,000 may be paid to the PRs before grant at the discretion of the building society, but this is not so if the whole sum exceeds 5,000. However, the building society could be approached and asked to consider whether it will send the 10,000 directly to the Inland Revenue (*see* 10.6.2).

If the building society and Charlotte Price are prepared to co-operate, this will leave a shortfall of 10,000. It should first be considered whether any of the assets of the estate can be sold without proof of title, and if not, a bank loan of 10,000 should be obtained.

4 *The position of the signature* raises the question as to whether the will has been properly executed. An affidavit of due execution will be required from the witnesses or from Norman (if present at the time of execution) to establish that the signature was intended to validate the will.

As the paper on which the will is written is torn an affidavit of attempted revocation will be needed to establish that the testator has not revoked the will. The more damaged the will is by the tearing the greater the presumption it has been revoked. It is unhelpful that Norman has no explanation for the tearing, but he should be questioned in order to ascertain whether anyone else can shed light on the condition of the will.

As the will is in Norman's handwriting and he is a major beneficiary under the will there is no presumption of knowledge and approval, so an affidavit of knowledge and approval will be required (*see* 10.6.2). It may also be necessary to query whether Cederic had testamentary capacity at the time the will was executed given that he is too weak to write.

The altered legacy will be invalid if the alteration was made after execution of the will. As an alteration of this kind is presumed to have been made after execution affidavit evidence will need to be obtained from the witnesses and/ or from Norman who wrote the will, to the effect that the alteration was made before execution.

5   *See* 10.8 and 10.9.

Chapter 11

Administration of an estate

Introduction

11.1

The aims of the chapter are to:

- Provide an overview of the duties of personal representatives (PRs) in relation to the administration of an estate;
- Explain the source and extent of the powers of PRs;
- Outline how PRs may protect themselves from liability;
- Outline how solicitors should organise the administration of an estate.

Duties of personal representatives

11.2

Broadly speaking PRs have three duties:

- To collect in the assets of the estate;
- To pay funeral, testamentary and administration expenses, all debts of the deceased, and tax for which they are liable; and
- Distribute the estate.

The payment of the debts is considered in Chapter 12, along with the inheritance tax and income tax liability of the PRs. Duties in relation to distribution of the estate are considered in Chapter 13. The duty to collect in the assets of the estate is considered in paragraph 11.3.

Duty to collect in assets

11.3

Section 25(a), Administration of Estates Act 1925 (as substituted by s.9, Administration of Estates Act 1971) provides that it is the duty of PRs to collect all the assets of the deceased's estate after a grant has been made to them.

In doing so, they must act with 'due diligence': *Re Tankard* (1942). This requires that they collect in the assets as quickly as is practically possible and take reasonable steps to collect all debts due to the deceased. The latter may involve bringing proceedings to recover money due to the deceased. If, for example, a PR without just excuse took so long to collect in the assets of the estate that a debtor of the deceased was able to plead the Limitation Act, they would be personally liable.

Upon death, immediate steps should be taken to safeguard valuables of the deceased by removing them to a place of safekeeping, eg. documents of title and valuable items of property left in an empty house.

Collecting in the assets of the deceased involves the PRs having all the personal property of the deceased transferred into their names, eg. bank accounts, building society deposits, stocks and shares.

The following assets of the deceased will *not* need to be collected in by the PRs as they will not be assets of the deceased's estate:

- *Insurance policies* written in trust for third parties under the Married Women's Property Act 1882. Such assets are payable to the trustees of the policy. However, if no trustees are named in the policy the proceeds will be paid to the PRs but will not be assets of the estate for tax purposes. If the PRs of the deceased are the trustees of the policy, they receive payment in the capacity of trustees and the assets do not form part of the deceased's estate.

- Interests in *property held as a joint tenant*. The rule of survivorship will have operated passing the deceased's interest by *right of survivorship* to the surviving joint tenant(s).

- Sums payable under *discretionary pension schemes*. The trustees of the pension scheme will make payment directly to the person(s) selected to benefit.

Property which is the subject of a nomination or a *donatio mortis causa* is treated as an asset of the deceased's estate but devolves directly on the nominee or donee immediately upon the deceased's death and as such does not become vested in the deceased's PRs.

11.3.1   Office copies of the grant

In most cases the PRs will need a grant as proof of their entitlement before they are able to collect the deceased's assets from the persons in possession of them at the time of the deceased's death. So, even though an executor has authority to deal with the deceased's estate from the date of death (*see* Chapter 8, para. 8.5.3), in practice they will not be able to collect in many of the assets of the estate until they have obtained a grant.

The original grant is a document of title. There is a risk of its loss if it has to be sent to many destinations as proof of the PRs' title. In addition, if the estate consists of many assets, it will take a long time to collect in if the PRs have to wait for the return of the original grant from each person from whom they seek to recover the deceased's assets. For these reasons, obtaining office copies of the original grant from the registry is good practice as they are adequate proof of entitlement for most types of property. A small fee has to be paid for each copy.

Note

Office copies of the original grant are not the same as a photocopy of the original grant made in the solicitor's office and the latter is not sufficient evidence of entitlement to a grant.

Implied powers of personal representatives 11.4

The Administration of Estates Act 1925, the Trustee Act 1925 and the Trustee Investment Act 1961 all give PRs various powers. However, in the circumstances of many wills, it is desirable to confer on the PR's powers additional to those implied by law and to extend the existing powers (*see* Chapter 4).

Here we consider the powers implied by law as these may well be important when the PR is acting on a home-made will and will be important where the deceased has died intestate where only the statutory powers will be available to an administrator.

Powers of sale, mortgage and leasing 11.4.1

Section 39(1), Administration of Estates Act 1925 gives PRs the same powers of *sale*, *mortgage* and *leasing* as those conferred upon trustees for sale of land. According to s.28(1), Law of Property Act 1925 trustees for sale have all the powers of the tenant for life and of the trustees of a settlement under the Settled Land Act 1925. These include the power to sell or exchange land, or any part thereof, or to grant easements, rights or privileges over or in relation to the land. In the case of a lease, it includes the power to lease and to accept a surrender of a lease.

The powers are necessarily very wide as the PRs may have to raise funds to pay funeral, testamentary and administration expenses; debts of the deceased; inheritance tax; or legacies. Which assets should be sold for these purposes may be a complex issue (*see* Chapter 12, para. 12.6).

Power to appropriate 11.4.2

Conditions
Section 41, Administration of Estates Act 1925 provides that PRs may appropriate any part of an estate in or towards the

satisfaction of a legacy or any other interest in the estate of the deceased subject to the following conditions:

- The appropriation must not prejudice a specific gift made by the deceased;
- Appropriate consents must be obtained. In the case of a *beneficiary absolutely entitled in possession* it is only necessary for the PRs to obtain the consent of that person.

Valuing the assets

For the purpose of the power of appropriation contained in s.41, the assets are valued at the date of appropriation rather than at the deceased's death (*Re Collins* (1975)) and the PRs have the power to ascertain and fix the value of the assets as they think fit (s.41(3)) but should employ a suitably qualified valuer where this is necessary.

Example

In *Re Bythway* (1911), it was considered that an executrix was not entitled to appropriate to herself unquoted company shares at her own valuation.

According to *Re Phelps* (1980), if the asset exceeds the value of the beneficiary's legacy or other interest in the estate, s.41 cannot be invoked as the assets must be appropriated *in or towards satisfaction* of the legacy or other interest. However, it will be possible for the PRs to use their power of sale (*see* 11.4.1) to sell the asset to the beneficiary, with the beneficiary providing cash insofar as the value of the asset exceeds their legacy or other interest in the estate. One possible drawback to this is it is likely that *ad valorem* stamp duty will be payable if an instrument is necessary to effect the sale and the transaction may be regraded as a sale for capital gains tax purposes.

Note

On intestacy a surviving spouse has a right to require the PRs to appropriate a dwelling house comprised in the deceased's estate in which the surviving spouse was resident at the time of the deceased's death in partial or total satisfaction of the surviving spouse's absolute and/or capitalised interest in the estate: Schedule 2, Intestates' Estates Act 1952 (*see* Chapter 7, para. 7.4.4).

11.4.3   Power to appoint trustees

Section 42, Administration of Estates Act 1925 provides that where a *minor* is absolutely entitled either under a will (in which no trustees are appointed of the gift to the minor) or under the rules of intestacy, the PRs may appoint a trust corporation or two or more individuals (to a maximum of four) to be trustees for the minor. The trustees may include the PRs.

The purpose of this section is to overcome the problem that a minor cannot give a good receipt to the PRs for money or securities, neither can a parent or guardian on behalf of the child, unless there is an express provision in the will to the contrary. If the PRs appoint trustees under s.42 and transfer property to the trustees, a receipt signed by the trustees will be a good discharge to the PRs.

This power only applies where the minor has an *absolute* interest under a will or the rules of intestacy. In view of the statutory trusts, whereby on intestacy a minor is only entitled to contingent interests on attaining 18 or marriage under that age, the circumstances in which s.42 applies on intestacy will be rare.

Note

If a minor beneficiary has only a *contingent interest* on intestacy or under a will and the will does not provide for the minor or parent or guardian thereof to give a good receipt to the trustees, the trustees will either have to exercise their power of appropriation under s.41, Administration of Estates Act 1925 (*see* 11.4.2) or pay into court money to which the minor is entitled. The receipt or certificate of the proper officer is then a discharge to the PRs: ss.63(1) and 68(17), Trustee Act 1925. Given trustees' wide power of appropriation, the option of payment into court is seldom used.

Power to postpone distribution   11.4.4

PRs are not bound to distribute the estate of the deceased before the expiration of one year from death: s.44, Administration of Estates Act 1925. This is often referred to as the 'executor's year'. They are, however, free to distribute the residuary estate before the expiration of the executor's year if they so choose, but they cannot be compelled to do so even if the will directs otherwise.

Note the following points:

- If a beneficiary under the deceased's estate is in need of *immediate financial assistance*, eg. the deceased's surviving spouse, the court can make an interim order in favour of an applicant under s.5(1), Inheritance (Provision for Family and Dependants) Act 1975.

- The PRs are not bound to distribute the deceased's estate at the expiration of the executor's year if the administration of the estate cannot reasonably be completed within this time. They may, however, be required to explain the delay and all pecuniary and general legatees (other than those with merely a contingent interest) will thereafter be entitled to interest at 6% per annum.

● The power to postpone *distribution* does not apply to payment of debts. These must be paid with due diligence. This may require payment before the expiration of the executor's year (*see* Chapter 12, para. 12.2).

11.4.5   Power to maintain minors

Section 31, Trustee Act gives PRs (and trustees) the power to apply income for the 'maintenance education or benefit' of an beneficiary under 18. The power operates, in the case of a will, so long as there is no contrary intention in the will.

Before the PRs can exercise their power, the gift must carry 'intermediate income', ie. the income produced from the property to which the minor is entitled must be intended by the testator to be part of the minor's entitlement. If the testator specifies in the will what is to be done with the intermediate income, the testator's intentions prevail. For example, the testator may expressly direct that the income is to be paid to a third party or is to be accumulated and added to capital. In either of these situations the gift will not carry intermediate income.

Where the will is silent, what is to be done with any intermediate income is governed either by s.175, Law of Property Act 1925 or the common law.

Most testamentary gifts do carry intermediate income, but contingent pecuniary legacies form an important exception to this general rule in that they do not carry intermediate income *unless*:

● The gift is made by a person *in loco parentis and* the contingency is attaining the age of 18 *and* there is no other fund set aside for the maintenance of the legatee; or

● The testator shows an intention to maintain: *see Re Churchill* (1909); or

● The testator directs the legacy to be paid out of property which does not form part of the residue of the estate.

Once it is established that the statutory power of maintenance is available, the PRs have discretion to apply the whole or part of the income for the minor's maintenance, education or benefit, as may in all the circumstance be reasonable having regard to the minor's age, actual requirements, and all the circumstances of the case. This is so even if there is another fund(s) applicable for the same purpose and even if there is someone bound by law to provide for the minor's maintenance.

The following points about the s.31 power of maintenance require special attention:

- If the PRs do not apply all the income for the maintenance of the minor beneficiary, it is to be *accumulated*, although the accumulated income may be used by the PRs in any subsequent year of infancy as if it was income arising from the current year;

- The trustee's power to apply income for maintenance is subject to the *objective test of reasonableness* and requires them to have regard to, *inter alia*, the existence of other funds available.

Note

The power of maintenance is often extended by an express clause in a will, giving the PRs (or trustees) absolute discretion on the application of income (*see* Chapter 4, para. 4.11.3).

PR's (and trustee's) powers of maintenance are particularly important:

- In relation to *accumulation and maintenance trusts* (*see* Chapter 5);

- Where a *statutory trust* arises in favour of a minor on intestacy – the minor is only entitled to their share contingent upon attaining 18 years or marriage under that age (*see* Chapter 7, para. 7.5.1);

- In the case of trustees, where an *absolute gift of money or securities* is made to a minor by will, and the will does not contain a receipt clause allowing a parent or guardian to receive the gift on the minor's behalf (*see* 11.4.3).

Power of advancement   11.4.6

Section 32, Trustee Act 1925, gives PRs (and trustees) a power to advance capital which applies so long as there is no contrary intention. Before the power will operate, the subject matter of the gift must be money or personal securities, or land held on trust for sale. Advancements may be made at the absolute discretion of the PRs (or trustees) for the benefit of any beneficiary with an interest in capital so long as the funds are applied for the 'advancement or benefit' of the beneficiary. This has been widely interpreted to mean 'any use of the money which will improve the material situation of the beneficiary': *Pilkington v IRC* (1964).

Note the three following important limitations on the statutory power:

- Before an advancement can be made, the PRs (or trustees) must obtain the *consent of any person entitled to a prior interest*, eg. a life tenant, before an advancement to a beneficiary entitled in remainder – such person may only give their consent if they are of full age and mental capacity;

- Although more than one advancement can be made, the PRs (or trustees) cannot advance *more than half the presumptive share of a beneficiary*;

- Advancements made must be *brought into account when the beneficiary becomes absolutely entitled*.

Note

Because of the limitations of the statutory power of advancement, it is usual for wills to contain an express power of advancement extending the statutory power (*see* Chapter 4, para. 4.11.4).

11.4.7   Power to insure

Section 19, Trustee Act 1925 gives PRs (and trustees) power to insure against loss or damage by *fire* for up to *three-quarters* of the value of the property, the premiums to be paid out of income. The power applies in the case of a will, so long as there is no contrary intention. However, the power does *not* apply if the PRs are bound immediately to convey the property absolutely to a beneficiary upon being requested to do so: s.19(2).

Note

Because of the serious limitations on the power, it is usual for wills to contain an express clause extending the power (*see* Chapter 4, para. 4.11.1).

11.4.8   Power to delegate

Extent of the power

Section 23(1), Trustee Act 1925 provides that PRs (and trustees) may employ an agent to transact any business or to do any act in the administration of the estate (trust) and may remunerate such agent out of the estate (trust fund).

In connection with the administration of estates, s.23(1) is most likely to be used to employ estate agents to sell land, or where it is necessary to engage a stockbroker to value shares, or a bank to act in relation to the administration of the estate.

Section 23(1) does not allow PRs (trustees) to delegate their *decision making powers* in respect of the administration of the estate (trust) but s.25(1) permits this in certain limited

circumstances, the most important of which is if the delegation is made by *power of attorney*. It is then possible to
delegate all matters in the administration of the estate
including decision making powers for a period (renewable)
not exceeding 12 months. The formalities for creating such a
power are contained in the Powers of Attorney Act 1971 and
the Enduring Powers of Attorney Act 1985.

PRs may wish to rely on a power of attorney where acts
need to be done in the administration of the estate and they
are temporarily absent, eg. on holiday, or abroad through
work commitments.

Liability for acts of agents appointed

Where a PR delegates under s.25(1) by means of a power of
attorney, they are liable for *all* acts done by the attorney.
Where the delegation is made under s.23(1) the position is
less clear. Provided they have appointed the agent in good
faith they will probably only be liable for the actions of the
agent if they fail to exercise reasonable supervision over
them but not beyond this. If the PR has not made an
appointment in good faith (probably the objective standard
of the reasonable man) they will be liable for *all* actions of
the agent.

Power of indemnity

11.4.9

Section 30(2), Trustee Act 1925 gives PRs (and trustees) the
power to reimburse themselves for all expenses incurred in
the execution of their powers and duties.

Power of investment

11.4.10

Most professionally drawn wills give the PRs extensive
powers of investment (*see* Chapter 4, para. 4.11.2). This is
because in the absence of such powers, the PRs will be
limited to investments permitted by the Trustee Investment
Act 1961, or by s.73, Settled Land Act 1925 and s.28, Law of
Property Act 1925.

Trustee Investment Act 1961

This Act sets out permitted types of investments for PRs
(and trustees) which apply so long as, in the case of a will,
there is no contrary intention. The investments permitted
are very limited and are not necessarily the best investments for the 1990s, added to which the scheme of the Act
is complex and expensive to administer.

Section 73, Settled Land Act 1925 and s.28, Law of Property Act 1925

The powers of investment contained in the Trustee Investment Act 1961 do not include the power to invest in land.

However, trustees of a strict settlement (s.73) and trustees of land held on trust for sale (s.28) have the power to reinvest in land so long as they retain some of the land held on trust (*Re Wakeman* (1945)) and possibly where all the land subject to the trust has been sold but the proceeds of sale remain identifiable (*Re Wellsted's Will Trusts* (1949)).

Remember that the statutory powers are to *invest* property. In *Re Wragg* (1919), it was said that 'investment' requires that the property is purchased for the sake of the income produced and for possible capital appreciation. Consequently, in *Re Power* (1947), it was said that the statutory power to invest did not include the purchase of a house for occupation by the beneficiaries. It has long been held that unsecured loans are not investments: *Khoo Tek Keong v Ch'ng Joo Tuan Neoh* (1934).

11.4.11   Power to run a business

The general rule is that the PRs have no power to carry on the deceased's business whatever form it takes.

If the deceased was a partner in a *partnership* they are generally under a duty to call in the deceased's share in the partnership. However, in the case of a *sole proprietor*, the PRs have implied authority to carry on the deceased's business with a view to the proper realisation of the deceased's estate. For example, they may carry out the deceased's obligations under a contract made before their death (*Marshall v Broadhurst* (1831)) or carry on the business to enable it to be sold as a going concern (*Dowse v Gorton* (1891)). Thus, if selling the business as a going concern is a proper method of realisation, PRs may carry on the deceased's business for such period of time as is reasonably necessary to enable them to effect a sale. This period will not normally exceed the executor's year: *Re Crowther* (1895).

Note

On the death of a sole proprietor, the assets of the business devolve on their PRs in the same way as their non-business assets.

Similarly, on the death of a partner, any assets of the partnership which were vested in the deceased (other than as a joint tenant) devolve on the deceased's PRs, although they remain assets of the partnership and the surviving partner(s) may deal with them for the purposes of the partnership.

In contrast, if the deceased ran a *company* business the deceased's *shares* in the business, but not the *assets* of the company, devolve on the deceased's PRs.

Devastavit and protection from liability   11.5

If a PR commits any breach of the duties of their office, causing a loss of assets, they are said to commit a *devastavit*, ie. a wasting of the assets of the deceased's estate, and are normally personally liable to the deceased's creditors and beneficiaries.

Where there is more than one PR, each PR is liable for their own breaches of duty but not for those of any other PRs unless:

- In failing to carry out their own duty the PR allows a breach of duty by another; or
- The PR acquiesces in a breach of duty by another PR.

Where a PR is in breach of duty they may be able to obtain relief from liability by:

- Placing reliance on *an express provision in a will* which limits the liability of the PRs;
- A *release obtained from the beneficiaries* affected by the breach;
- Obtaining *relief from the court*;
- Pleading the *defence of limitation*;
- Advertising under *s.27, Trustee Act 1925* or by obtaining a *Benjamin Order*.

Express provision in a will   11.5.1

It is common for a will appointing professional persons as PRs to protect them from liability for all but acts of dishonesty.

Release obtained from the beneficiaries   11.5.2

A release obtained from the beneficiaries affected by the breach will only be possible if either the beneficiaries are of full age and mental capacity and have full knowledge of the breach, or if the beneficiaries have induced the PRs to effect the breach.

Obtaining relief from the court   11.5.3

Section 61, Trustee Act 1925 provides that the court may relieve a PR (or trustee) in whole or in part if it appears to the court that the PR has acted 'honestly and reasonably and ought fairly to be excused'.

Note

It is unlikely that the court will grant relief under this provision to a professional trustee.

11.5.4   Pleading the defence of limitation

Claim by a creditor

A PR can plead the defence of limitation for non-payment of a debt at the expiration of six years from the date of distribution of the estate: s.2, Limitation Act 1980.

Claim by a beneficiary

A PR can generally plead the defence of limitation in respect of a claim to the deceased's personal property (s.22) or land (s.15(1)) after the expiration of 12 years from the date on which the right of action accrued. However, no limitation period applies where the PRs has either committed a fraudulent breach of duty or where they have converted the assets of the estate to their own use: s.21.

Note

In the case of a claim by either a creditor or a beneficiary, the period of limitation may be extended for a wide variety of reasons, eg. disability of the claimant or fraudulent concealment of the claim.

11.5.5   Advertising under s.27, Trustee Act 1925 or by obtaining a Benjamin Order

Section 27, Trustee Act 1925 and Benjamin Orders provide protection for PRs against an innocent, but wrongful, distribution of the estate as a result of being unaware of the existence or whereabouts of a creditor or beneficiary (*see* Chapter 13, paras. 13.4.1–2).

11.6   Organisation of the administration of an estate

In administering estates, you should:

- Ensure good file management;
- Organise time properly; and
- Keep adequate records.

11.6.1   Ensuring good file management

As probate work involves considerable paperwork, and the administration of a complex estate can take months or even years, you must file:

- Letters received (in date order);
- Copies of letters sent;
- Notes of meetings;
- Notes made of telephone calls; and
- Keep a checklist at the top of the client's file and review it regularly.

Checklists should contain:

- Relevant names and addresses;
- Lists of assets and liabilities;
- The steps which need to be taken in the administration of the estate.

Organisation of time   11.6.2

Administration of an estate goes through stages which involve many actions to be taken all at once, with 'quieter' periods in between. For example, there is much to be done immediately after receiving instructions on death (*see* Chapter 8) and later, once the grant of representation has been obtained, when you have to collect in the assets. You must anticipate when 'peaks' of activity are likely to occur and to make time available to deal with them.

Keeping adequate records   11.6.3

In the final stages, estate accounts will need to be prepared (*see* Chapter 13, para. 13.11.4). To make this task easier, you must keep proper records from the very outset of the administration period.

Self-assessment questions

1 What are office copies of the original grant and why may they be needed?

2 Helen is entitled under a will to a legacy of £10,000 absolutely. The will contains no express power of appropriation. Helen wishes the PRs to transfer a painting worth £9,000 to her in partial satisfaction of her legacy. Is this possible? Would your answer be different if the painting was worth £11,000?

3 By a home-made will containing no express powers for PRs, Tom leaves a legacy of £50,000 to his nephew Simon (who is at the present time aged four). How should the PRs deal with the legacy in distributing the estate? Would your answer be different if Simon was only entitled contingent upon reaching 18?

4 Your client's husband died a month ago leaving a will which appoints his two brothers as executors and which leaves his (substantial) residuary estate to your client. Her brother-in-laws have told her that they have no intention of giving her anything from her husband's estate for at least two years. Advise her.

5 You are approached by Mrs Smith whose husband died intestate three months ago leaving an estate worth ap-

proximately £250,000 and three children (aged eight, 12 and 18). She wishes to know whether assets can be made available from the estate to pay the school fees of the two younger children and to provide a deposit on a house for the eldest child. Advise Mrs Smith.

6 Billy, the sole proprietor of a business known as 'Billy's Bar', died intestate last month. Advise his PRs as to their position in relation to the business.

Answer guidance to self-assessment questions

1 *See* 11.2.

2 Painting worth £9,000 – this is possible with Helen's consent: s.41, AEA power of appropriation (*see* 11.3.2).

Painting is worth £11,000 – this is not possible as it cannot be said to be 'in or towards satisfaction' within s.41. However, the PRs may make use of their power of sale (*see* 11.3.2 and 11.3.1).

3 Absolute gift – the PRs can appoint trustees under s.42, AEA (*see* 11.3.3).

Contingent gift – s.42, AEA does not apply, the PRs will either have to exercise their power of appropriation under s.41 or pay the money into court (*see* 11.3.3).

4 *See* 11.3.4. PRs have a power to postpone the distribution of the estate until one year has passed since the deceased's death. Even then, they need not distribute the estate if the administration of the estate cannot reasonably be completed within this time. However, they can be called upon to explain the delay.

Depending on the severity of the client's financial problems, it may be appropriate to apply for an interim payment under s.5(1), Inheritance (Provision for Family and Dependants) Act 1975.

5 The statutory power of maintenance is available for the school fees: s.31, Trustee Act 1925 (*see* 11.3.5).

The power of advancement is available for the deposit on the house s.32, Trustee Act 1925 (*see* 11.3.6).

Both the exercise of the power of maintenance and advancement are at the discretion of the PRs.

6 *See* 11.3.11. The business devolves on the PRs, but they only have the power to carry it on for the purpose of realisation.

Chapter 12

Payment of expenses and discharge of liabilities

Introduction 12.1

The aim of the chapter is to explain:

- The rules which apply to the payment of the deceased's funeral and testamentary expenses and the discharge of the deceased's debts whether the deceased dies leaving a valid will or intestate;

- How to decide which assets of the estate should be sold to pay the various debts and other liabilities;

- How personal representatives (PRs) can protect themselves from liability for non-payment of unknown debts.

General points 12.2

PRs are under a duty to pay the deceased's funeral and testamentary expenses and discharge all debts incurred by the deceased before death with 'due diligence' having regard to the assets in their hands which are properly applicable for the payment of debts: *Re Tankard* (1942). The duty does not depend on the PRs being aware of the existence of the debts, although there are certain steps PRs can take to protect themselves from liability for debts of which they are unaware (*see* 12.6).

Different rules apply for payment of debts depending on whether the estate is solvent (*see* 12.4) or insolvent (*see* 12.5).

The duty to pay debts is owed to the creditors and the beneficiaries under the estate. If the PRs do not pay debts 'with due diligence' they will be personally liable for any consequential loss suffered by the creditors or beneficiaries.

There is no rule which requires payment of debts within a particular time, eg. one year, but the duty to act 'with due diligence' may, in the circumstances, require the PRs to make payment quite soon after the deceased's death. As soon as the various monies forming part of the deceased's estate can be collected in, the PRs should begin to pay the deceased's debts and funeral expenses.

Note

It may be necessary to obtain a bank loan in order to raise the IHT to obtain a grant of representation. If this is the case, it is likely that the bank will, under the terms of the loan, require a

> 'first proceeds' undertaking. This means that the PRs will be under an obligation to use the money first realised by them to repay the bank.

The PRs may have to sell assets of the estate to pay expenses and discharge liabilities. If this is so, the PRs will need to consider which assets should be sold (*see* 12.6).

12.3   Funeral, testamentary and administration expenses

'Reasonable' funeral expenses are payable from the deceased's estate. What are 'reasonable' funeral expenses is a question of fact in each case.

The terms 'testamentary' and 'administration' used in relation to expenses are not defined by statute but case-law establishes that both terms refer to expenses incurred by the PRs in the proper performance of their duties. The terms include the:

- Cost of *obtaining a grant*;
- Costs of *collecting in the assets* of the deceased's estate;
- *IHT* payable on death on UK property which vests in the PRs;
- *Administration expenses*, such as solicitors' fees for acting for the PRs and valuers' fees.

12.4   Payment of debts – solvent estates

An estate is solvent if there are sufficient assets to pay expenses and all other debts in full. An estate is not insolvent simply because *legacies* cannot be paid or paid in full.

In deciding which property is available for payment of debts in a solvent estate, you must distinguish between debts charged on property during the deceased's lifetime and all other debts. Debts charged on the deceased's property *during the lifetime* of the deceased are governed by s.35, Administration of Estates Act 1925 unless a contrary intention is expressed in the will (*see* 12.4.1).

Property to be used for the payment of *other debts* is, in the absence of any contrary intention in the will, governed by the statutory order set down in Part II of the First Schedule of the Administration of Estates Act 1925 (*see* 12.4.2).

12.4.1   Property charged with a debt during the deceased's lifetime

The most common type of debt in this category is a *mortgage debt* charged on the family home. However, the charge need not necessarily have been created by the deceased, as in the case of a mortgage, but may arise by operation of the law.

Charges arising during the deceased's lifetime include:

- All *mortgages*, whether legal or equitable, over land held by the deceased;
- *Charges imposed by the court on land* to satisfy a judgment debt;
- An *Inland Revenue charge* imposed as IHT remains unpaid.

Section 35, Administration of Estates Act 1925 provides that where a debt is charged on property during the deceased's lifetime, the property charged will be liable for payment of the debt unless a contrary intention is shown.

Example

A testatrix leaves her holiday cottage 'Balmoral' to her nephew. The cottage is subject to a mortgage of £6,000. There is no provision in the will as to how the mortgage debt is to be discharged. The nephew will take 'Balmoral' subject to the mortgage.

What amounts to a contrary intention?

The effect of s.35 may be varied by a contrary intention expressed in the will (or any other document). The following are sufficient to show a contrary intention:

- In making the specific gift which is subject to the debt, it is expressed to be given free from the debt.

Specimen clause

I give my holiday cottage 'Balmoral', Seaview Road, Bognor Regis, to my nephew Charles Small free of mortgage ...

- Where the residuary gift is expressly made to be subject to debts charged on property during the deceased's lifetime.

Specimen clause

I GIVE the residue of my estate SUBJECT TO the payment of my debts, funeral, testamentary and administrative expenses including any mortgage or charge affecting my freehold property ...

- Where the testator provides that debts are to be paid from a special fund other than residue. In this case, without specific reference to debts charged on property during the deceased's lifetime, the direction will be construed as extending to all debts.

Example

A testator directs that all his debts are to be paid from the proceeds of sale of the business he ran as a sole trader. At his death, the testator's house is still subject to a mortgage. The mortgage debt should be discharged from the proceeds of sale of the business along with any other debts. If this special fund is insufficient to pay all the debts, the property remains subject to the charge to the extent that the charge cannot be paid from the fund: *Re Fegan* (1928).

Note

A clause in a will which simply states that debts etc are to be paid out of the residue is *not sufficient* to amount to a contrary intention: s.35(2).

The rights of creditors

Section 35 only regulates the incidence of secured debts as between the *beneficiaries* of the estate. It does not affect the rights of the creditors, who may pursue whatever remedy is available to them.

Example

A personal action may be brought by a secured creditor and in consequence the PRs may make payment from the general estate rather than from the charged property. If this happens the doctrine of marshalling will apply to ensure that the debt is borne by the correct beneficiary.

12.4.2   The statutory order for unsecured debts

Section 34(3), Administration of Estates Act 1925 provides that the statutory order of application of assets set out in Part II of the First Schedule to the Act applies to unsecured debts of a solvent estate in so far as there is no contrary intention expressed in the will. The order is:

1   *Property of the deceased undisposed of by will, subject to the retention thereout of a fund to meet any pecuniary legacies.* Undisposed of property will arise where the will does not deal with all the assets of the deceased and consequently there is a partial intestacy.

2   *Property of the deceased not specifically devised or bequeathed but included (either by specific or general description) in a residuary gift, subject to the retention thereout of a fund sufficient to meet any pecuniary legacies, so far as it is not already provided for.* For this purpose, any gift of property which is not a specific gift (*see* Chapter 4, para. 4.5.1) is regarded as a residuary gift.

Example

In *Re Wilson* (1967) a testator made some specific gifts and pecuniary legacies and then made a gift of 'all my real estate and the residue of my personal estate'. It was held that the real estate fell within paragraph 2 above.

3   *Property of the deceased given for the payment of debts.* This occurs where the testator directs in the will that the property is to be used for the payment of debts and leaves no directions as to what is to happen if there is any property left over after the debts have been paid.

Example

A testator provides 'all my debts are to be paid from the proceeds of the sale of my shares in British Telecom'. The will does not go on to say what is to happen if the proceeds of sale exceed the testator's debts.

4   *Property of the deceased charged with the payment of debts.* Property is said to be charged with the payment of debts, as opposed to given for the payment of debts, where the testator provides that the debts are to be paid out of a specified property and also provides in the will what is to happen to the balance (if any) of the proceeds of sale of the property.

Example

A testator provides 'all my debts are to be paid from the proceeds of sale of my shares in British Telecom and any balance is to go to my niece Margaret Beeson'.

5   *The fund, if any, retained to meet pecuniary legacies.* This fund may be from the undisposed of property and/or from the residue.

Note

1   'Pecuniary legacy' is defined by s.55(1)(ix), Administration of Estates Act 1925, and is wider than the normal meaning (*see* 4.5.1).

2   Where funds made available for pecuniary legacies have to be used for payment of debts, the pecuniary legacies abate proportionally unless the deceased directed that certain legacies be paid in priority to others.

6   *Property specifically devised or bequeathed rateably according to value.* Note here that when valuing the property to use for payment of debts rateably, the amount of any charge created on the property during the deceased's lifetime and not discharged upon the deceased's death, should be taken into account.

Example

A testator makes specific gifts of (a) his house 'Greenwood' worth £200,000 but subject at his death to a mortgage of £100,000; and (b) his Rolls Royce motor car worth £50,000. Debts of £90,000 have to be paid from the specific gifts.

In discharging the debts rateably from the specific gifts, 'Greenwood' is valued at £100,000. As 'Greenwood' is worth twice as much as the Rolls Royce, it bears £60,000, while the gift of the Rolls Royce bears £30,000.

7   *Property appointed by will under a general power* (including a statutory power to dispose of entailed interests) rateably according to value. This occurs where a testator has a power to appoint to anyone they wish and exercises the power expressly in the will.

Note

Property which is the subject of a *donatio mortis causa* or a statutory nomination, although outside the statutory order, is available for payment of debts once property within this statutory order has been exhausted.

Example of the application of the statutory order
By his will Thomas left his MG motor car (registration number MG I234) worth £7000 to Mary, pecuniary legacies to various different beneficiaries, to the total of £8000, and the residue of his estate to Nancy who survives Thomas. There is no contrary intention to the statutory order in the will. The residue before debts etc totals £66,000. The debts etc are £12,000.

As there is no undisposed of property as per category 1 (above), the PRs should pay the debts etc out of the residuary estate, but subject to a fund sufficient to pay the pecuniary legacies, ie. as per category 2 (above).

The distribution will be as follows.

MG motor car (specific gift)	£7,000	
Residue before debts etc		£66,000
Less pecuniary legacies		£8,000
		£58,000
Less debts		£12,000
To Nancy		£46,000

12.4.3   Variations of the statutory order

As the application of the statutory order is complex, it is normally excluded when drafting a will. The most common way in which this is done is by making a gift of the residue expressly 'subject to' or 'after' payment of debts. This is taken as a direction to pay all debts from the whole of the residue before it is given to the beneficiary(ies) of the residue.

Specimen clause

If my husband survives me by 28 days I GIVE to him absolutely but subject to the payment of debts, funeral and testamentary expenses the residue of my estate ...

Example

By his will Tom leaves the residue of his estate to his brothers in equal shares. Tom has two brothers Adam and Bernard of whom Adam predeceases him. The residuary gift is expressly stated to be made after payment of debts etc.

As Adam predeceases Tom and the brothers take as tenants in common, Adam's share in the residuary estate lapses leaving undisposed of property. However, because of the express words providing for payment of debts from the residue, the debts etc are paid *before* the division of the residue between Adam (whose share passes in partial intestacy) and Bernard. (If the statutory order had been applied, the residuary estate would have been divided in half and the debts paid out of A's undisposed of half.)

Payment of debts – insolvent estates 12.5

Meaning of insolvent estate 12.5.1

An estate is insolvent if the assets are not sufficient to pay *all* funeral, testamentary and administration expenses, and debts and liabilities. If an estate is insolvent, creditors will not be paid in full and the beneficiaries under the estate will receive nothing.

The order in which creditors are to be paid is determined by statute and if the PRs do not follow this order they will incur personal liability for 'superior' debts which are left unpaid. If the PRs are uncertain whether an estate is insolvent they should administer the estate as if it were insolvent to avoid personal liability.

Note

There is some limited protection for PRs who pay a debt in full at a time when they are not aware the estate is insolvent (*see* s.10(2), Administration of Estates Act 1925).

Order for distribution of assets 12.5.2

Normally the following order of distribution of assets

applies: Administration of Insolvent Estates of Deceased Persons Order 1986.

1 *Reasonable funeral, testamentary and administration expenses.* Where an estate is insolvent, 'reasonable' funeral expenses are on a lower scale than in the case of a solvent estate.

2 *Specially preferred debts,* eg. money being held by the deceased belonging to a friendly society.

3 *Preferential debts.* These include:

- Wages or salary and/or accrued holiday pay owed by the deceased to an employee in respect of the whole/part of a period of *four* months prior to deceased's death up to a specified maximum (currently £800);

- Sums due from the deceased in the 12 months before death in respect of Class 1 or Class 2 contributions under the Social Security Act 1975;

- Sums due from the deceased in respect of contributions to occupational pension schemes and the State pension schemes (under Schedule 3, Social Security Pensions Act 1975);

- Sums due to the Inland Revenue for PAYE deducted from employees' remuneration in the 12 months before death;

- Sums due to HM Customs and Excise for VAT for the six months before death.

Note

Preferential debts rank equally (*pari passu*) and abate proportionately.

4 *Ordinary debts.* These are all other debts which are not deferred. They rank equally and abate proportionately.

5 *Interest on preferential and ordinary debts.*

6 *Deferred debts.* These are debts owed in respect of credit given by a person who was the deceased's *spouse* at the *date of death*. It is irrelevant that the creditor was not the deceased's spouse when the loan was given.

Note

A secured creditor, eg. a mortgagee, will normally be able to rely upon their security and not prove for the debt at all. If this is done, the secured creditor will take priority over all unsecured creditors and over payment of funeral, testamentary and administration expenses. However, if the security is not sufficient to cover the debt, the secured creditor will have to prove for any balance as an unsecured creditor in the order set out above.

Sale of assets 12.6

The PRs may have to sell assets to pay funeral, testamentary expenses, debts and other liabilities. If this is so, they will have to take into account the following in deciding which to sell:

- The terms of the will;
- The wishes of the beneficiaries;
- The tax consequences;
- The provisions of the Financial Services Act 1986 and the Solicitors' Investment Business Rules 1990.

The terms of will 12.6.1

If the will has been professionally drafted it is likely to include provisions as to which part of the deceased's estate is to be used for the payment of debts etc – it is usual to provide that debts are to be paid from the residue (*see* 12.4.3). Where there is no such provision, the statutory order applies (*see* 12.4.2). Whether the statutory order applies or not, the normal position is that assets which are the subject matter of specific gifts should *not* be sold unless all other assets in the estate have been exhausted.

The wishes of the beneficiaries 12.6.2

Wherever possible the PRs should consider the wishes and needs of the beneficiaries in deciding which assets to sell. Although they have power to sell any assets of the estate, if, for example, a residuary beneficiary particularly wishes to keep a painting which is comprised in the residuary estate, all other things being equal, the PRs should respect their wish.

Tax consequences 12.6.3

In selecting which assets to sell, the PRs should take into account any Capital Gains Tax or IHT consequences of the sale.

Capital gains tax

CGT is *prima facie* payable by PRs at 25% on any gains made on the disposal of assets of the estate *during the period of administration*.

> *Note* _____
>
> Tax is only chargeable on gains *arising since death*, death itself is not a disposal for CGT purposes (*see* Chapter 9, para. 10.11) and an exemption or relief may be available.

The rights of PRs to claim exemptions and reliefs are more limited than that for individuals, ie:

- The annual exemption is only available in the tax year of death and the two following tax years;
- The main residence exemption does not apply unless before and after death the residence has been used as a main or only residence by a person(s) who, under the will or rules of intestacy, is entitled to the whole or substantially the whole of the proceeds of sale of the house.

Note

When calculating the value of a chargeable gain, the PRs may deduct the incidental costs of disposal, eg. commission to a stockbroker on the sale of shares, and a proportion of the cost of valuing the deceased's estate for probate purposes.

When deciding from the CGT point of view whether an asset which has increased in value since death should be sold, the PRs should ask themselves the following questions:

- *Can we take advantage of the annual exemption?* The annual exemption (currently £5,800) is available in the tax year of death and the two following years. For this reason, sales of assets which have risen in value should be spread over two or more tax years wherever possible so that more than one annual exemption can be used;
- *Can we claim an indexation allowance?* This applies in the same way as for individuals.
- *Have other assets of the estate been sold at a loss?* If so, loss relief can be claimed. A loss must be set off against any gains which the PRs realise in the same tax year but to the extent that this is not possible, a loss can be carried forward and set off against gains made by the PRs in future tax years.

Note

If PRs have made losses on their disposals but have insufficient gains to set them against, the unabsorbed losses *cannot* be passed on to the beneficiaries. Consequently, if the PRs are unlikely to make future gains they should consider whether the loss-making asset(s) should be vested in any beneficiary with a large CGT liability rather than sold in order to enable that beneficiary to sell the asset and set off the loss against their own future gains. Conversely, if a beneficiary has unrelieved losses it may be that such a beneficiary will want an appreciating asset vested in them rather than sold.

- *Are any of the beneficiaries higher rate tax payers?* A beneficiary who is a *higher rate tax payer* who has no exemptions or reliefs available to them and who has had a specific asset of the estate which is increasing in value left to them, may prefer the PRs to sell the asset and pay the proceeds to the beneficiary. This is because PRs pay CGT at a rate equivalent to the basic rate of income tax.

Inheritance tax

Sections 178–98, Inheritance Tax Act 1984 give relief where certain assets are sold within given periods of the date of death for less than their *market value at the date of death*. These are certain categories of shares and land.

Shares If 'qualifying investments' are sold by the 'appropriate person' within *12 months of the death* at less than their market value at the date of death, the sale price can be substituted for the market value at the date of death.

'Qualifying investments' are:

- Shares and securities which were *quoted* at the date of death on a recognised stock exchange or unlisted securities market; and

- Units in *authorised unit trusts* (s.178(1), Inheritance Tax Act 1984): s.272, Finance Act 1987; and

- Investments held in a *settlement* of which the deceased was a *life tenant*.

The 'appropriate person' is 'the person liable for the tax attributable to the value of those investments or, if there is more than one such person, and one of them is paying the tax, that person': s.178(1).

This means if the PRs have paid the tax on, say, quoted shares, relief would not be available to a specific legatee if the PRs vested the shares in the beneficiary who sold the shares at a loss within the 12-month period.

Calculation of the loss *Prima facie* the sale price is deducted from the market value at the date of death, ie. the probate value. However, the Revenue have the power to substitute the best consideration which could reasonably have been obtained: s.179(1)(b).

Note

1 Expenses incurred as a result of sale cannot be used to increase the loss.

2 If sale proceeds of qualifying investments are reinvested in other qualifying investments within *two months* of the last sale, the loss relief available will be reduced or extinguished: s.180(1).

3 If the PRs make more than one sale of qualifying investments within the 12-month period, the aggregate of the sale proceeds

over the whole period must be taken into account in calculating whether there has been a loss and, if so, the extent of the loss.

Example

Paula dies leaving quoted shares in X plc with a probate value of £20,000 and quoted shares in Y plc with a probate value of £30,000. Four months after her death the PRs of her estate sell the shares in X plc for £15,000 and six months after her death the shares in Y plc for £32,000. The *overall* loss is £3,000 and it is on this sum that the loss relief can be claimed (and not the £5,000 loss on the sale of X plc shares).

Inter-relationship between IHT loss relief and CGT If the PRs sell assets at a loss they will realise an allowable loss for CGT purposes (*see* above). However, if the PRs elect for IHT relief, the sale price becomes the acquisition value for CGT purposes: s.187, Inheritance Tax Act 1984; s.274, Taxation of Chargeable Gains Act 1992. The consequence of this is that the PRs will not be able to claim a CGT loss, neither will there be a gain, as the sale price is treated as the acquisition value.

Example

Janice dies leaving quoted shares in X Plc with a probate value of £10,000. Four months after her death her PRs sell the shares in X Plc for £6000.

If IHT Loss Relief is claimed the sale price of £6000 is treated for CGT purposes as the acquisition cost of the shares in X Plc (instead of the original probate value of £10,000). This being so, there is no loss or gain for CGT purposes.

If no IHT Loss Relief is claimed the probate value of the shares in X Plc, ie. £10,000, is treated as the acquisition cost, and there is a loss of £4000 for CGT purposes.

In the light of the above, should the PRs therefore claim IHT loss relief or CGT loss relief? It will always be better to claim IHT loss relief unless the CGT loss is more than the amount by which the nil rate band for IHT purposes is exceeded, *and* there are likely to be future gains to set the loss against taking into account CGT exemptions and reliefs. This is because IHT is chargeable at 40% on the value of the estate exceeding the nil rate band, while CGT payable by PRs is only 25% of the chargeable gain.

If there is no IHT payable on the estate because, for example, of the spouse or charity exemption, or because the estate falls within the nil rate band, there can be no IHT losses. In these circumstances CGT Loss Relief may be more valuable to the PRs.

Sale of land Similar provisions as to those explained for quoted shares etc apply to sales of land within *four years* of death at a loss: ss.190–8, Inheritance Tax Act 1984.

The provisions differ to the position outlined for quoted shares etc in the following ways:

- Where there is a small decrease in value, ie. of less than either £1,000 or 5% of its value on death, whichever is the lesser, relief is not available: s.191;

- If sale proceeds of land are reinvested in any other interest in land *within four months* of the last qualifying sale, relief may be lost or extinguished;

- There is no provision which expressly states that the CGT acquisition value is to be substituted for the sale price when IHT loss relief is claimed. However, s.274, Taxation of Chargeable Gains Act 1992 *probably* has this effect.

The Financial Services Act 1986 and the Solicitors' Investment Rules 1990   12.6.4

The points made in this section assume a prior knowledge and understanding of the essential terminology and framework of the law relating to financial services. It is intended only to explain here how the law relating to financial services may affect solicitors either acting as PRs or for PRs when they sell assets of an estate to raise money to pay the deceased's debts, funeral and other testamentary expenses. Additionally, the position of PRs and trustees who are not solicitors is considered. (For an explanation of the basics of the law relating to financial services *see* the *Pervasives* Companion.)

In the administration of most estates it is likely that assets will have to be sold in order to pay debts etc, including raising money to pay the necessary IHT in order to gain a grant of representation. But not all sales will come within the Financial Services Act 1986 (FSA), and be covered by the Solicitors' Investment Business Rules 1990 (SIBR). To decide whether the FSA or SIBR apply, you must consider:

- The asset to be sold; and
- Who is doing the selling?

The asset to be sold
Not all assets of an estate will constitute investments for the purposes of the FSA. For example, jewellery, antique furniture, works of art and some insurance policies are not investments.

The sale may be an 'excluded activity' within Schedule

1 Part III, FSA, eg. arrangements made or advice given about acquisition or disposals of shares in a private company where 75% or more of the voting rights are involved.

Who is doing the selling?

Personal representative (and trustee) who is not a solicitor PRs and trustees who are not solicitors and who are acting for themselves, rather than having a solicitor act on their behalf, will not be caught by the FSA unless they are remunerated. This is because 'arranging deals', 'managing investments' etc within the FSA involves carrying on a business as such.

Solicitors Potentially, sales of assets by solicitors may fall within the FSA as they will involve:

- 'Managing investments on behalf of another' where investments are sold in the exercise of their discretionary powers as PRs;

- 'Arranging deals in investments' where, for example, they engage a stockbroker to sell shares;

- Giving 'investment advice' where, for example, they need to exercise expertise to decide which investments should be sold.

However, we must distinguish between a solicitor(s) in a firm acting *as* a PR as opposed to a solicitor(s) merely acting *for* the PR. In the former case, a sale of assets by the solicitor(s) will be an excluded 'activity' within the FSA and as such not regulated by the Act.

Where the sale does not fall within the excluded activity provision, you must decide whether the activity is *non-discrete investment business* (non-DIB) or *discrete investment business* (DIB). If the activity is DIB, full compliance with the SIBR is required whereas non-DIB only requires very limited compliance, the most onerous requirement being that relating to record-keeping (r.12(5), SIBR).

Investment business within estate administration can normally be conducted as non-DIB should the firm so desire. An activity will be non-DIB if the solicitor is:

- Personally acting *as* PR (r.(2)(3)(a), SIBR);

- Acting for lay PRs provided the activity is *incidental* (r(2)(2), SIBR). This will normally be the case.

Note

1 In the case of PRs the incidental exclusion is available despite the fact that the investment, eg. in unit trusts, is a 'specified investment' within the SIBR, such investments not normally being able to benefit from the exclusion.

2 Once the PRs have ceased to be PRs and have become trustees, the activity will not be regarded as 'incidental'.

Apart from the situation where a solicitor is giving advice to a beneficiary about the investment of their inheritance (*see* Chapter 13, para. 13.9), investment business is only likely to be DIB where the firm has a specialist financial services department. In such a case, it would be difficult to describe the activity as being 'incidental' as the firm would be holding itself out as a provide of financial services.

Protection against unknown creditors   12.7

As a general rule PRs are liable to the beneficiaries and creditors for unpaid debts and liabilities of the deceased even if they are unaware of them. However, the PRs can acquire statutory protection from liability by advertising for claimants in accordance with s.27, Trustee Act 1925.

To obtain protection under s.27 the PRs must:

1 *Advertise* their intention to distribute the estate requiring any person interested to send particulars of their claim within a stated time, at least two months from the date of the notice. The advertisement must be placed in:

● The *London Gazette*; and

● A newspaper circulated in the district in which any land to be distributed is situated; and

● Such other places, 'including notices elsewhere than in England and Wales, as would, in any special case have been directed by a court of competent jurisdiction in an action for administration'. A court would normally order the placing of such advertisements as are appropriate to the circumstances of the case.

Note

1 If the PRs are uncertain what a court might regard as 'appropriate', they should apply to the court for direction or risk losing the protection of the section.

2 Printed forms for the advertisements can be obtained from legal stationers.

2 *Carry out appropriate searches.* Section 27(2) requires the PRs to make such searches of land as a prudent purchaser of land would make, the purpose being to reveal the existence of any liability in relation to the deceased's land, eg. a second mortgage.

Note

The subsection does not list the searches which are to be made but searches should be made in HM Land Registry, HM Land Charges Department and local land charges register as appropriate.

3 *Distribute the estate only after the notice period has expired.* Only when the time limit has expired can the PRs can distribute the estate with regard only to the claims of which they have notice. The PRs are not personally liable if a claim is made after the expiry of the notice period. However, the disappointed beneficiary can recover the assets by tracing into the hands of beneficiaries who have received them from the PRs.

Note

1 To avoid delay in the administration of the estate the advertisements should be placed and the searches made as early as possible in the process of administration.

2 Section 27 does not relieve the PRs from liability for claims of which they have *actual notice* even if the claimant does not respond to the advertisement.

12.8   Contingent liabilities

A contingent liability is one which may or may not arise in the future. Common examples are where the deceased has guaranteed the repayment of a debt by a third party or where there is a threat of a legal action against the estate. The problem for the PRs is that they will not know whether the guarantee will ever be enforced against the estate or whether the legal action will be pursued. In such circumstances the PRs have four options. They can:

- *Set aside assets* from the estate sufficient to meet the contingent liability if it arises;
- *Obtain an indemnity from the beneficiaries* to cover the possibility of the liability materialising, and then distribute the estate. (It is, of course, unwise to deal with the problem in this way if the beneficiaries are not sufficiently financially secure to make the indemnity of value.
- If possible, *insure* against the risk of the liability occurring;
- *Apply to the court for directions.* This may be appropriate where the contingent liability is great and insurance cover is not available. It will protect the PRs from personal liability if they act in accordance with the directions.

Note

The first option is likely to be unpopular with the beneficiaries. The third, if available, is usually the best.

Inheritance tax liability on potentially exempt transfers 12.8.1

Where a potentially exempt transfer becomes chargeable the *inter vivos* transferee is primarily liable for the tax but the PRs of the transferor become liable if the tax remains unpaid for 12 months. As there is no obligation to inform the PRs of a potentially exempt transfer, they may not learn about it until they have distributed the assets of the estate. Moreover, the amount of IHT payable on death may be increased because the nil rate band has been wholly or partly lost.

PRs who are solicitors may be protected in either of these circumstances out of the Solicitors' Indemnity Fund (*see* Law Society's *Gazette*, 7 March 1990). *PRs who are not solicitors* have no such protection but the Revenue has said (*see* Law Society's *Gazette* 13 March 1991) that they will not usually pursue an IHT claim against PRs in these circumstances if:

- They have made the *fullest enquiries* reasonably practicable in the circumstances to discover lifetime transfers; and so

- Have done all in their power to make *full disclosure* of them to the Inland Revenue; and

- Have obtained a *certificate of discharge* (*see* Chapter 13, para. 13.11.1) and distributed the estate before the chargeable transfer came to light.

Self-assessment questions

1 By her will Moira left a specific gift of 7 Waverley Road, Oxshott (valued at £100,000) to her daughter Lucy and her residuary estate (valued at £200,000) to her sons Michael and Simon in equal shares. Simon predeceased Moira leaving no children. The property 7 Waverley Road is subject to a mortgage of £40,000. Moira died leaving other debts totalling £60,000. There are no express provisions in Moira's will concerning payment of debts. Out of which part of the estate should the mortgage and other debts be paid?

Would your answer be different if the residuary clause of Moira's will provided:

I GIVE my residuary estate after payment of my funeral, testamentary, administration expenses, debts and other liabilities ...?

2   The PRs of Max's estate need to sell certain assets comprised in the residuary estate to raise money for payment of debts. They are considering selling some shares in two quoted companies:

(a) Hascott Trust plc, the shares of which were valued at £18,000 at Max's death nine months ago, but which are now worth £14,000; and

(b) Pendow plc, the shares of which were valued at £20,000 at Max's death, but which are now worth £23,000.

Explain the potential IHT and CGT consequences of these sales, if any.

3   How should PRs protect themselves against the possibility of creditors of an estate unknown to them coming forward and making a personal claim against them after they have distributed the estate?

4   You are the PRs of Maxime Cross who died leaving an estate of £300,000. During her lifetime she guaranteed a loan of £100,000 made to Cyril, a friend, who is not a beneficiary under her will. The loan has to date not been repaid. What action, if any, should you take in administering the estate in the light of the continuing existence of the guarantee?

Answer guidance to self-assessment questions

1   As Michael and Simon take the residuary estate in equal shares they are tenants in common. Consequently, as there is no substitutional gift there is a partial intestacy of Simon's half share.

Mortgage debt There being no contrary intention, 7 Waverley Road bears the mortgage: s.35, AEA (*see* 12.4.1).

Other debts As there is no express provision in the will about payment of debts etc, the statutory order (*see* 12.4.2) applies. The debts will be paid out of Simon's undisposed of share.

Would your answer be different ...?

The express words included would amount to a variation of the statutory order (*see* 12.4.3). Consequently, the general debts would be paid out of the residue before it is divided in half between Michael and Simon's undisposed of share. However, the words are not sufficient to show a contrary intention to s.35, AEA (*see* 12.4.1); therefore 7 Waverley Road still bears the mortgage debt.

2   *IHT* The PRs may be able to claim IHT loss relief on the Hascott plc shares (*see* 12.6.3). However, as all sales of

qualifying investments within the 12-month period are aggregated in calculating the loss, they can only claim on the basis of £1,000 as the Pendow plc shares have risen in value.

CGT The sale of the shares is a disposal for CGT purposes and therefore as a gain has been made on the Pendow plc shares, *prima facie*, tax is payable. However, it may be possible to set the gain off against the loss on the Hascott plc shares and the annual exemption may also be available (*see* 12.6.3).

If CGT loss relief is claimed on the Pendow plc shares, then IHT loss relief cannot be claimed as the sale price is treated as the acquisition value for IHT purposes.

In the light of the likely availability of the annual exemption for CGT purposes (currently £5,800) and the fact that IHT is chargeable at 40% in excess of the nil rate band while CGT is only at 25%, it would be better to claim IHT loss relief.

3   *See* 12.7.

4   *See* 12.8.

Chapter 13

Distribution of the estate

Introduction 13.1

The aim of the chapter is to explain:

- The steps that the personal representatives (PRs) should take to ascertain the beneficial entitlement to the deceased's estate;
- How they should go about distributing the estate; and
- The steps to be taken in completing the administration of the estate.

Beneficiaries under a will or the rules of intestacy may not necessarily wish to take all or part of the property to which they are entitled. The reasons for this are explained at 13.10, along with the tax and other consequences of either disclaiming a gift or effecting a variation.

Ascertaining the beneficial entitlement 13.2

Once the funeral, testamentary and administration expenses, debts and other liabilities have either been paid or sufficient assets set aside for their payment, the PRs should begin distributing the gifts made in the will. They should distribute non-residuary gifts first, although they may need to consider the making of interim distributions to residuary beneficiaries.

In distributing legacies, the PRs should:

- Identify correctly the beneficiaries entitled to the gifts made in the will;
- Identify the property which forms the subject matter of each beneficiary's gift;
- Establish the nature and extent of each beneficiary's entitlement.

Where the deceased dies leaving a *valid will*, the PRs will need to construe the terms of the will to achieve this. Aspects of construction of wills are explained in paragraph 13.3. They will also have to be sure that each gift made has not failed for any reason – possible reasons for failure of a gift by will are explained in paragraph 13.5.

If the deceased has died wholly or partly *intestate*, the PRs must apply the rules of intestacy (*see* 13.6 and Chapter 7).

PRs may also need to take steps to ascertain the whereabouts or existence, or otherwise, of potential beneficiaries under the will or on intestacy (*see* 13.4).

13.3   Construction of wills

13.3.1   Construction summons

If the PRs cannot establish the true meaning of the deceased's will, they should take out a construction summons to have the issue determined by the court. An application is normally made to the Chancery Division of the High Court, but the County Court has jurisdiction where the estate is worth less than £30,000.

13.3.2   Extrinsic evidence

The object of constructing a will is to ascertain the testator's intention as expressed in the will. The court is not generally permitted to speculate upon what the testator may actually have intended. However, extrinsic evidence is permitted under s.21, Administration of Justice Act 1982.

Section 21, Administration of Justice Act 1982
Section 21 provides that extrinsic evidence including evidence of declarations as to the testator's intention may be admitted to assist in the construction of a will in so far as:

(a) Any part of it is meaningless;

Example

In *Kell v Charmer* (1856) a jeweller left by will to one son 'the sum of i.x.x', and to another 'the sum of o.x.x.' Evidence was admitted to show that the testator used this 'code' to denote his prices in his business.

(b) The language used in any part of it is, on the face of it, ambiguous, eg. a gift of 'my assets', 'my money';

(c) Evidence, other than evidence of the testator's intention, shows that the language used in any part of it is ambiguous in the light of the surrounding circumstances. This includes a latent ambiguity – one which becomes apparent when the PRs go to distribute the estate.

Example

If a testator makes a gift 'to my niece Jane' and the testator has two nieces called Jane, or if a testator makes a gift of 'my stamp album' and has two stamp albums, there is a latent ambiguity. In these cases extrinsic evidence, including evidence of the testator's intention, is admissible.

Note

In relation to (c) above:

1   Evidence of surrounding circumstances can be admitted to raise the possibility that an ambiguity exists.

2   Although evidence of the testator's intention cannot be introduced to raise an ambiguity (only circumstantial evidence is admissible for this purpose), once an ambiguity is established, evidence of the testator's intention is admissible to assist in resolving the ambiguity.

A will speaks from death as regards property   13.3.3

Section 24, Wills Act 1837 provides that a will speaks from death as regards property unless a contrary intention appears in the will. For example, a gift of 'all my estate' passes all property owned by the testator at the date of their death.

Certain words and phrases are often found to show a contrary intention, for example:

- 'My' coupled with a gift of a single specific item, eg. 'my sideboard', 'my gold ring'. This is *not* so, however if the word 'my' is coupled with a general description of property, such as 'all my shares' or where the specific description refers to a collection which may increase or decrease such as a stamp collection.

- 'Now' or 'at present', eg. 'my house where I now reside'.

Note

Section 24 only applies to property, not to the beneficiaries. As regards the beneficiaries a will is construed at the date it is made (or republished), unless a contrary intention is shown. Thus, a gift to the eldest child of my sister Natasha will be construed as a gift to Natasha's eldest child at the date the will is executed; if that child predeceases the testator, the gift will lapse and not take effect to Natasha's eldest child at the date of death.

Gifts to children   13.3.4

When identifying family relationships referred to in wills executed after 3 April 1988, references to any relationship between two persons shall be construed without regard to whether or not the father and mother of either of them or the father and mother of any person through whom the relationship is deduced, have or had been married to each other at any time: ss.1(1) and 19(1), Family Law Reform Act 1987. Thus, a gift to 'my children' includes illegitimate children and a gift to 'my grandchildren' includes the children of the testator's children, whether or not the testator's children or the grandchildren are legitimate.

Adopted children are treated as the children of their adoptive parents and not the children of their natural parents: s.39, Adoption Act 1976.

Where a gift in a will depends on the date of birth of a child or children, the gift is to be construed in the absence of a contrary intention, as if:

- An adopted child had been born on the date of the adoption; and

- Two or more children adopted on the same date had been born on that date in the order of their actual births.

Example _____

Tom makes a gift to the children of Adam living 'at the date of my death'. Tom dies in 1994. In 1995 Adam adopts Peter who was born in 1992. Peter is treated as born in 1995 and therefore cannot take under Tom's will.

_____

This rule does *not* affect any reference to the age of a child.

Example _____

Tom makes a gift 'to the first child of Adam to reach twenty-one years'. Adam has a natural child born in 1986 (Bernard), and an adopted child (Christopher) adopted in 1987 at aged three. It is the adopted child who will reach age 21 first and therefore becomes entitled to the gift.

However, if the gift was made to the 'eldest child of Adam', this would not be a gift made by reference to the age of the child, and Christopher would be treated as born on the date of adoption, making Bernard the eldest child of Adam.

_____

13.3.5   Class closing rules

A class gift is a gift to be divided among individuals who fulfil a general description where the size of any individual's share depends upon the number of persons falling within the class, eg. a gift to 'the children of X'.

Class gifts could (but for the class closing rules) make it difficult for PRs to distribute the estate. Taking the example of the gift made by Y 'to the children of X', but for the class closing rules, the PRs would have to wait until the death of X to ascertain the number of children falling within the class.

The class closing rules close a class at an artificially early date. They are rules of construction based on the need for convenience in the administration of the estate. How the rules operate depends on the nature of gift, *see* Table 13.1.

Table 13.1 Class closing rules

Type of gift	Closing date
Immediate class gift, eg. to the children of X.	If X has a child living at the testator's death the class closes at the testator's death and includes all children alive at the testator's death. If X has no children, the class remains open until X dies.
Deferred class gift, eg. to Y for life, with remainder to the children of X.	Provided that X has a child before the death of Y, the class closes either at the death of the testator, if Y predeceases the testator, or on the death of Y, if Y survives the testator, and includes all children of X alive at the death of the testator or Y (whichever is appropriate). If X has no children at the testator's death or at the death of Y if later, the class remains open until X dies.
Contingent class gift, eg. to the children of X who reach 21.	If any child of X has reached 21 at the testator's death, the class closes and includes all children alive at the testator's death who subsequently reach 21. If no child of X has reached 21 at the testator's death, the class closes when the first child of X reaches 21 and includes all children of X alive at that date who subsequently reach 21.
Contingent and deferred class gift, eg. to Y for life, with remainder to the children of X who reach 21.	The class closes at the testator's death if any child of X has reached 21 before the testator's death and Y has predeceased the testator. It closes at Y's death if Y survives the testator and a child of X has reached 21 by Y's death. The class includes all children alive at the death of the testator or Y (whichever is appropriate) who subsequently reach 21. If no child of X has reached 21 by the death of the testator or the death of Y, if later, the class remains open until the first child of X reaches 21 and includes all children alive at that date who subsequently reach 21.

13.4   Protecting personal representatives from unknown beneficiaries and beneficiaries who cannot be found

PRs who distribute the deceased's estate to the wrong beneficiaries are generally personally liable to the true beneficiaries. However, there are steps which the PRs can take to protect themselves from beneficiaries later coming forward and claiming a share in the estate, both where they were unknown to the PRs and where the PRs were aware of the claimant's rights but simply could not find them.

13.4.1   Statutory advertisements

Section 27, Trustee Act 1925 sets out a procedure to be followed before distributing the assets of an estate in order to protect the PRs from both *unknown beneficiaries and creditors*. The procedure was explained fully in relation to creditors in Chapter 12; it is identical for potential beneficiaries (*see* Chapter 12, para. 12.7).

13.4.2   Benjamin Orders

PRs cannot obtain protection from s.27 (*see* 13.4.1) if they are *aware* of the existence of a particular beneficiary but simply cannot find them. It may be that they are unsure whether a given beneficiary is dead or alive. In these circumstances the PRs must apply to the court for a Benjamin Order allowing them to distribute the estate on the assumption that the beneficiary is dead, or on the basis of some other assumption, eg. in one case, on the basis that a child who predeceased the testatrix left no child who survived the testatrix. If the person concerned is later proved to have survived the deceased, they, or their PRs, may recover their share of the estate from the other beneficiaries by means of a tracing claim, but the PRs will be protected from personal liability on the basis of the court order.

The court will only make a Benjamin Order once it is satisfied that the fullest possible enquiries have been made to find the missing claimant. Although the making of any order is not conditional on the PRs having placed statutory advertisements (as per s.27), a Benjamin Order *may* only be granted without further advertising if the court considers that this is unlikely to prove successful in tracing the missing beneficiary.

Note _____

Appropriate alternatives to a Benjamin Order may be for the PRs to obtain insurance cover or to seek an indemnity from the beneficiaries. An insurance company is likely to require the same sort of enquiries as for the granting of a Benjamin order.

Illegitimate and adopted beneficiaries   13.4.3

Illegitimate persons

In the case of a will, references to children include illegitimate and adopted children unless there is an express contrary intention (*see* 13.3.4). This may make it difficult for PRs to ascertain the deceased's children. PRs generally have no statutory protection from overlooking the existence of an illegitimate child. They should therefore:

- Make enquiries of the testator's relatives and known beneficiaries to ascertain whether illegitimate children exist; and

- Place statutory advertisements (as per s.27).

If they consider they may still be at risk, they should take out insurance cover or seek an indemnity from the known beneficiaries.

Note

For the purpose of distribution on intestacy, there is a rebuttable presumption that a child (whether of the deceased or of any other relative) whose mother or father were not married to each other at the time of the child's birth is not survived by his father or anyone claiming through him (*see* Chapter 7, para. 7.6.3).

Adopted children

Section 45, Adoption Act 1976 gives statutory protection to PRs if they distribute an estate in ignorance of an adoption of which they did not have notice.

PRs are not under a duty to enquire whether an adoption has been effected and therefore need not take any special steps to protect themselves.

Failure of gifts made by will   13.5

In ascertaining the beneficial entitlement, the PRs must consider whether any of the gifts made by will have failed for any one of the following reasons:

- Doctrine of lapse;
- Mistake, fraud or undue influence;
- Uncertainty;
- Divorce/nullity of marriage;
- Beneficiary or spouse has witnessed the will;
- Ademption;
- Failure to satisfy a contingency;
- Perpetuity;

- Abatement;
- Disclaimer.

13.5.1 Doctrine of lapse

As a general rule, if a beneficiary under a will predeceases the testator their gift will lapse. If the gift is a non-residuary gift, the property will fall into residue. If the gift is a residuary gift, the property will pass according to the rules of intestacy unless there is a substitutional gift. A gift will not lapse if the beneficiary can be shown to have survived the testator, for however short a period. Where the circumstances of death make it uncertain whether the beneficiary survived the testator, a beneficiary may be deemed to have either survived or predeceased the testator under the doctrine of commorientes (*see* 13.5.2).

Joint tenants

If a gift is made to beneficiaries as joint tenants, the gift will not lapse unless *all* the joint tenants predecease the testator as a surviving joint tenant(s) takes the share of a deceased joint tenant by survivorship.

Example

X leaves her residuary estate to 'A and B jointly'. A predeceases the testator. B takes the whole gift by survivorship.

Tenants in common

If a gift is made to beneficiaries as tenants in common, the share of any beneficiary who predeceases the testator will lapse. For a tenancy in common 'words of severance' will need to be present, eg. 'equally', 'equal shares', 'to be divided between', 'to share amongst'.

Example

X leaves her residuary estate to 'A and B in equal shares'. A predeceases X. A's gift lapses and B takes his half share.

Class gifts

If a gift is a class gift it will not lapse unless all the members of the class predecease the testator.

Example

X leaves her residuary estate to 'my children in equal shares'. The gift will not lapse unless all the children of X have predeceased her.

Survivorship clauses

A testator may wish to prevent a beneficiary from receiving their gift if they survive them for only a very short period, eg. because both die as a result of a common accident. A survivorship clause requires a beneficiary (normally a spouse) to survive the testator by a certain period of time (usually 28 or 30 days). If the beneficiary does not survive the period their gift will lapse (*see* Chapter 4, para. 4.10).

Section 33, Wills Act 1837

Section 33, Wills Act 1837 (as substituted by the Administration of Justice Act 1982) may save gifts made to the testator's children or remoter issue from lapse if the children or remoter issue predecease the testator. It may also alter the effect of class gifts to children or remoter issue where a child or remoter issue predeceases the testator.

Section 33 operates, unless there is *a contrary intention* in the will, and provides that where:

- A will contains a gift to a child or remoter descendant of the testator; *and*
- The intended beneficiary dies before the testator, leaving issue; *and*
- Issue of the intended beneficiary are living at the testator's death;

the gift shall take effect as a gift to the issue living at the time of the testator's death. Section 33(3) further provides that such issue take according to their stock, in equal shares if more than one, any gift or share which their parent would have taken.

Example

Tessa leaves her daughter Una and her son Victor each £10,000 in her will. Una predeceases Tessa leaving, William and Xavier, but Victor survives Tessa. The distribution of the legacy will be as follows.

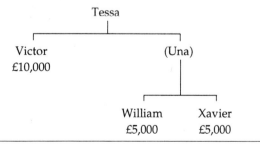

Note that s.33(3) provides that no issue shall take whose parent is living at the testator's death and is so capable of taking.

Example

Ann by her will leaves her daughter Betty, who predeceases

her, a gift of £10,000. Betty had two sons Christopher and David, of whom David also predeceased Ann. Christopher has a daughter Esther, and David died leaving two sons Frederick and George. The distribution of the legacy will be as follows.

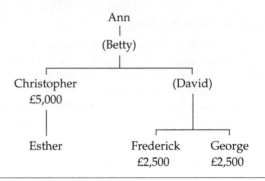

Section 33(2) deals with *class gifts* and provides that, unless there is *a contrary intention* in the will, where:

- A will contains a gift to a class of persons consisting of children or remoter descendants of the testator; and
- A member of the class dies before the testator leaving issue; and
- Issue of that member are living at the testator's death;

the gift takes effect as if the class includes the issue of the deceased member living at the testator's death. The issue take *per stirpes* according to their stock – if more than one in equal shares – the share which their parent would have taken.

Example

By her will Harriet leaves £15,000 'to be shared among all my children'. Harriet has three children, Ian, John and Kate, of whom Kate predeceased her. Kate died leaving two children, Liam and Mandy, who were both alive at Harriet's death and Ian has two children, Nicholas and Olivier. The £15,000 will be distributed as follows:

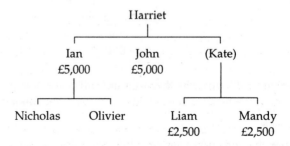

Note that Nicholas and Olivier get nothing as their parent Ian has survived the testatrix Harriet: s.33(3).

Note

In applying s.33 remember that:

● It is irrelevant that the child in question is illegitimate; and

● A child *en ventre sa mere* is treated as living for the purposes of the section.

Commorientes

If the death of the testator and a beneficiary under the will occur close together you must try to establish who died first. If evidence exists that the beneficiary predeceased the testator, however close the deaths, the doctrine of lapse will normally apply.

Where there is no evidence as to the order of death because, for example, the deaths were as a result of a common accident, s.184, Law of Property Act 1925 provides that for the purposes of succession of property the deaths are presumed to have occurred in order of seniority. Thus, the elder is presumed to have died first.

Example

Harry (aged 60) and Wendy (aged 47) die in a car crash leaving their estates to one another. It is uncertain who died first. They had no children and made no substitutional gifts. As Harry is the older, he is presumed to have died first and his estate passes into Wendy's estate. The gift to Harry in Wendy's will lapses as he is deemed to have predeceased her. Her estate passes according to the rules of intestacy.

Note

Section 184 equally applies on intestacy subject to one exception (*see* Chapter 7, para. 7.4.6).

Mistake/fraud and undue influence   13.5.2

Mistake

The knowledge and approval of the testator is required for a valid will (*see* Chapter 1, para. 1.4). This may be absent because of a mistake of the testator or of a draftsman employed by the testator. The mistake may relate to the whole of the will or only to part of it.

Example

In *In the goods of Hunt* (1875) a woman who was living with her sister prepared two wills in similar terms for their respective execution and, by mistake, executed the will of her sister rather than the one she had prepared for herself. Probate of the will was refused as the testatrix would not have executed the sister's will had she known of the contents.

Where a testator includes words they do not know and approve, that part of the will will be omitted from probate.

Example

In *Re Phelan* (1972) a testator executed a home-made will using printed will forms, one of which contained a revocation clause which the testator did not delete. He wrote each disposition on a separate form (in total four) and executed them in succession. It was held that all four wills should be admitted to probate but with the revocation clause in the last three omitted as the testator had inadvertently included the revocation clause in each will.

Similarly, if a draftsman by inadvertence or clerical error, includes words which are contrary to the testator's instructions, those words may be omitted from probate.

If the mistake is as to the *legal effect* of the words used as opposed to the use of the words themselves, the words are admissible to probate. This is so whether the mistake is by the testator or the draftsman.

Rectification

Section 20, Administration of Justice Act 1982 allows the court to order that a will is rectified, either by omitting or inserting words, where it fails to carry out the testator's intentions because of a:

- Clerical error; or
- Failure to understand his instructions.

An application for rectification should be made:

- Within six months of the grant of representation or leave of the court will be required before an application can be made – if the PRs distribute the estate after the expiration of six months, they will not be liable even if the rectification alters the proper distribution of the estate;
- To the registrar; and
- Should be supported by an affidavit setting out the grounds for rectification.

Notice of the application for rectification normally needs to be given to all persons having an interest under the will whose interest might be prejudiced and any written comment of such persons have to be exhibited to the affidavit in support of the application: Rule 55, Non-contentious Probate Rules 1987.

> *Note*
> An application for rectification cannot be made where a probate action has been commenced.

Fraud and undue influence
See Chapter 1, para. 1.5.

Uncertainty   13.5.3

A gift will fail unless the subject matter of the gift and the beneficiaries are identified with sufficient certainty. For example, in one case a gift of 'my blue-chip securities' failed for uncertainty of subject matter and in another, a gift of 'some of my best table linen' likewise failed. A gift to my 'friends' may well fail for uncertainty of objects, as possibly would a gift to 'the son of A' where A had more than one son.

> *Note*
> Some gifts may now be saved from uncertainty by the effects of the s.21, Administration of Justice Act 1982 (*see* 13.3).

Ademption   13.5.4

Where a specific gift is made the gift will fail if the subject matter of the gift does not form part of the testator's estate at the date of their death (*see* Chapter 4, para. 4.5.1). Ademption is likely to occur because the property has either been sold, given away, or destroyed during the testator's lifetime.

Problems may occur if the property has changed in nature since the will was made. This is a particular problem with shares unless the will had been carefully drafted (*see* Chapter 4, para. 4.5.1). If, for instance, the company in which the testator held shares had been taken over since the execution of the will but before the testator's death, it must be decided whether the asset has merely changed in form or whether it has changed in substance. If the latter, the gift will adeem.

Divorce/nullity of marriage   13.5.5

Section 18A, Wills Act 1837 (as substituted by the Administration of Justice Act 1982) provides that where a testator's marriage is dissolved or annulled or declared void after the date of the will, any gift to a former spouse shall lapse except in so far as a contrary intention appears in the will (*see* Chapter 6, paras. 6.7.2–3).

Beneficiary or spouse witnesses the will   13.5.6

Section 15, Wills Act 1837 provides that a gift made to a beneficiary will fail if either the beneficiary or their spouse witness the will. The validity of the will is not affected.

Note that:

- Section 15 only applies to *beneficial gifts*. Thus, if a trustee of a gift or their spouse witness the will, the gift will not fail.

- For s.15 to operate in respect of a spouse of a beneficiary, the person must be the spouse of the beneficiary *at the time the will is executed*. Thus, if, for example, a beneficiary under a will later marries someone who has witnessed the will, s.15 will not invalidate the gift.

- A gift will not fail if there is a *codicil* which confirms the will and which was *not witnessed* by the beneficiary or their spouse.

- Section 1, Wills Act 1968 provides that the attestation of a will by any beneficiaries or their spouses is to be disregarded if without them the will is duly executed.

Example

1 A will is witnessed by Bill, Chris and Davina. Davina is a spouse of a beneficiary, Bill and Chris are neither beneficiaries nor spouses of beneficiaries. Davina's spouse can take their gift.

2 A will is witnessed by Bettina, Charles and Di. Bettina is an independent witness but Charles and Di are beneficiaries under the will. As there is only one independent witness, neither Charles nor Di can take their gifts. They cannot agree, say, that Charles will forfeit his gift and Di will then share his gift with Bettina.

- A charging clause is treated as a legacy in a will. Consequently, if a professional executor witnesses the will they lose their entitlement to charge (*see* Chapter 6, para. 6.1.4).

13.5.7 Failure to satisfy a contingency

Where a gift is contingent, the PRs must ensure that the beneficiary has satisfied the contingency before they transfer their gift to them.

If the beneficiary dies after the testator but before they justify the contingency, the gift will lapse.

13.5.8 Perpetuity

A gift will fail if it infringes the rules against perpetuity or accumulations.

13.5.9 Abatement

A gift will abate wholly or partly if the estate is not large enough to pay all debts and legacies (*see* 13.8.1).

Disclaimer   13.5.10

A beneficiary may decide not to accept the gift which is made to them by will and disclaim the gift (*see* 13.10.1). If the gift is a non-residuary gift it will then pass into residue. If the gift disclaimed is one of residue, it will pass according to the rules of intestacy.

Total and partial intestacy   13.6

The beneficial entitlement on total or partial intestacy has been fully explained in Chapter 7. After payment of funeral, testamentary and administration expenses and debts and other liabilities, the property must be distributed according to the appropriate provisions of the Administration of Estates Act 1925.

Time for distribution of the estate   13.7

PRs are not bound to distribute the estate of the deceased to the beneficiaries before the expiration of one year from the death: s.44, Administration of Estates Act 1925. Thus, although the PR may distribute within one year they cannot be compelled to do so. Thus, even if the will directs that a given legacy is to be paid within, say, six months of the deceased's death, the executors are not bound to pay it until the executor's year has passed – although interest may be payable on a pecuniary legacy (*see* 13.8.2).

PRs should be wary of distributing before the expiration of six months from the date of the testator's death, in case there are claims under the Inheritance (Provision for Family and Dependants) Act 1975 (*see* Chapter 14, para. 14.3).

Pecuniary legacies   13.8

Incidence of pecuniary legacies   13.8.1

If the will expressly provides which part of the estate is to be used for the payment of pecuniary legacies, they should be paid out of that part of the estate.

Most commonly wills expressly provide for pecuniary legacies to be paid out of the *residuary estate*, but there may be an express provision making them payable from elsewhere.

Wills should contain an express provision as to the source of payment of pecuniary legacies because in the absence of such a provision the statutory or common law provisions apply. These are complex and obscure. To understand them we have to distinguish between the situation where a will disposes fully of the testator's property and the situation where a partial intestacy occurs.

Property fully disposed of by will

Here, in the absence of an express provision, the position is governed by the common law. This provides that in the absence of a contrary intention pecuniary legacies are payable from *personalty* comprised in a gift of residue. If there is insufficient personalty, the legacies will abate proportionally.

Realty is not available for payment of pecuniary legacies unless there is an implied contrary intention shown in the will. Such an implied contrary intention will exist if a testator leaves the residue of their estate, both real and personal, to one beneficiary, eg. 'I give all my real and personal property ... to X'. In this situation realty can be used for payment of legacies but only in so far as the personalty has been exhausted: the rule in *Greville v Brown* (1859).

Partial intestacy

Here, in the absence of an express provision in the will providing for payment of legacies, the position depends on whether or not s.33(2), Administration of Estates Act 1925 operates. Section 33(2) will apply if there is a *statutory* trust for sale of the undisposed of share of the residue and the section provides that legacies should be paid out of the undisposed of share.

Example

Tom's will leaves a legacy of £10,000 to James. The residue of Tom's estate is to be divided equally between William and Charlotte. There is no substitutional gift. Charlotte's gift lapses. Ignoring debts, Tom's estate is valued at £100,000. On the assumption that the will contained no express trust for sale of residue and that there is no provision for payment of legacies, William gets £50,000 and the legacy of £10,000 is paid out of Charlotte's half share which passes on intestacy as her gift as lapsed.

However, s.33(2) does *not* apply where there is an *express trust for sale* contained in the will as a statutory and express trust cannot apply to the same property and s.33(7) provides that the statutory trust in s.33 is subject to the express provisions of the will.

Where s.33(2) does not apply, the law is very uncertain.

One argument is that the statutory order for payment of debts (*see* Chapter 12, para. 12.3.2) should be applied to pecuniary legacies, another is that the common law existing before 1925 should be applied under which legacies should be paid from the general estate and not primarily out of undisposed of property.

As the situation is so complex and uncertain it is essential that a will should contain an express provision as to the payment of pecuniary legacies. A will should, in any event, be drafted so as to avoid a partial intestacy!

Interest on pecuniary legacies   13.8.2

The rule that the PRs are not bound to distribute the estate before the expiration of one year from the testator's death (*see* 13.7) applies equally to pecuniary legacies. However, it is often difficult to make payment even within a year and thus, in order to compensate the beneficiaries of pecuniary legacies, if payment is delayed beyond a year they are entitled to interest at 6% per annum unless some other rate of interest is prescribed by the will. Interest will *not* automatically be available, however, once the year has expired if the will provides that the legacy is to be payable subject to a contingency not satisfied at the expiration of one year or where the legacy is payable on a future date not reached at the expiration of one year. In these cases interest is payable from the date when the contingency is satisfied or the specified date is reached.

By way of exception, interest is payable from the date of death where:

- The will stipulates that the legacy is to be *paid immediately* on death;

Note

Such an instruction does not compel the PRs to pay the legacy before the expiration of the executor's year.

- The legacy is paid to *satisfy a debt* owed by the testator;
- The legacy is *charged on real property* owned by the testator;
- The legacy made to a *child of the testator who is under 18* at the testator's death, provided that there exists no other fund for the maintenance;
- The legacy is made to *any minor* (not necessarily being a child of the testator or a child to whom the testator is *in loco parentis*) provided that the will shows an intention to provide for the maintenance of that child.

13.9   Advice on investments and the law on financial services

When you advise about investment, beneficiaries who have received money or other property from an estate, either under a will or the rules of intestacy, you must ensure that you do not infringe the law relating to financial services in giving the advice.

Note

For an explanation of the basics of the law relating to financial services, you must consult the *Pervasives* Companion. The points made here assume prior knowledge and understanding of the essential terminology and framework of the relevant law and are intended only to explain the impact of the Financial Services Act 1986 (FSA) and the Solicitors' Investment Business Rules 1990 (SIBR) on a solicitor who is advising a beneficiary as to how to invest their inheritance.

Where you give advice to a beneficiary who has inherited from an estate of which you are either the PR or acting for the PRs, the advice given is not an act done in the administration of the estate. Consequently, a solicitor/client relationship arises between you and the beneficiary.

Where you personally provide advice and make arrangements to invest the beneficiary's inheritance, this will constitute 'discrete investment business (DIB) with the consequence that you must be authorised to conduct investment business and full compliance with the SIBR is required.

Note

1   DIB will not be involved if an exclusion to the FSA applies, eg. because the proposed investment is not an investment within the Act, or because the activity is an excluded activity listed in Sched. 1, Part III.

2   If you obtain investment advice for a beneficiary through a PTP (Permitted Third party), eg. a stockbroker, most of the SIBR will be avoided. To avoid the obligations of the SIBR by this means, if the beneficiary accepts the advice, the PTP should be instructed to implement the advice on behalf of the beneficiary.

13.10   Post-mortem alterations

It is possible that a person who has been left property by will or who becomes entitled to property under the rules of intestacy may not wish to take the property which has been left to them. This is especially true of entitlement on intestacy because the arbitrary division of an estate in accordance with the provisions of the Administration of Estates Act 1925 may be inappropriate to the circumstances of the deceased's family.

A beneficiary may not wish to take the property because they have sufficient assets of their own and it is better from the tax point of view that the property which is their entitlement passes elsewhere and/or because someone else associated with the deceased is left 'short' due to the benefit which they are to receive. Where this is so, it may be possible to alter the effects of a will or the rules of intestacy by means of either:

- A 'disclaimer'; or
- A 'variation'.

Alterations to the precise entitlement of the beneficiaries may also occur:

- On intestacy when a surviving spouse exercises their right to capitalise their life interest (*see* Chapter 7, para. 7.4.4); or
- Where an order is made in favour of a claimant under the Inheritance (Provision for Family and Dependants) Act 1975 (*see* Chapter 14).

Disclaimer   13.10.1

A disclaimer is simply a rejection by the beneficiary of property left to them under a will or to which they become entitled under the rules of intestacy.

How should a beneficiary disclaim?
The beneficiary need only inform the PRs of their intention to disclaim the property to which they are entitled. This can be done orally, although it is better to give notice in writing. The consent of the PRs is not required.

Note _____

If the tax benefits of a disclaimer are to be claimed, certain formalities must be complied with (*see* below).

Limitations on the right to disclaim
There are three limitations on the right to disclaim:

- A beneficiary cannot disclaim *once they have accepted their entitlement*, eg. by having the property transferred to them or receiving interest or income from the property;
- A beneficiary must disclaim the *whole of their entitlement* under the rules of intestacy or an *entire gift* under a will; it is not possible to disclaim part only;

- If a beneficiary disclaims their gift under a will or their entitlement under the rules of intestacy they *cannot select the person(s) to whom their entitlement should pass in their place*. If a beneficiary disclaims property, the property passes as if the gift to them had failed. Thus, if the property is a *non-residuary gift* in a will, the property will pass into residue. If it is a *residuary gift* it will pass on intestacy unless it forms a class gift or a gift to joint tenants, in which case it will pass to the remaining members of the class/joint tenant(s). If the property is part of the *beneficiary's entitlement on intestacy*, it will either pass to other members of the same class or, if there are none, to the next class of persons entitled.

Example

Andrew is entitled to part of his father's estate on intestacy along with his brothers Bob and Zach. Andrew disclaims his entitlement, Bob and Zach will get a larger share.

If Andrew had no brothers or sisters and disclaimed, and his father left a widow, she would take an enlarged share of the estate as a result of Andrew's disclaimer.

Note

If a beneficiary disclaims a gift made in a will, this does not prevent them from taking on a partial intestacy. They will need to disclaim in both capacities.

A major disadvantage of a disclaimer therefore, is that the beneficiary loses control over the final destination of the property which they have disclaimed. It is often the case that the beneficiary wishes to select the person(s) to take in their place. This can be achieved by means of a *variation* (see 13.10.2).

Taxation aspects

IHT As a general principle, a beneficiary who disclaims their entitlement is treated as having made a transfer of value for IHT purposes. The transfer is a potentially exempt transfer. Thus, subject to exemptions and reliefs, IHT will be payable if the beneficiary dies within seven years of disclaiming. However, if the following conditions are satisfied a disclaimer will not be treated as a transfer of value but instead the deceased will be treated as having left their property to the person(s) entitled once the disclaimer has taken effect: s.142, Inheritance Tax Act 1984:

- The disclaimer must not be made for *consideration in money or money's worth* (other than the making of a disclaimer or variation in respect of another disposition); and
- The disclaimer must be *in writing*; and
- The disclaimer must be made *within two years* of the death.

It may be that the effect of a disclaimer will either increase or decrease the IHT liability of the deceased.

Example _____

A testator leaves a legacy of £100,000 to his spouse. She disclaims the gift which falls into residue, the residuary beneficiaries being the children of the deceased. The legacy to the spouse would have been spouse exempt but as the £100,000 falls into residue and the residuary beneficiaries are non-exempt, more tax will be payable.

_____

CGT Under normal principles a disclaimer constitutes to a disposal by the original beneficiary for CGT purposes. However, provided the conditions set out above for IHT have been satisfied, the property is treated as if left by the deceased to the person(s) entitled once this disclaimer has taken effect: s.62(6), Chargeable Gains Act 1992. As death is not a disposal, no CGT is payable.

Variations   13.10.2

A variation is a direction from a beneficiary to the PRs to transfer some or all of the gifted property to someone other than the original beneficiary. In effect it amounts to an *inter vivos* gift by the original beneficiary to another and as such no formalities need to be satisfied.

A variation *differs* from a disclaimer in that:

- The original beneficiary can *control the final destination* of the property;
- Whereas it is not possible to disclaim part of a gift, it is possible to make a *partial variation*;
- A variation is still possible even where the beneficiary has *accepted the gift*, and even when the administration of the estate is complete.

Taxation aspects

Variations play a very important role in tax planning. Although they are used to redirect property to a family member who is inadequately provided for, they are most likely to be used to reduce the burden of IHT. Common uses are to enable full advantage to be made of the nil-rate band and to avoid 'bunching' of estates.

Example

Wilma has left all her estate to her husband Fred. At Wilma's death, Fred is able to afford to redirect part of his entitlement in Wilma's estate to their children. He effects a variation equivalent to the nil-rate band to be shared among their children immediately.

However, before tax savings are achieved, as with disclaimers, certain conditions have to be satisfied (*see* below).

IHT Normally, as a variation is in effect an *inter vivos* gift by the original beneficiary to another, it is treated as a potentially exempt transfer of the original beneficiary and tax will be payable if the original beneficiary dies within seven years (subject to exemptions and reliefs). However, if the three conditions outlined for disclaimers (*see* IHT disclaimers above) plus the following two further conditions are satisfied, IHT is calculated as if the deceased had left that property to the person to whom it has been directed as a result of the variation. The two further conditions are:

- The beneficiary making the variation must give *written notice* of the election to the Inland Revenue within six months of the variation; and

- If the variation results in *additional tax* being payable by the PRs, the PRs must join the election.

Example

Kirit died leaving all his estate to Hansa. Hansa has sufficient wealth of her own to manage on only part of Kirit's estate. She therefore decides to redirect part of Kirit's estate to her grandchildren.

If the above conditions are not satisfied, Hansa is treated as making a potentially exempt transfer and IHT could become payable if she dies within seven years. However, if the conditions are satisfied, IHT is calculated as if Kirit made a transfer of the part of the estate elected by Hansa to the grandchildren. As Hansa (being a spouse) was an exempt beneficiary, no tax would have been payable but for the variation. As the grandchildren are non-exempt beneficiaries, IHT may become payable on the part of the estate transferred to them and so the PRs must join the election.

CGT As a variation is in effect an *inter vivos* gift of the original beneficiary to another, it is a disposal for CGT purposes. However, if the same conditions as are required for IHT purposes (*see* above) are satisfied, apart from the requirement of the PRs joining the election, the variation will not be treated as a disposal but as if the deceased had left the property to the person entitled under the variation (death not being a disposal).

Note

It is possible to make an election for CGT purposes and not for IHT purposes or vice versa.

It may be advisable not to make an election for CGT purposes if:

- The property, the subject of the gift to the original beneficiary, *decreases in value* as it may amount to a loss which can be set off against other gains of the original beneficiary;

- The property has *increased in value* but not above the annual exemption (currently £5,800) as the person benefiting from the variation can take the benefit of the increased acquisition value. If an election is made, this acquisition value would be the value at the deceased's death.

Note

The indexation allowance may mean there is no chargeable gain. If this is so it does not matter whether or not an election is made.

The final stages of administration   13.11

Having paid the deceased's funeral, testamentary and administration expenses, debts and any legacies given by any will left by the deceased, the PRs will have reached the final stages of administration.

These involve the final distribution of the residuary estate to the beneficiaries entitled (interim payments may well have been made earlier) after making any adjustments to the IHT assessment and paying any income tax and CGT for which the PRs are liable.

Once these tax matters have been dealt with and the residuary estate has been distributed the estate accounts can be drawn up.

IHT   13.11.1

Before they can obtain a grant of representation, the PRs will have to submit an Inland Revenue account and pay the IHT on non-instalment option property (*see* Chapter 10, para. 10.4.2). The Inland Revenue account amounts to self-assessment of the IHT liability due on death. However, during the course of administration the assessment may need adjusting as either additional tax becomes payable or a refund is needed for one or more of the following reasons:

- *Lifetime transfers* made by the deceased within seven years of death come to light;
- *Further assets* of the deceased are discovered after submitting the Inland Revenue account;
- *Further liabilities* of the deceased are discovered after submitting the Inland Revenue account;
- The *tax liability* (income tax or CGT) of the deceased as entered in the Inland Revenue account is altered after negotiation between the PRs and the Inland Revenue and this decreases the deceased's liability;
- *Formal valuations* may differ from the provisionally estimated values entered in the Inland Revenue account. There is often protracted negotiation on the value of assets such as shares in a private company (negotiated with the shares valuation division of the Inland Revenue) and land (negotiated with the district valuer);
- *Sales* made by the PRs have given rise to IHT 'loss relief' (*see* Chapter 12, para. 12.6.3);
- A post-death *disclaimer or variation* has resulted in an alteration in the liability to pay IHT (*see* 13.10).

Inland Revenue corrective account
Once any adjustments have been made to the IHT liability because of the factors listed above, the PRs must submit a corrective account on form CAPD-3 (unless only very minor adjustments are to be made, where a letter to the Capital Taxes Office is sufficient). Form CAPD-3 does not involve a self-assessment of the IHT but is simply a form signed by the PRs disclosing all matters resulting in the need to make adjustments. On submission, the Capital Taxes Office makes a final IHT assessment. If any further IHT is payable, this should then be paid by the PRs. Conversely, if the PRs have overpaid, repayment should be requested.

IHT clearance certificate
The final step to be taken is to obtain from the Capital Taxes Office a certificate of discharge from any further claim to IHT. The effect of the certificate is to:

- *Discharge* the PRs (and all other persons liable for IHT) from further liability to IHT unless there has been fraud or non-disclosure of material facts; and

- *Extinguish* any Inland Revenue charge which has been imposed on the deceased's property for IHT.

The certificate of discharge is obtained by the PRs completing IHT Form CAP 30 and submitting it to the Capital Taxes Office.

Where IHT is being paid by instalments, the PRs cannot obtain a certificate of discharge with respect to the instalment option property. Such a certificate can be obtained for the rest of the property and once the instalments have been paid the PRs can apply for a full certificate of discharge.

Note

As the PRs are liable for outstanding instalments on instalment option property, they will have to make arrangements for the payments to be made before distributing the rest of the residuary estate.

Income tax and CGT   13.11.2

Income tax
The PRs must submit a return for each income tax year (or part) during the administration period for income they receive on the deceased's assets. Before the residuary estate is fully distributed, the PRs must ensure such tax has been paid.

CGT
Although on death there is no disposal for CGT purposes, if the PRs sell chargeable assets in the course of the administration of the deceased's estate, they will be liable for CGT on any chargeable gains they make (*see* Chapter 12.6.3). Such liability must also be discharged before the residuary estate is fully distributed.

Transfer of assets to residuary beneficiaries   13.11.3

If the residuary beneficiaries are adults and they have a *vested interest* in the residuary estate, their entitlement can be transferred to them. If they have only a *contingent interest*, the property must be transferred to trustees to hold on their behalf.

Where the beneficiary is a *minor*, whether their interest is vested or contingent, the property will normally be held by the PRs on trust for them until they reach 18 and any contingency is satisfied. However, the following alternative options are available in the following circumstances:

- Where the gift is one made by will and the will contains a *minor receipt clause* (*see* Chapter 4, para. 4.11.3), the PRs may be able to transfer the minor's share to the beneficiary themselves (usually only if aged 16 or over) or to a parent or guardian of the minor.

- Where the *minor has a vested interest in the residuary estate*, the PRs may transfer the subject matter of the minor's gift to two trustees or a trust corporation to hold until the beneficiary reaches 18: s.42, Administration of Estates Act 1925 (*see* Chapter 11, para. 11.4.3). It is common to use this provision to transfer the minor beneficiary's gift to their parents to hold on trust for them until they reach 18.

Method of transfer

The method of transfer to a residuary beneficiary (under a will or through the operation of the rules of intestacy) or to trustees on their behalf, depends upon the nature of the property comprised in the residuary estate.

1   *Personal property* In relation to personal property the general rule is that no particular form of transfer is required. Thus, if the property is given *in specie*, it can simply be handed over (delivered) to the beneficiary.

The following items of personal property do require specific steps to be taken:

- *Money* left in the estate is transferred by means of a cheque drawn on the PRs' bank account or solicitor's cheque account (as appropriate);
- *National Saving certificates* and *money from National Saving accounts* require special withdrawal forms;
- *Company shares* require a share transfer form – the beneficiary then applies to be registered as a shareholder in the company in the place of the deceased.

2   *Freehold and leasehold land* The PRs should vest the legal estate in the person entitled (whether as trustee or beneficially) by means of an assent. By s.36(4), Administration of Estates Act 1925 an assent must:

- Be *in writing*;
- Be *signed by the PRs*;
- *Name* the person in whose favour it is made.

Note ─────────────────────────────

1   A deed is unnecessary to pass the legal estate but the PRs must use a deed if they wish to obtain an *indemnity covenant* from the beneficiary. This they will want to protect themselves if they will remain liable on the covenants, eg. where the deceased was an original lessee or where indemnity covenants have been made.

2   If the PRs are to continue to hold the property in the *capacity of trustees*, they should vest the property in themselves in the changed capacity by means of an assent. (The law is unclear

whether this is, in fact, necessary, but to avoid any doubt it is wise to take this simple step.)

3   If the title to the land is *registered*, the assent must be in the form specified by the Land Registration Rules 1925.

Estate accounts   13.11.4

The PRs must produce estate accounts for the residuary beneficiaries. The purpose is to show what is available to the residuary beneficiaries after the payment of all the expenses, debts and other liabilities. The accounts will show how the entitlement of each beneficiary is to be paid, ie. whether in cash or *in specie* or in a combination of both.

The estate accounts are presented to the residuary beneficiaries for approval. If they approve, the residuary beneficiaries sign and acknowledge receipt of the amount due. The effect of this is to discharge the PRs from further liability to the beneficiaries in the absence of fraud or failure to disclose assets.

There is no prescribed form for estate accounts. However, it is important that they are set out in a clear and simple manner so that they can be understood by the residuary beneficiaries. The accounts usually start with a narrative to make them easier to follow. This normally includes the following issues:

- Deceased's date of death;
- Date of grant of representation;
- Summary of gifts in the will (or of the effect of the rules of intestacy);
- Value of gross and net estate;
- Details of interim payment received by residuary beneficiaries;
- How the beneficiaries are to be paid (cash/*in specie*).

The accounts may be presented vertically, ie. showing assets less liabilities, or they may be horizontal showing receipts on one side and payments on the other. The accounts are usually divided into a capital account and an income account. This may not be so in the case of a very small estate unless a life interest or minority interest has been created in the residue so that the beneficiaries entitlement is divided between capital and income.

Self-assessment questions

1   You are acting for the PRs of the estate of Joan Clark who died leaving the following gifts by a home-made will:

'(1) I leave my Morris Minor to my nephew Ted.'

(2) I leave my money to father.'

You are told that:

● Joan Clark owns two Morris Minor cars at the date of her death; and

● She has two nephews by the name of Ted alive at her death; and

6   Cederic dies leaving a home-made will as follows:

'£500 to Cancer Research.'

'£2,000 to my niece Annabel.'

'The rest of my estate to be divided between my two sons, Brian and Charles.'

Brian predeceases his father. Out of which part of the estate will the legacies be paid?

Would your answer be different if Brian had not predeceased Cederic?

7   Barry died leaving £100,000 to each of his two sons Christopher and John, the residue to pass to his spouse, Eileen. Christopher had tried to persuade his father to leave his share of the estate to his children as he thought this would be better in the long run from the tax point of view.

Is there any way in which Christopher's wishes can be given effect to now that his father is dead? Explain your answer.

8   What is, and what is the effect of, an IHT clearance certificate.

Answer guidance to self-assessment questions

1   *Gift (1)*

There are latent ambiguities in describing both the Morris Minor and the nephew Ted (*see* 13.3.2). Extrinsic evidence of the testator's intention is admissible to explain which Morris Minor and which nephew Joan Clark was referring to. If no evidence is available the gift will fail for uncertainty.

Gift (2)

'Father' The armchair principle (*see* 13.3.2) can be applied to allow extrinsic evidence to be admitted to explain that the reference to 'father' was in fact intended to refer to the close uncle of Jean.

'My money' This term is *prima facie* uncertain and will cause the gift to fail unless extrinsic evidence is available under s.21, Administration of Justice Act 1982 (*see* 13.3.2) to explain how Jean Clark used the term.

2   (a) The class closes at A's death and includes only the one child of B alive at that date.

(b) The class closes at A's death if B has predeceased A or at B's death if B survives A and includes only children alive at the relevant date.

(c) The class closes at A's death and includes the three children of B alive at that date, in the case of the younger two if they reach 25.

(d) The class closes at A's death if B predeceased A and includes the same beneficiaries as in (c). If B survives A the class closes at B's death if one child of B is aged 25 and includes all the children of B alive who may attain 25.

3   *See* 13.4.2.

4   Section 33 will operate (*see* 13.5.1; s.33, Wills Act 1837). The distribution of the gifts is shown below.

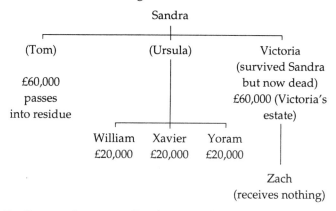

5   Commorientes applies (*see* 13.5.1).

Paul, being the older, is presumed to have predeceased Simon. His property therefore passes into the estate of Simon. As Paul predeceases Simon the gift of property in Paul's will to Simon lapses and Paul's estate is distributed according to the rules of intestacy.

6   *See* 13.8.1.

As Brian and Charles take as tenants in common, there is a partial intestacy. Section 33(2) operates and the legacies are paid out of the residue of the estate before the division to Brian and Charles is made.

If Brian did not predecease his father, the estate would be fully disposed of by will and the common law would apply to make the legacies payable out of residuary personalty. If there is insufficient personalty, the legacies will abate proportionately.

7   Discuss a variation (*see* 13.10.2). Explain that a disclaimer (*see* 13.10.1) will not achieve Christopher's aims as he cannot control the destination of the property. If he disclaims, his share will pass into residue.

Explain the steps which need to be taken from the IHT point of view so that the variation does not operate as a PET of Christopher.

8   *See* 13.11.1.

Chapter 14

Family provision

Introduction

As a general principle people can dispose of their property on death as they like. Not even the closest of relatives has a *right* to a testator's property. However, the Inheritance (Provision for Family and Dependants) Act 1975 (I(PFD)A) limits testamentary freedom to a certain extent. The court has power to order financial provision

out of the net estate of the deceased for the benefit of persons falling within the Act. The Act also applies where the rules of intestacy fail to make 'reasonable financial provision' for persons falling within the Act's protection.

The aims of this chapter are to:

● Outline the categories of applicants protected by the I(PFD)A; and

● Explain the circumstances in which an application by such persons is likely to be successful.

We also consider:

● What property is available for the grant of financial provision under the Act;

● The form that such provision may take, and:

● What provisions exist to prevent evasion of the Act.

Relevance of the Act in practice

You need to be aware of the provisions of the I(PFD)A in three distinct types of circumstances:

1   *In advising clients on the making of a will.* You should make a client aware of the possible effects of the I(PFD)A where you believe that the testator's proposals may expose their estate to a successful claim under the I(PFD)A following their death (*see* 14.4).

2   *In advising personal representatives in the administration of an estate.* Personal representatives need to consider the possibility of a claim on an estate and should not distribute the estate until the time limit for applications under the I(PFD)A has expired (*see* 14.3).

3   In order to act *for a claimant under the I(PFD)A against an estate.* In this situation you must remember the *rules of professional conduct.* A solicitor cannot act for a claimant under the Act if they or their firm is already acting for the

personal representatives of the estate or if they or their firm advised the testator in connection with the will. This is because a clear conflict of duty and interest will arise.

Note

All references in this chapter are to Inheritance (Provision for Family and Dependants) Act 1975 unless otherwise stated.

14.2   Jurisdiction and choice of court

14.2.1   Out of court settlements

If all the beneficiaries under the will and/or rules of intestacy are *sui juris* when the claim under the I(PFD)A is brought against the estate, they can try to reach agreement with any claimant under the Act. Obviously out of court settlements are to be encouraged because of the cost of litigation, potential delay in the distribution of the estate, and the bitterness which may result from ongoing litigation. Having said this, it is often difficult to advise clients as to level of awards because of the limited number of reported cases.

If the firm is acting for the claimant and the claim cannot be settled out of court, the matter will normally be put in the hands of the firm's litigation department.

14.2.2   Jurisdiction

The Act only applies where the deceased died domiciled in England and Wales after 31 March 1976: s.1(1). It does not apply to persons who die domiciled in Scotland.

14.2.3   Choice of court

An application under the Act may be made either to the Chancery Division or to the Family Division of the High Court, which have unlimited jurisdiction, or to the County Court, for which there is now no financial limit.

Where an application is made to the High Court it does not normally matter whether the application is made in the Chancery or the Family Division. However, there may be instances where there is a particular advantage in choosing. For example, if the validity of the will which is alleged not to make 'reasonable financial provision' for applicants within the Act is also in dispute, the Chancery Division would be more appropriate.

14.3   Time limits for applications

Applications must normally be made within six months of the date of the first effective grant of representation: s.4. The time limit is relatively short in order to enable the personal representatives to distribute the estate.

Practical implications

The Act provides that personal representatives can distribute the estate after the six months without personal liability: s.20. Caution is therefore required in distributing an estate before the expiry of the six month period but personal representatives will normally be safe in paying a legacy to a beneficiary who is making an application under the Act to obtain more (unless there are stronger applications likely from others) and it will probably be safe to distribute assets to a beneficiary who has a strong moral claim on the deceased, especially where such person has an urgent need. Personal representatives may also pay funeral, testamentary, and administration expenses, debts and liabilities, including tax due on the estate before the expiry of six months, as claims under the Act are only payable out of the deceased's *net* estate (*see* 14.7).

Late applications

The court has discretion to allow applications outside the normal six month period. The Act gives no guidance as to how the court should exercise its discretion, but the following guidelines (which were not intended to be exhaustive) were laid down in *Re Dennis* (1981). The court will:

- Require applicants to show that they have an *arguable case* under the Act, ie. 'a case fit to go to trial';
- Place the onus on the applicant to show *special reasons* (which must be substantial) for taking the matter out of the general six months time limit;
- Consider the *circumstances surrounding the delay* and how promptly and in what circumstances the application has been made after the time has expired;
- Consider whether *negotiations* have started within the six month period;
- Take into account whether the estate has been *distributed* before the claim under the Act was notified?
- Consider whether refusal of leave to bring proceedings out of time will leave the applicant *without recourse* to anyone else, eg. possibly, a negligent solicitor.

Where the court extends the time limit for an application the personal representatives will not be personally liable if the assets of the estate have already been distributed (s.20) but there is a power to recover from the beneficiaries any part of the estate already distributed.

14.3.3   Standing search

When acting for a claimant under the I(PFD)A, to ensure that the claim is brought within the proper time limit you can make a standing search to the probate registry. This will reveal the issue of any grant with respect to the estate in question during the preceding six months and ensure that the claimant is notified of any grant issued in the following 12 months.

A standing search will enable the claimant to discover the names and addresses of the PRs (and of any solicitor acting for them) and will also ensure knowledge of the date by which a claim should be brought.

14.4   Categories of applicant

Section 1(1) allows five categories of applicant to apply to the court on the grounds that either the deceased's will or the rules of intestacy or a combination of both, do not make reasonable financial provision for the applicant.

- The spouse of the deceased.
- A former spouse who has not remarried.
- A child of the deceased.
- A person (not being a child of the deceased) who is treated by the deceased as a *child of the family* in connection with a marriage to which the deceased was a party.
- Any person (not being a person included in the foregoing paragraphs) who immediately before the death of the deceased was being maintained wholly or partly by the deceased, ie. a *dependant*.

14.4.1   The spouse of the deceased

This category includes a *judicially separated* spouse and a party to a *voidable marriage* which has not been annulled prior to the deceased's death.

It also includes a party to a *void marriage* so long as that the applicant entered into the marriage in good faith unless, during the deceased's lifetime:

- The marriage was dissolved or annulled; or
- The applicant entered a later marriage.

Note

A judicially separated spouse may be barred from applying for provision by an order of the court made on the application of the other spouse on or after the decree of judicial separation: s.15.

A former spouse who has not remarried

A former spouse is a person whose marriage with the deceased was dissolved or annulled during the deceased's lifetime either:

- By a decree of divorce or nullity granted under the law of any part of the British Islands; or
- Overseas, by a divorce or annulment recognised as valid by English law.

Either party to a marriage may ask the court in divorce or nullity proceedings to ban the other party from bringing a claim under the Act: s.15 and s.15A (as amended by Matrimonial and Family Proceeding Act 1984). If such an order is made, the court may not entertain an application.

In *Re Fullard* (1982) the Court of Appeal pointed out that in view of the court's powers to make appropriate financial provision in matrimonial proceedings, including capital adjustments between spouses, there will be comparatively few cases where a former spouse will succeed in an application under the Act. Circumstances where a former spouse might succeed include situations where substantial capital is released by the death of the deceased, eg. insurance or pension policies, or where the deceased has only been ordered to make periodic payments to the spouse on matrimonial proceedings, but the deceased leaves a reasonable amount of capital.

A child of the deceased

This category includes a child *en ventre sa mere*, a child of a relationship outside marriage, a legitimated child or an adopted child, although an adopted child cannot make a claim against a natural parent: *Re Collins dec'd* (1991). There is no age restriction and marriage is not, of itself, a bar to a claim.

Note _____

The courts will not look sympathetically upon an application from adult able-bodied children (whether male or female) who are capable of earning their own living: *Re Coventry* (1980); *Williams v Johns* (1988).

A child of the family

The principle of a 'child of the family' comes from family law although to 'qualify' under the Act a child need only be treated as a child of the family by the *deceased*, and not by both parties as in matrimonial legislation.

Treatment of a person as a child of the family refers to the behaviour of the deceased towards that person and involves the assuming of the position of a parent towards the applicant in terms of the responsibilities and privileges of the parent/child relationship. Mere displays of affection or hospitality are not sufficient.

Note

The category is not restricted to minor or dependent children, and applies even to persons who are adults when the deceased married their parent: *Re Callaghan* (1985).

14.4.5   A dependant

This category is not confined to relatives of the deceased or even members of the deceased's household, and it covers persons who had no enforceable right to maintenance against the deceased during the deceased's lifetime.

No minimum period of dependence on the deceased is prescribed by the Act, but the length of dependence is a matter to which the court must have regard in deciding whether and in what manner to make an order (*see* 14.6).

The maintenance must be immediately before the death of the deceased. However, this requirement is fairly liberally interpreted.

Example

In *Re Beaumont* (1980) the requirement was found to be satisfied where the deceased had habitually maintained the applicant but had not been able to do so while in hospital for a number of weeks immediately before her death. Megarry VC said that the court must look at 'the settled basis or ... general arrangement between the parties'.

The maintenance of the applicant may be in whole or in part, but s.1(3) provides that a person is only treated as maintained by the deceased 'if the deceased otherwise than for full valuable consideration was making a *substantial* contribution in money or money's worth towards the reasonable needs of that person'.

Note the following points about this requirement.

- The *burden of proof* lies on the applicant to establish that this requirement has been satisfied: *Re Wilkinson* (1978).
- The contribution must be *'a substantial contribution'* either in money or *'money's worth'*. In *Jelley v Iliffe* (1981), for example, the Court of Appeal held that the provision of rent free accommodation was substantial.
- Once it has been established that the contribution is substantial, the applicant must next show that it was *'other-*

wise than for full valuable consideration'. Note that the consideration may be full valuable consideration even if it is not provided under a contract: *Re Beaumont* (1980); *Jelley v Iliffe* (1981). Services to the deceased, including companionship are capable of amounting to full valuable consideration. The question to be decided is, do the services rendered by the applicant to the deceased outweigh the contribution made by the deceased to the applicant's maintenance? It is a question of fact in each case.

Example

In *Bishop v Plumley* (1991) the Court of Appeal held that the devoted care and nursing provided by the applicant did not amount to full valuable consideration for the rent free accommodation of the deceased.

The test of reasonable financial provision   14.5

The court may only order provision for an applicant under the Act if it is satisfied that either the will, or the rules of intestacy, or a combination of both do not make 'reasonable financial provision' for the applicant: s.2(1).

Section 1(2) sets down two different standards of financial provision:

- The *surviving spouse standard*; and
- The *maintenance standard*.

The Act sets down some guidelines common to all applicants (*see* 14.5.3) and guidelines limited to a particular category to assist in determining whether there is 'reasonable financial provision' (*see* 14.5.4).

The test of whether reasonable financial provision has been made is an objective test. It is therefore irrelevant to consider whether the deceased acted reasonably and consequently it is irrelevant whether the deceased knew all the material facts. However, if a testator has reasons for making no provision, or limited provision, for a relative or dependent, they should give details of those reasons with their will. These will then be considered by the court which take them into account to the extent that they are valid.

In deciding whether reasonable financial provision has been made the court takes into account the facts as known to the court at the date of the hearing: s.3(5). This, therefore, includes events occurring after the deceased's death.

The surviving spouse standard   14.5.1

Reasonable financial provision at the surviving spouse

standard is 'such financial provision as it would be reasonable in all the circumstances of the case for a husband or wife to receive whether or not that provision is required for his or her maintenance': s.1(2)(a). This standard is more generous than the maintenance standard applying to other applicants and is broadly that which a spouse would expect to obtain if the marriage had been ended by divorce, rather than death.

The surviving spouse standard is applicable to the deceased husband or wife. The court has discretion to apply this standard where a decree of divorce, nullity or judicial separation has been made within 12 months of the deceased's death and no order for financial provision has been made or refused in matrimonial proceedings: s.14.

14.5.2 The maintenance standard

Reasonable financial provision at the maintenance standard means 'such financial provision as it would be reasonable in all the circumstances of the case for the applicant to receive for his maintenance': s.1(2)(b).

The term 'maintenance' is not on the one hand confined to provision at a subsistence level, but on the other hand 'it does not mean anything which may be regarded as reasonably desirable for (the applicant's) general benefit or welfare': per Goff LJ in *Re Coventry* (1980). Buckley LJ in *Re Coventry*, suggested that it means 'such provision as would be reasonable in all the circumstances of the case to enable the applicant to maintain himself in a manner suitable to those circumstances'. In *Re Dennis* (1981) Browne-Wilkinson J described the maintenance standard as enabling the applicant 'to discharge the cost of his daily living at whatever standard of living is appropriate to him'.

14.5.3 The common guidelines

Section 3(1) sets down guidelines common to all applicants to assist the court in deciding whether the deceased has made 'reasonable financial provision' for the applicant, and also to help the court to decide whether to exercise its discretion under the Act to make an order (*see* 14.6).

Under s.3(1) the court must have regard to the following matters:

1   The financial resources and needs of the applicant, any other applicant, and any beneficiary now or in the foreseeable future: s.3(1)(a)–(c).

Earning capacity, pensions and social security benefits are all relevant, as are the applicant's capital assets. In considering an applicant's financial needs the court must take into account their financial obligations and responsibilities: s.3(6).

Note
The guideline refers not only to present financial needs but also those likely in the foreseeable future.

2   Any obligations and responsibilities of the deceased towards the applicant or any beneficiary: s.3(1)(d). If the estate is not large enough for the deceased to discharge all their obligations, the court will have to weigh up conflicting claims.

3   The size and nature of the net estate of the deceased. In *Re Fullard* (1982) Ormrod LJ suggested that, in order to discourage applications in respect of very small estates, where the cost of the action may exhaust a large part of the assets of the estate, judges should consider ordering the costs of an unsuccessful application to be borne by the applicant rather than as normal, by the estate.

Note
In the light of the above you should consider the question of costs when advising clients who wish to make an application under the Act, especially against a small estate; legal aid authorities should be informed of the likely effects of an application and an appeal on an estate in cases where legal aid has been applied for.

4   Any physical or mental disability of any applicant or any beneficiary: s.3(1)(f). The availability of state aid, such as free hospital accommodation, is a factor to be taken into account: *Re Watkins* (1949).

5   Any other matter including the conduct of the applicant or any other person: s.3(1)(g). This covers the conduct of the deceased as well as that of any applicant or any beneficiary. In *Williams v Johns* (1988) the applicant's conduct which caused shame and emotional distress to her adoptive mother was taken into account in dismissing her claim.

The particular guidelines   14.5.4

Section 3 also provides that without prejudice to the common guidelines the court will consider the following additional guidelines in relation to particular categories.

1   *The surviving spouse.* The court will consider the:

● Age of the applicant and the duration of the marriage; and

- Contribution made by the applicant to the welfare of the family of the deceased, including any contribution made in looking after the home or caring for the family; and

- Provision that the applicant might reasonably have expected to receive if on the day on which the deceased died, the marriage, instead of being terminated by death, had been terminated by a decree of divorce: s.3(2).

2 *Former spouse*. The court will consider the first two guidelines above as for a surviving spouse, but only the third if the court has exercised its discretion to apply the surviving spouse standard (*see* 14.5.1).

3 *A child of the deceased*. The only particular guideline here is the manner in which the applicant was being, or in which they might be expected, to be educated or trained: s.3(3).

4 *A child of the family*. In addition to the education guideline applying to a child of the deceased, the following particular guidelines are set down:

- Whether the deceased had assumed any responsibility for the applicant's maintenance and, if so, the extent to which and the basis on which the deceased assumed that responsibility and the length of time for which the deceased discharged that responsibility; and

- Whether in assuming and discharging the responsibility the deceased knew that the applicant was not his own child; and

- The liability of any other person to maintain the applicant: s.3(3).

5 *A person maintained by the deceased*. The particular guideline for this category of applicant is the extent to which and the basis upon which the deceased had assumed responsibility for the maintenance of the applicant and the length of time for which the deceased discharged that responsibility: s.3(4).

In *Re Beaumont* (1980), Megarry VC expressed the view that this guideline required proof that the deceased has assumed responsibility before an application could be made. However, in *Jelley v Iliffe* (1981), the Court of Appeal decided that no overt act is necessary to raise the presumption that the deceased has assumed responsibility; as a general rule, proof that the deceased was maintaining the applicant raises a presumption that responsibility had been assumed. Nevertheless, the presumption of assumed responsibility can be rebutted, it would seem, by the testator leaving a statement to the effect that there has been no assumption of responsibility for maintenance.

Criteria for deciding whether and in what manner to make an order   14.6

If the court decides using the common and particular guidelines that the will or rules of intestacy or a combination of both do not make 'reasonable financial provision' for the applicant at the appropriate standard (either the surviving spouse standard or the maintenance standard), the court must still decide whether or not to make provision and, if so, the manner in which provision should be ordered. This is a question of discretion which the court decides upon by using the same common and particular guidelines and standards used to decide whether there is 'reasonable financial provision' in the first place.

As with ascertaining whether reasonable financial provision has been made, when deciding whether and in what manner to make an order, the court takes into account facts known to the court at the date of the hearing: s.3(5).

Property available for financial provision   14.7

If the court decides to make an order in favour of a person falling within the categories of applicant set out in s.1(1), the order is made against the 'net estate' of the deceased. Section 25 defines 'net estate'.

Assets can be divided for the purpose of s.25 into property which is always included in the net estate, and property included only if the court so orders.

Property always included in net estate   14.7.1

1   Property which the deceased had power to dispose by his will (otherwise than by virtue of a special power of appointment) less the amount of his funeral, testamentary and administration expenses, debts and liabilities including any inheritance tax payable out of his estate on death.

Note _____

This category does not include benefits under assurance policies on the life of the deceased where the proceeds are payable directly to the beneficiary rather than to the estate. However, category 2 in 14.7.2 below may be applicable to such assets.

_____

2   Property in respect of which the deceased held a general power of appointment (not being a power exercisable by will) which has not been exercised. If the power is exercisable by will, the property falls within 1 above, whether or not the deceased has exercised the power.

3 Any sum of money or other property nominated to any person by the deceased under a statutory nomination or received by any person from the deceased as a *donatio mortis causa* less any inheritance tax payable in respect of such property and borne by the nominee or donee: ss.8 and 25(1).

14.7.2   Property included in 'net estate' only if the court so orders

1 The deceased's severable share of any property of which they were a beneficial joint tenant immediately before death. The court shall to such an extent as it appears to the court to be just in the circumstances (and after allowing for any inheritance tax payable) treat the deceased's severable share as part of the net estate.

> *Note*
>
> The discretion only exists where the application has been made within the normal time limit (*see* 14.3). Section 9(4) expressly provides that for the purposes of the section there may be a joint tenancy of a chose in action, eg. an account at a bank.

2 Any property which the court directs shall be available as a result of its powers to prevent evasion of the Act (*see* 14.8).

14.8   Forms of provision which the court may make

Under s.2(1) the court may make any one or more of the following orders once it is satisfied that the disposition of the deceased's estate does not make 'reasonable financial provision' for the applicant:

1 *Periodic payments* – such an order may provide for periodical payments:

- Of a specified sum, or
- Equal to the whole, or a specific part of the income of the net estate; or
- Equal to the whole of the income of such part of the net estate as the court directs to be set aside or appropriated; or
- To be determined in any way the court thinks fit.

Periodic payments are payable for the period specified in the court order. In the case of a former spouse the Act provides that an order shall cease to have effect on the remarriage of the former spouse: s.19(2). In any other case the court must lay down the date of termination when it makes the order.

2 A *lump sum payment* (such payments may be by instalments).

3 To *transfer a particular asset* of the deceased's net estate to the applicant, eg. the family home.

4 An *order to settle property* comprised in the deceased's net estate, for the benefit of the applicant. (This is particularly likely where the applicant is a minor or is otherwise in need of protection.)

5 The *acquisition of property* for transfer or for settlement.

6 The *variation of an ante-nuptial or post-nuptial settlement* (including one made by will) made on the parties to a marriage of the deceased.

Note that orders for periodic payments and amounts and dates for payments where a lump sum payment is payable by instalments may be varied, but apart from this an order once made cannot be varied: s.6.

Note _____

1 The most common types of order in practice are orders for a lump sum payment or for the transfer of a particular asset to the claimant.

2 If the court makes a periodic payments order or a lump sum order it may direct which part of the estate is to bear the burden.

3 The court has power to make an interim order in favour of an applicant if it appears to the court that the applicant is in immediate need of financial assistance but it is not yet possible to determine what order (if any) should be made; and property forming part of the net estate of the deceased is or can be made available to meet the needs of the applicant: s.5(1).

Burden of the order   14.9

Where the court makes an order under the Act, it can make the order against any part of the net estate of the deceased. The order is not automatically made out of the residue of the estate. Where a beneficiary loses out because the order of the court is made against their share of the estate, the court may order that other beneficiaries of the estate hand over part of their entitlement to the beneficiary who has lost out on account of the claim.

Example _____

Sam has left a house worth £75,000 to Bryony. He has also left a legacy of £70,000 to Bill and the residue of his estate to Frank. Judith makes a successful claim against Sam's estate under the Act. The court orders that the house left to Bryony be transferred to Judith. It may also order that Bill pay part of his legacy, or Frank part of his share in the residue to Bryony.

14.10   Inheritance tax consequences of orders

The court is deemed to have altered the disposition of the estate of the deceased from the date of death of the deceased for all purposes including the payment of inheritance tax. Thus, for example, if an order increases the amount passing to a child of the deceased at the expense of the surviving spouse, the chargeable value of the estate will be increased as part of the spouse exemption will be lost.

14.11   Anti-avoidance provisions

In order to defeat an application made under the Act a person may attempt to give away property *inter vivos* so as to reduce the value of their net estate at death, or to enter into a binding contract to leave property by will and so reduce the value of their net estate. Sections 10–13 give the court power to stop an evasion of claims for provision by either of these methods.

Applicants who apply to the court for an order making provision for them, may also apply in the same proceedings for an anti-evasion order compelling the 'donee' under such a disposition or contract to provide money or other property for the purpose of making financial provision for the applicant.

An anti-evasion order can also be made against the 'donee's' PR or trustee.

14.11.1   Requirements before an anti-evasion order can be made

Before the court can make an anti-evasion order the court must be satisfied on the following three matters.

> *Note*
>
> The requirement is one of the alternatives in 1 below *plus* 2, *plus* 3.

1   *Either* of the following exists:

- An *inter vivos* disposition was made less than six years before the date of the death of the deceased for less than full valuable consideration; *or*

- A contract entered into after 31 March 1976 whereby the deceased agreed to leave money or other property by will or agreed that money or other property would be paid or transferred to any person from his estate, and when the contract was made full valuable consideration was not given or promised.

Note

An *inter vivos* disposition here includes any payment of money and any conveyance of property whether or not made by instrument, but does not include:

- A statutory nomination;

- A *donatio mortis causa*; or

- An appointment of property under a special power.

2   The disposition or contract was made with the intention of defeating an application under the Act. Section 12 provides that this requirement is satisfied if the court is of the opinion on a balance of probabilities that the deceased's intention (though not necessarily his sole intention) in making the disposition or contract, was to prevent an order for financial provision being made or to reduce the amount of provision that might otherwise be ordered.

Section 12(2) provides that where a contract is made for no valuable consideration at all there will be a presumption that the deceased's intention was to defeat an application under the Act.

3   That use of its anti-avoidance powers will facilitate the making of financial provision for the applicant.

The Court's discretion in making an order   14.11.2

Once the court is satisfied that the requirements set out in 14.11.1 have been satisfied it may make an order against the donee. However, in deciding whether or not to exercise its discretion it must consider:

- The circumstances in which the disposition or contract was made;

- Any valuable consideration given;

- The relationship (if any) of the donee to the deceased;

- The conduct and financial resources of the donee; and

- All the circumstances of the case: s.10(6) and s.11(4).

Orders which can be made   14.11.3

In the case of a donee of a disposition the court may order a donee to provide such sum of money or other property as it may specify (s.10(2)) subject to two limitations:

- Donees given money cannot be ordered to provide more than the money paid by the deceased to them less any inheritance tax borne by the donee on the payment: s.10(3);

- Donees given property cannot be ordered to provide more than the value of the property at the deceased's date of death (or the date of disposal of the property by the donee, if earlier) less inheritance tax borne by the donee in respect of the property: s.10(4).

Where an order is made against a 'donee' under a contract and the personal representatives of the deceased have not transferred the money or other property to the 'donee' before the date of the application, the court may order them:

- Not to make such payment or transfer; or
- To make no further payment or transfer;
- To make only a reduced payment or transfer: s.11(2)(ii).

If the personal representatives have already paid the money or transferred the property to the 'donee' before the date of application, the court may order the donee to provide such sum of money or such other property as it may specify which has been paid to the donee under the contract: s.11(2)(i). However, the court may only make such orders to the extent that the property transferred under the contract exceeds the value of the consideration given: s.11(3).

Self-assessment questions

1   Mrs Court is seeking your advice as to whether she has a claim under the Inheritance (Provision for Family and Dependants) Act 1975 against the estate of Mr Oddy. She tells you Mr Oddy died in Scotland a year ago.

    What preliminary matters must you consider?

2   You are advising Geraldine and Jessica Short about a possible application under the Inheritance (Provision for Family and Dependants) Act 1975. Geraldine cohabited with Tom Sharpe between 1970–90. Jessica is a child of the relationship and was born in 1971. She is currently training to be an accountant.

    After leaving Geraldine in 1990, Tom married Priscilla and by his will left all his estate (valued at £200,000) to her.

    Geraldine still lives in the house, of which Tom was the sole legal and beneficial owner, and in which she cohabited with Tom. From the date of leaving Geraldine, Tom paid no maintenance to her although he did make irregular payments, averaging about £50 a month to Jessica, until his death.

    (a) On the information you have, is it likely that Geraldine and/or Jessica will have a valid claim under the Act?

    (b) Make a note of further information you will need to acquire from Geraldine and Jessica before advising them of their chances of success.

3 Mr Ox wishes to make an application under the Inheritance (Provision for Family and Dependants) Act 1975
against the estate of his wife, Mrs Ox, who died leaving
all her estate (valued at £40,000) by a valid will to the
League Against Cruel Sports.

Mr and Mrs Ox, although not judicially separated, were
not on good terms during the two years prior to Mrs Ox's
death. Mr Ox was, before his wife's death, sole legal and
beneficial owner of the matrimonial home. Apart from
this, his assets are worth only about £12,000.

Shortly before her death Mrs Ox sold all her shares in
Sainsbury's plc and gave the proceeds of sale (£50,000)
to the League Against Cruel Sports. There are no other
likely applicants under the I(PFD)A.

Advise Mr Ox on his chances of a successful claim.

Answer guidance to self-assessment questions

1 • Did Mr Oddy die domiciled in England and Wales
    (*see* 14.2.2)?

   • An application can be made within six months of the
    date of the first effective grant of representation? If
    not, might the court exercise its discretion to allow an
    application outside this period (*see* 14.3)?

2 (a) *Geraldine*. Category 5 is appropriate – probably making a substantial contribution to her maintenance in the
form of accommodation.

It is necessary to decide whether the will makes 'reasonable financial provision' for her – the maintenance standard
(*see* 14.5.2) is the appropriate standard. In deciding this the
common guidelines should be applied (*see* 14.5.3) as well as
the particular guideline to category 5 applicants (*see* 14.5.4).

If the court decides that the will does not make reasonable financial provision for Geraldine, it will then be necessary for it to decide whether to exercise its discretion and
make an order and if so, the type of order will have to be
decided. Here again the common guidelines and the particular guideline appropriate to category 5 applicants will
be applied.

Jessica. Category 3 is appropriate to her application.

The same two stage process as for Geraldine must be
applied, ie. (i) the court decides whether the will makes
reasonable financial provision for Jessica and, if not, (ii)
whether to exercise its discretion and in what manner.

At both stages, in addition to the common guidelines the

particular guidelines of the manner in which the applicant was being, or in which she might be expected to be, educated or trained, should be applied.

Remember that the courts are unlikely to look sympathetically upon applications from adult able-bodied children. So, in the long term, her chances of obtaining maintenance from the estate do not look good.

(b) • Date of Tom's death – relevant to time limit (*see* 14.3).

   • Financial resources and needs of Geraldine and Jessica.

   • Any physical/mental disability suffered by Geraldine/Jessica.

   • Relationship Jessica had with her father (may be relevant to common guideline 5).

   • Factors which led to the breakdown of relationship between Geraldine and Tom (may find information relevant to common guideline 5).

   • Do they know of any other likely applicants under the I(PFD)A against the estate of Tom?

3   Mr Ox falls within category 1. Therefore the surviving spouse standard (*see* 14.5.1) is appropriate in deciding upon whether there has been 'reasonable financial provision'). The common guidelines and the particular guideline appropriate to the surviving spouse will be considered, both in deciding whether reasonable financial provision has been made, and whether or not to make an order under the Act.

Mrs Ox's estate is very small, but Mr Ox is clearly not wealthy. It might be worth considering whether the sale of the shares and transfer of the proceeds to the League Against Cruel Sports were made to defeat a claim under the Act (*see* 14.11). Although use of the court's anti-avoidance powers would probably facilitate the making of financial provision for the applicant, it may be difficult to prove an intention on Mrs Ox's part to defeat a claim under the Act.